THE POWER TO KEEP PEACE

A Study from the Arms Control Project

Center for International Studies

Massachusetts Institute of Technology

THE POWER TO KEEP PEACE

Today and in a World Without War

by Lincoln P. Bloomfield

with

Hans J. Morgenthau   Thomas C. Schelling

Stanley Hoffmann   Henry V. Dicks

U Thant   Dag Hammarskjöld

World Without War Council

This book was first published as **International Military Forces, The
Question of Peacekeeping in an Armed and Disarming World**. Part I has
been substantially revised and updated. Stanley Hoffmann and Henry V.
Dicks revised their contributions to Part II.

The World Without War Council is grateful to Little, Brown and Company
for permission to publish a revised version of this study and to the Editors
of *International Organization* for permission to reprint a revised version of
"The United States, the Soviet Union, and the Prospects for Peacekeeping" which appeared in Volume XXIV, Number 3, 1970 of that periodical.

Printed in the U.S.A.

World Without War Council Publications

1730 Grove Street, Berkeley, California 94709

FOREWORD

THIS BOOK—a comprehensive revision of a work published in 1964[1]—is designed for scholars, students of international relations and concerned citizens interested in improving the international community's peace-keeping abilities in the 1970's. It focuses on one problem: what sort of police or military force should be at the disposal of the United Nations, given today's institutions, ideological divisions and political realities? This book asks: "If some form of police force is required, how can it be organized, maintained, controlled, and deployed?"; and "What would have to change before such a force could become a genuinely effective keeper of the peace?"

When the first edition of this book was published, the possibility of the United Nations developing a stand-by police force capability was not great. On the face of it, it is even less promising today. While there is a growing community of scholars in the U.S. and around the world who are committed to the idea of multilateral peacekeeping, their influence in governmental circles, with the public, and it might be added, even in the peace movement, is not strong. Most of the opposition to American policy in Vietnam has been built around criticism of misuse of military power, not around establishing international institutions or procedures for controlling that or new conflicts. The central reason for the lack of interest is not far to seek: we live in a deeply divided world in which agreement between adversaries seems more lacking than ever before. No abstract conception of community or brotherhood, whether expressed in political or moral terms, by itself carries anywhere enough authority to restrain contemporary belligerents.

Even so, exclusive reliance on national military power to achieve national security may be on the wane. The arms race has spiraled to the point where both the super-powers have a paramount interest in arms control, if not in general disarmament agreements. War, despite its recurrence, seems to be regarded by a growing fraction of mankind as obsolete. World travel, communication, health, and trade patterns point to increasing functional inter-relatedness, and there are growing signs that

[1] International Military Forces—The Question of Peacekeeping in an Armed and Disarming World (Boston: Little, Brown, 1964) by the present author and others.

organizations will be established or strengthened to meet insistent needs. The new dimension of outer space and new access to the immense riches of the sea-beds have already opened two new areas to international regimes that transcend national sovereignty.

It is thus tragic that, despite the obvious shrinkage of our globe, and in the face of these new and powerful reasons for common global action, the nations still do not supply the political, financial and moral backing required for success in international peacekeeping. Yet the issue is far from dead, and pessimism is not universal. In recent times two panels of leading citizens, scholars, and government officials, one privately organized by the United Nations Association of U.S.A.[2] the other by President Nixon[3] (on both of which the author was privileged to serve) have recommended that the U.S. support the development of a United Nations force. Steps have been taken toward establishing an international peace academy which could help to train the necessary skills.[4] Studies of the causes of conflict, and organizations engaged in peace research (such as the organization sponsoring this publication) may increase the credibility of ways of prosecuting conflict that do not lead to war, as well as aiding in ending wars if they occur.[5]

The decade of the 1970's offers no dearth of cases in which international peacekeeping is relevant. It is not inconceivable that a multilateral presence could play a useful role in Vietnam and in other South East Asian states after a ceasefire (and a strong case can be made for having done so many years earlier). The persistent Middle East conflict probably cannot be resolved without some strengthened form of international observer/peacemaking function.

The past usefulness of U.N. police forces in Suez, the Congo, India-Pakistan and Cyprus indicates the range of future problem areas in which it could prove indispensable to make progress on organizing, maintaining and controlling an international force.

The overall problem of peace is circular. The development of a significant international peacekeeping capability cannot be meaningfully considered outside the wider context of strengthening international institutions, developing genuine and workable instruments of world law, pursuing substantial disarmament agreements, promoting world economic development, and achieving an enforcement capability for broadly defined conceptions of human rights.[6] At the same time progress toward

---

[2]See Appendix 1

[3]See Appendix 2

[4]See Appendix 7

[5]See *Controlling Small Wars* (New York: Alfred A. Knopf, 1969) by the present author and Amelia C. Leiss.

[6]I have elaborated on these other goals in *The United Nations and U.S. Foreign Policy* (Boston: Little Brown, rev. ed. 1967). Also *The U.N. and World Order* (Head-

any of these goals falters in the absence of adequate procedures in the political security field reflecting at least "second order" agreements between adversary political systems. One element in such a "second order" agreement between the United States, the Soviet Union, and the People's Republic of China would be a workable international peacekeeping system in operation. Few other devices would as greatly increase the credibility of those advocating limitation of international conflicts. The alternative is to see such conflicts become even more unmanageable, violent, longlasting and destructive.

Admittedly, a generalized sense of short-run caution verging on pessimism limits my own hospitality at the present for more elaborate, expensive, or revolutionary schemes for an international force. But it is a sense of greater optimism for the longer run that inspires the search for politically acceptable solutions which have a chance of fulfillment. My own position rests on the belief that this prospect is denied to utopias, whether they commit the Marxist's sin of abolishing history or the Western visionary's sin of abolishing man.

In this quest I also enlisted the talents of several highly qualified colleagues. One chief purpose in commissioning their papers was to have the benefit of the thinking of some who had not particularly focused their professional attention on international forces but who *had* thought deeply in other contexts about such subjects as military strategy and logistics, police functions, and the psychology of the soldier. Within these covers they share common quarters with others who have distinguished themselves in the area of international organization and politics.

Since the purpose is to illuminate the issues, their approach, like my own, is generally friendly but critical. Each author has imposed his own particular logic on the material. The method was designed to scrutinize the problem through a variety of lenses, and the result, hopefully, is to open widely varying angles of vision into it.

The symposium in Part II of the book looks ahead to the possibility of international forces in a changed political and military environment brought about by a disarmament agreement. In the first and second papers two distinguished political scientists probe into some of the key theoretical issues in the complex relation of force and politics that are raised by any real-life version of international force. Hans J. Morgenthau focuses on those things that distinguish international "police" operations from the traditional concept of police in a community. Stanley Hoffmann[7] tackles the problem through fundamental questions of political authority and loyalty in a political system.

line Series 197, Oct. 1969). Also see *To End War* Robert Pickus and Robert Woito (New York: Harper & Row 1970), which provides a laymen's introduction to work for a world without war.

[7]Stanley Hoffmann and Henry Dicks have revised and updated their contributions for this edition.

Moving still closer to the so-far non-existent world in which armaments are significantly reduced, an imaginative analysis by Thomas C. Schelling speculates on the strategic problems that an international force would doubtless face whatever the national level of arms.

Finally, in considering a special aspect of international forces rarely investigated in the public print (or, for that matter, by governments) Henry V. Dicks reflects on his notable wartime psychiatric work with national soldiers to raise profound questions about international recruits.

The Appendix includes the essential documents for anyone studying the subject. Appendixes one and two present recommendations of two important commissions, both concluding that a standby U.N. force is needed now and that the U.S. should seek its establishment. Appendixes three and four present the view of two U.N. Secretaries General on this question, Appendix five the most recent U.N. reviews of Peacekeeping operations and Appendix six the U.N. Charter articles related to peacekeeping. Appendixes seven and eight describe a variety of private efforts designed to improve the U.N.'s peacekeeping capability.

Lincoln P. Bloomfield
Cambridge, Massachusetts
September 1971

TABLE OF CONTENTS

PART I

International Forces
Today and Tomorrow

One

THE MEANINGS OF INTERNATIONAL FORCE

Two sets of events in modern times have combined to give the subject of international military force prime importance. One was the dramatic creation of the several UN emergency forces. From the midst of the Suez crisis came the first true international force—the UN Emergency Force (UNEF). Two years after Suez, in the tense summer of 1958, the UN Observation Group in Lebanon (UNOGIL) was created. In July 1960 came the UN force in the Congo (ONUC). ONUC brought the United Nations to the verge of bankruptcy even as it was at the time containing the forces seeking to rend that turbulent land. And in 1964, after realizing that no alternative to war was available to the torn island republic of Cyprus, the UN Force in Cyprus (UNFICYP) was set up and still keeps apart the impassioned Greek and Turkish Cypriot adversaries.

None of these developments was precisely envisaged in 1945 when the UN Charter was written with the expectation that the great powers would themselves furnish forces to the Security Council; it turned out that forces enlisted from the lesser, non-great powers were not only the best obtainable under the circumstances but also a potentially indispensable addition to the arts of peacekeeping.

This invention of a new form of military presence—the non- (or almost non-) fighting UN force contributed by the smaller powers—posed a host of questions for the foreign policy and strategy of the principal members. It has already stimulated some (but not enough) fresh analysis of the need for stand-by forces and for improved international observation and fact-finding resources.[1] The Congo experience

---

[1]See particularly the panel report by the United Nations Association of the USA entitled *Controlling Conflicts in the 1970's* (UNA-USA 1969) and the *Report of President Nixon's Commission for the Observance of the Twenty-Fifth Anniversary of the United Nations* (Washington: G.P.O., 1971) (on both of which the present author was privileged to serve).

alone has supplied material for permanent controversy—certainly enough to fill several volumes.[2]

Alongside the UN problem another major political development has raised still broader questions about the concept of international forces. Western acceptance of the package approach to "general and complete disarmament" carried with it a portentous corollary that both illuminates and bedevils the disarmament dialogue. The corollary, first enunciated by Secretary of State Herter in early 1960, has since become embedded in Western policy. Simply stated, it holds that general disarmament must be accompanied by a significant degree of world authority which in turn must have at its disposal a military capability that would grow during the disarming process to the point where, by the end of stage III, no state would be in a position to challenge it. In a word, it calls for limited world government (without labeling it that), backed by military power at the center designed ultimately to supplant national military power.

This revolutionary concept was advanced, one suspects, without full comprehension of its implications. Initially left unanswered were questions ranging from broad and obvious ones such as the kind of political world in which a world peace force could function, to the lesser but no less crucial ones about the sorts of people one could envisage serving in such a force, the kinds of real-life chores such a force would probably have to take on, and such possibly decisive issues as command and location (and thus vulnerability to control or seizure by individual nations).

There are, then, two large parts to the question of international force, one involving the painfully familiar armed world of self-help, nuclear deterrence, endemic crises, and weak international authority; the other the unfamiliar one of vastly reduced armaments, *detente*, quantum increases in international authority (and, it is argued here, nuclear deterrence and endemic crises as before).

As one tackles the several meanings of "international force" it is striking how little experience the world has actually had that could illuminate the future. Paradoxically, the type of international force that is most *avant-garde*, so to speak, is the type with the longest history. Groups of military men truly mixed down to the squad of foot soldiers, or the crew of a man o'war, have sometimes put in dazzling performances. Englishmen will not forget that Admiral Nelson's own flagship

---

[2]Notably Ernest W. Lefever, *Crisis in the Congo—A UN Force in Action* (Washington: Brookings Institution, 1965) and *Uncertain Mandate* (Baltimore: Johns Hopkins Press, 1967); also King Gordon, *UN in the Congo* (New York: Carnegie Endowment, 1962), Conor Cruise O'Brien, *To Katanga and Back* (New York: Simon and Shuster, 1962).

at the Battle of Trafalgar—H.M.S. *Victory*—was crewed by Englishmen, Scotsmen, Irishmen, Welshmen and various islanders, and the following: twenty-two Americans, seven Dutchmen, six Swedes, three Frenchmen, two Danes, three Norwegians, one Russian, three Germans, two Swiss, two Portuguese, four Italians, two Indians, one African, nine West Indians, and four Maltese.

Some would see the collective use of national power to suppress threats to the status quo of 1815 as an analogy to the world today: to others it would be ideologically far-fetched. Perhaps the six-nation international force that captured Peking from the Boxer rebels on August 14, 1900 is closer to the mark, even to its non-Western participants (the Japanese).

In 1910 the United States Congress suggested creating a commission which would study "constituting the combined navies of the world [into] an international force for the preservation of universal peace" in connection with arms limitation.[3] This early linkage of peacekeeping with disarmament reappeared in the aftermath of World War I in a French proposal for a joint military force under an international general staff, later renewed in more detail in 1932. It showed up in the closing months of World War II at the Dumbarton Oaks Conference of 1944 in proposals by both the Soviet Union and China for an international air force.

In pre-UN days the need for international enforcement power of some variety was sometimes voiced. But in the absence of any suitable international institutions individual nations sometimes believed themselves to be acting in the name of the non-existent—or at any rate non-operative—community. Theodore Roosevelt told the Congress that

> Chronic wrongdoing, or an impotence which results in a general lessening of the ties of civilized society, may in America, as elsewhere, ultimately require intervention by some civilized nation, and in the Western Hemisphere the adherence of the United States, however reluctantly, in flagrant cases of such wrongdoing or impotence, to the exercise of an international police power.[4]

The closest thing to a genuine international force the world saw before the UN era was the 3300-man, four-nation force set up by the League of Nations to supervise the 1934 Saar Plebiscite.

The UN Charter, with its limited version of an "international police power," represented a shift in the legalistic, pacifistic, even millenial thinking that characterized the peace movement of the early 20th

[3] Cited by Arthur Larson in *When Nations Disagree* (Louisiana State University Press, 1961), p. 209.
[4] House Documents (4780), 58th Congress, 3rd Session, No. 1, p. XLI-II.

century. Whatever other misguided notions about the international political process the Charter may have embodied, it did incorporate some fresh insights into the relationship between peacekeeping and military power, insights the League of Nations Covenant had largely neglected in its preoccupation with disarmament. The 1945 Charter said a modest "Yes, but—" to disarmament. At the time it seemed sophisticated indeed in its acceptance of the legitimized role of force in support of the Charter principles.

The overwhelming obstacle this time was, we now know so well, the Charter's expectation of great-power collaboration in keeping the peace, combining elements of their military establishments on call of the Security Council for enforcement purposes. We have learned to live with the disparity between that hope and the reemergent reality of massive political warfare among the great-power blocs. The "Article 43 forces" were never placed at the disposal of the Security Council because such an act would have had to rest on a consensus that did not exist. From the onset there was thus not the single indispensable basis for the employment by the UN of significant force. It would have taken a politically cohesive directing body whose collective decisions would furnish the "law" in whose name the forces would act. (When the same organization, resting on the same fragments of true community, was required to deal with the Congo as though such an integrated system existed in fact, the complications were evident.)

It is generally supposed that if the superpowers had shared a common view of the established order in 1945 and had been prepared to defend outrages against it, the system would have worked. But one may fairly suspect that, even in such an unlikely event, the relationship between disarmament and international forces, between peacekeeping and enforcement, and between national sovereignty and multilateral power would still have been insufficiently understood—as it is today—to the detriment of clear national policy and sensible international negotiations on the subject.

But that is in the realm of might-have-been. As it was, the Soviet leadership in the mid-1940's saw in the very notion of an international force in a predominantly non-Communist world a *prima facie* threat. There is evidence that this view still persists relatively unchanged. It is also likely that the fears of the then Communist minority of 1946 were magnified by the position taken by United States representatives in the UN Military Staff Committee which met in 1946 to negotiate the levels for the promised Article 43 forces. Even by contrast with its closest allies the United States seemed to be asking for an inordinately large force (e.g., 3,800 planes against the 1,200 proposed by the United

Kingdom and France; 90 submarines against 12; 84 destroyers against 24).[5]

According to one observer these grandiose U.S. demands, coupled with the simultaneous American attack on the veto power, made the effort fruitless, particularly when the U.S. representative refused to discuss the forces question in conjunction with disarmament.[6] This is not to blame the collapse of Article 43 on the United States. It is to indicate the breadth of the gap that separated the two sides.

As virtually everybody knows, "UN forces" of one sort or another have been used in a dozen major postwar crises, and the statistics tell of both the modesty of scale of effort and the rather marvellous growth of wide-ranging peacekeeping activities. Fifteen countries contributed troops to the Korean action. Twenty-four offered units to the UN Emergency Force created in 1956 to enforce the ceasefire following the Suez invasion, and ten were finally accepted, supplying an average of one 500-man battalion apiece. Around 600 observers patrolled the Lebanese-Syrian border in 1958, with seventy observers of nine nationalities doing the same in Kashmir. Three hundred officer members of UN Truce teams observed the Palestine War armistice in its earliest aspects from 1948 (and nineteen years later additional UN observers were dispatched to stand hazardous watch along the Suez Canal ceasefire line after the 1967 June war had again torn the fabric of peace in the Middle East). Twenty-nine countries offered troops to the ONUC force; at its peak strength of 19,000 or so in early 1963 ONUC contained elements from ten countries—predominantly African—plus supporting personnel from ten others. The UN Security Force in West New Guinea in 1962 consisted of 1,485 Pakistani ground forces and a small U.S. and Canadian air and sea support component. Two hundred observers served in Yemen in 1963.

It can be seen that these "forces" run from a handful of observers, to a military body greater than division strength. Some missions did their turn and were dissolved, others changed shape as conflicts themselves changed. (For example, after the 1965 fighting between India and Pakistan UNIPOM was created, involving 89 military observers from 17 countries, as a kind of semi-autonomous extension of UNMOGIP.)

In attempting to approach systematically the problem of international forces one confronts an extraordinarily varied range of greater-than-national forces and their possible missions. If for the sake of analysis

[5]*UN Security Council Official Records*, Second Year, No. 50, 149th Mtg. (June 30, 1947), p. 1177.

[6]Bernhard Bechhoefer, *Postwar Negotiations for Arms Control* (Washington: Brookings Institution, 1961), pp. 97, 98.

one accepts the concept of a continuum (without necessarily beliving that one level will automatically lead to the next), the scale includes significant intermediate levels between the extremes of "the man with the binoculars" along the road between Damascus and Beirut, or in Kashmir or Yemen, and a world force possessing that paramount attribute of political authority, a relative monopoly of the means of physical coercion—Tennyson's "airy navies" in UN blue, as it were.[7]

The very sharpness of the dividing lines on our hypothetical scale of international forces is the crucial point. For the chief threshold lies between the familiar kind of world of nation-states, each disposing of armed forces and subject only in limited ways to a higher law, and that very different political never-never land in which genuine power is centered in a supranational authority.

If one looks closely at the spectrum of international forces, six basic types seem to emerge: (1) the type or types that one thinks of as likely and politically feasible today; (2) a force organized on regional rather than global principles; (3) a stand-by UN observation and patrol-type force; (4) a standing UN observation and patrol-type force; (5) a stand-by fighting force; and (6) a standing fighting force. The last one can be divided into two basic sub-types: (a) a great-power contributed force with veto—an extension of what was put in the UN Charter in 1945 under Article 43; and (b) a force recruited from all sources, with no great-power veto. The last one is the model of the force that represents a true monopoly of coercive power in the hands of a central authority, i.e. world government. One can of course think of almost infinite variations on each basic model. And one can discern even more clearly both the salient thresholds and the discontinuities that represent sharp breaks with both past and present.

Some additional light is cast by considering the missions for which an international force might be designed, remaining attentive to the kinds of missions that represent the familiar and those calling for a revolutionary transformation in power and politics. Here also there is a range from minor to major, from cheap to expensive, from uncontroversial to bitterly contested.

(1) At the bottom of the scale are what can be called guard duties—policing the UN buildings and meeting rooms, including installations in the field; or bodyguard to the Secretary General (UN Field Service personnel so served in the Congo and a personal guard was killed with Dag Hammarskjöld).

---

[7]"Heard the heavens fill with shouting and there rain'd a ghastly dew/From the nations' airy navies grappling in the central blue" from "Locksley Hall" by Alfred, Lord Tennyson.

(2) Next is the function of observation and patrol. The man with the binoculars is a uniquely valuable asset, often worth as much as a platoon of infantry; but he is usable only when conflict has been suspended or stopped by agreement of the parties (or never really broke out). Here is the "eye-balling" task exemplified by the lonely sentries on the postwar border watches in Northern Greece, the Middle East, Kashmir, Lebanon; the "presences" so useful for their psychological value, as in Laos and Jordan, and, some day, Berlin. (The UN today calls this 'Model I').

(3) Next is more militant enforcement of ceasefires and truces, for keeping the armed parties apart (but with far less actual military power than would be needed if they resumed hostilities). Here is the Palestine of 1949, Suez of 1956, the Yemen effort commencing in June, 1963, and UNFICYP on Cyprus.

(4) Another brand of mission is internal policing and order-keeping, as in the Congo. It is guaranteed to be controversial because of inescapable involvement in internal partisan politics. It may keep the United Nations in turmoil because of great-power differences. East Africa and South Africa may be on this list.

Under the guidelines first established by Secretary General Dag Hammarskjöld, initially for the UNEF operation, forces would be drawn for functions (2), (3), and (4), exclusively from middle and smaller powers. Moreover, they would be sent to a nation's territory, and retained there, *only* on the sufferance of the "host" country.

On the first of these major points, the growing crisis in the Middle East in the late 1960's and early 1970's brought a change in the public positions of the two superpowers. Both the Soviet Union and the United States in 1970 and 1971 indicated that they envisaged the possibility of their own armed forces participating in any new Mid-East peacekeeping force. Although ruling out a joint Soviet-American force,[8] the United States indicated an open mind on the subject:

> The United States has indicated, and will continue to indicate, a willingness to play a responsible role in a peacekeeping force or an observer force. We have not gone beyond that. Obviously, any such role would require the approval of all the nations concerned. So that we have offered and continue to say that assuming an agreement can be reached, we are prepared to consider playing a role in an observer force or any other force. We don't demand it. We are not sure that is the best system. We are perfectly happy if the parties could agree on some other kind of a force. But we do

[8]Secretary of State William Rogers at news conference Dec. 23, 1970, reported in *New York Times*, Dec. 24, 1970.

not want to back away from what we consider responsibility to try to bring about a peaceful settlement in the area.[9]

Moscow in mid-June 1969 had implied its support for great-power participation in such a force, by speaking of troops from countries chosen by the UN Security Council on "a balanced political and geographically just representation."[10]

As for host country permission, the precipitate withdrawal of UNEF in 1967 raised the issue sharply, and I discuss the matter in Chapter VI.

Returning to our scale of missions for any international force, it is clear that anything beyond that described in our first four categories implies that another crucially important threshold is crossed. For from (5) on, the missions involve *combat* for an international force. At the more modest end of this scale are internal disorder and civil war, and so far the United States, wisely or not, has not wished to entrust to the United Nations situations such as the Nigerian Civil War and the Indochina War. The scale ascends through the familiar categories of limited conventional war to local nuclear and eventually world-wide strategic war.

[9]Secretary Rogers in news conference April 23, 1971, Department of State *Bulletin,* May 10, 1971, p. 597.
[10]See *New York Times,* Oct. 19, 1969.

Two

WORLD FORCE AND WORLD ORDER

Western diplomacy has consistently insisted upon a close connection between disarmament and an international military force sufficient eventually to enforce with coercive power the will of an as yet unspecified central authority.

In February 1960 the American policy was established when, as we have noted, the then Secretary of State Christian Herter responded to Khrushchev's call the previous fall for "general and complete disarmament." Mr. Herter first sought to place disarmament in the setting of a "more stable military environment." This goal called, he asserted, for measures to control two types of dangers of a continuing arms race: the danger of surprise attack, and the promiscuous spread of nuclear weapons. These initial arms-control measures would pave the way to "progressive, gradual, and balanced reductions" in national military forces. With the military environment thus stabilized, a "second stage of general disarmament" would be approached. Here the crucial political and institutional corollary to "GCD" emerges, and it is worth quoting in full:

Our objective in this second stage should be twofold:

First, to create certain universally accepted rules of law which, if followed, would prevent all nations from attacking other nations. Such rules of law should be backed by a world court and by effective means of enforcement—that is, by international armed force.

Second, to reduce national armed forces, under safeguarded and verified arrangements, to the point where no single nation or group of nations could effectively oppose this enforcement of international law by international machinery.[1]

[1]Address to the National Press Club at Washington, D.C. on February 18, 1960, *Department of State Bulletin*, March 7, 1960, p. 357.

In the fall of 1961 the United States and the Soviet Union undertook bilateral negotiations whose result, considered quite extraordinary at the time, was a "Joint Statement of Agreed Principles for Disarmament Negotiations" which was circulated to all UN Members on September 20, 1961. The relevant sections for our purposes were these:

2. The programme for general and complete disarmament shall ensure that States will have at their disposal only those non-nuclear armaments, forces, facilities, and establishments as are agreed to be necessary to maintain internal order and protect the personal security of citizens; and that States shall support and provide agreed manpower for a United Nations peace force.

7. Progress in disarmament should be accompanied by measures to strengthen institutions for maintaining peace and the settlement of international disputes by peaceful means. During and after the implementation of the programme of general and complete disarmament, there should be taken, in accordance with the principles of the United Nations Charter, the necessary measures to maintain international peace and security, including the obligation of States to place at the disposal of the United Nations agreed manpower necessary for an international peace force to be equipped with agreed types of armaments. Arrangements for the use of this force should ensure that the United Nations can effectively deter or suppress any threat of use of arms in violation of the purposes and principles of the United Nations.[2]

That fall the United States submitted its own proposal for "General and Complete Disarmament" to the UN Assembly. In it were these provisions for the contemplated three stages of disarmament.

A. States shall develop arrangements in Stage I for the establishment in Stage II of a United Nations peace force.

B. During Stage II, States shall develop further the peacekeeping processes of the United Nations, to the end that the United Nations can effectively in Stage III deter or suppress any threat or use of force in violation of the purposes and principles of the United Nations:

(a) States shall agree upon strengthening the structure, authority, and operation of the United Nations so as to assure that the United Nations will be able effectively to protect States against threats to or breaches of the peace.

[2]UN Document A/4879, 20 September 1961.

(b) The United Nations peace force shall be established and progressively strengthened.

C. In Stage III, progressive controlled disarmament and continuously developing principles and procedures of international law would proceed to a point where no State would have the military power to challenge the progressively strengthened United Nations Peace Force and all international disputes would be settled according to the agreed principles of international conduct.

The progressive steps to be taken during the final phase of the disarmament programme would be directed toward the attainment of a world in which:

(a) States would retain only those forces, non-nuclear armaments, and establishments required for the purpose of maintaining internal order; they would also support and provide agreed manpower for a United Nations Peace Force.

(b) The United Nations Peace Force, equipped with agreed types and quantitites of armaments, would be fully functioning.

(c) The manufacture of armaments would be prohibited except for those of agreed types and quantitites to be used by the United Nations Peace Force and those required to maintain internal order. All other armaments would be destroyed or converted to peaceful purposes.

(d) The peacekeeping capabilities of the United Nations would be sufficiently strong and the obligations of all States under such arrangements sufficiently far-reaching as to assure peace and the just settlement of differences in a disarmed world.[3]

When subsequently at Geneva the United States presented a treaty outline in detail, the same themes carried over. The outline specified a "United Nations Peace Force, which would be equipped with agreed types of armaments and would be supplied agreed manpower by states, would be progressively strengthened until, in Stage III, it would be fully capable of insuring international security in a disarmed world."

In detail, under Stage I the parties would agree on these measures:

(a) Examination of the experience of the United Nations leading to a further strengthening of United Nations forces for keeping the peace.

---

[3]*Department of State Bulletin,* October 16, 1961, pp. 653, 654.

(b) Examination of the feasibility of concluding promptly the agreements envisaged in Article 43 of the United Nations Charter.

(c) Conclusion of an agreement for the establishment of a United Nations Peace Force in Stage II, including definitions of its purpose, mission, composition and strength, disposition, command and control, training, logistical support, financing, equipment and armaments.

Under "United Nations Peace Force" in the Stage II section of the plan:

> The United Nations Peace Force to be established as the result of the agreement reached during Stage I would come into being within the first year of Stage II and would be progressively strengthened during Stage II.

And under Stage III,

> The Parties to the Treaty would progressively strengthen the United Nations Peace Force established in Stage II until it had sufficient armed forces and armaments so that no state could challenge it.[4]

Since Secretary Herter's speech, there has been little public exposition or exegesis by government officials of the official policy toward international forces in a disarming or disarmed world. Such references as there have been are typically in the context of modest urgings that the United Nations develop further its present capabilities for peacekeeping. One of the rare references to the longer-range proposal was made by Assistant Secretary of State Cleveland in 1962:

> At a later stage a larger international peace force with some experience behind it might be able to cope with actual hostilities between well-armed secondary powers.
>
> Only in the final and faraway stage of general and complete disarmament could an international force interpose itself in a conflict between great powers. But by making it more difficult for brush fires to break out, and by reducing the temptation for big powers to intervene when brush fires do break out, even a small, highly mobile police force could render more unlikely the escalation of little wars into big ones.[5]

[4]*Blueprint for the Peace Race,* USACDA Publication 4, General Series 3, May, 1962.

[5]Press release 160, March 12, 1962, see *Department of State Bulletin,* April 9, 1962.

The Western commitment is thus to some a form of world government, however ill-formed the notions of some of those pressing this policy. But the implications of such a policy are so far-reaching that they require the most searching scrutiny, leading either to an informed opinion that would support the policy if it ever became operative, or to scrapping the present policy if upon analysis it is untenable.

The matter has been faced before in lesser form. The 1946 United States plan for the international control of atomic energy assigned the proposed international agency managerial control or ownership of "all atomic energy activities potentially dangerous to world security," plus "power to control, inspect, and license all other atomic activities." To carry this out would have required extraordinary powers at the center. But it was still some distance from even the Baruch Plan to the implications of political control of the world as a whole in present Western disarmament proposals. Throughout the postwar negotiating period, even when programs were advanced for drastic reduction and limitation of armaments, there is no record of any concrete suggestion or even discussion of a supranational political organization that would exercise effective control in the world.

The proposals for international peace forces backed by governmental-type powers, with all their unmistakable implications of an authentic world order, may not be taken seriously by many. Indeed, the usual responses to the idea on the part of politically sophisticated people are so invariably negative that the only wonder is that the United States thought it would make good propaganda to enunciate it. Some who are skeptical about disarmament will accept the troublesome political and institutional corollaries on the ground that "if you can believe that, you can believe anything."

But if one believes that significant moderation of the arms race is far too serious a matter to consign to a utopian paradise in which modern history reaches an end and a completely new political universe is wished into being, one will not accept such glib dialectics. It is worth while for three reasons to subject the proposals to serious analysis. On policy grounds it would be well to spell out with greater precision, if only for our own better understanding, that to which this country has committed itself. On grounds of sound scholarship it may be worthwhile to apply analytical methods to a problem commonly approached on the basis of hunch alone. Finally, there is always the possibility that sophisticated people will turn out to have been wrong.

What, in the highly unlikely event that United States disarmament proposals and, consequently, an effective world force were accepted, might it look like?[6]

---

[6]Thomas C. Schelling systematically explores the possible appearance, composition, and strategic problems of such a force in his essay in Part Two.

To accomplish its mission, the international force, compounded appropriately of ground, sea, air, and outer-space elements, would have to consist of at least 500,000 men, recruited individually and wearing the international uniform. It would control a nuclear force consisting of 50-100 mixed land-mobile and undersea missiles averaging 1 megaton per weapon. The force would be stationed and deployed in territorial enclaves equitably allocated among continents and areas for minimum temptation and likelihood of seizure by any single nation. Ten airtransportable divisions trained for vertical envelopment, armed with the latest field weapons (including a modest supply of tactical nuclear weapons), and provided with transport and communications facilities should be able to counter an aggressive thrust across one nation's borders of the dimensions likely under the circumstances. Beyond that, the strategic nuclear deterrent in the hands of the central authority would presumably deter conventional attack on a massive scale in the same fashion as in American hands it presumably deterred Soviet conventional aggression in Europe in the late 1940's and early 1950's. (The latter analogy rests of course on an unproved hypothesis, as does the whole doctrine of retaliation associated with strategic nuclear weapons.) We must also assume the force's ability to deal with guerrilla activities, but without high confidence.

It is obvious that an international force would be decreasingly capable of coping with higher levels of aggression involving several countries up to a point describable as true international civil war. It should, however, be understood that the choice is not between an international system incapable of coping with important threats and one that can deal successfully with every contingency in the spectrum. At one end of the scale the present international system has some capacity to cope. At the other end of the scale we can guess that there would be finite limits to the capacity of a supranational system to handle such maximum challenges as international civil war. A civil war, domestic or international, can gather such force as to end the preponderance at the center. The hypothetical system, while its capacities go significantly beyond those presently in sight, remains subject to the basic laws of political life.

What is the basis for the apportionment of forces that I have suggested between center and parts? Here strategic analysis supplies tentative answers.

Effective capacity to fulfill its mission connotes a relative monopoly of political power, accompanied by preponderant military force, at the center of the system. The word "relative" indicates that the power relationship between the center and the parts is one of degree. Some examples illustrate the equation. In the United States the people have the constitutional right to "keep and bear arms"; the government monopoly is legally abridged to this extent. In the Congo Republic during the most politically disturbed period the central army was outnumbered by the provincial forces, putting into question the existence of effective central rule. In Kuomintang China the military power of the national government was often balanced by the military power of the warlords; the writ of the government hence could not extend uniformly through the country. Thus under a supranational government the degrees of relative power as between center and parts can occupy a wide range. The most logical combination of forces poses at once the question of nuclear weapons. One fundamental consideration seems overriding.

Modern science and technology are essentially irreversible. They can perhaps be slowed down or even stopped either by some universal catastrophe or under a disarmament agreement that curtails the intensive allocation of economic and human resources to armaments. But the processes of fission and fusion and the design of engines of delivery cannot be unlearned. Moreover, assuming as we must that fission power may become increasingly economical, and fusion power—when harnessed—more so, even under total disarmament all of these technologies will be practiced in their peaceable aspects. Thus, however comprehensive the disarmament agreements, however much political power is transferred to a world government, and even if no significant amount of manpower is actually working on nuclear, chemical, and bacteriological weapons or on constructing military aircraft, ships, rockets, or space vehicles, there will always remain implicit in technically advanced societies the capacity to turn again to the production and fabrication of engines of war, probably with fair rapidity.

The very logic of effectiveness requires placing in the hands of the central authority military forces adequate to deal with breaches of the peace and acts of aggression through whatever means are necessary to preserve a preponderance of power at the center, even against the contingency of clandestine production of nuclear weapons. The conclusion is inescapable that the central authority, in addition to its conventional military capacity, will have to offset the inherent possibility of evasion by being equipped with nuclear weapons along with delivery systems adequate to deter any reasonable expectation of clandestine violation and attempt to destabilize or even destroy the new system.

It can be seen that even under a radically designed system of authority in a disarmed world the problem of deterrence would persist, including some of the features that characterize it today. The situation facing the central authority would not be very different from that confronting a traditional great power in its need to be equipped with forces adequate to deter any likely combination of hostile forces. Indeed, this is the problem *inside* any society. But the special feature in the new situation would be an element of profound uncertainty. Today national military forces are designed to deter known quantities or qualities of war-making capability in the arsenals of other nations. But our postulated regime, even with a good inspection system, would be to a degree uncertain whether nuclear weapons were hidden or being secretly made, or some highly potent bacteriological agent being developed in an isolated laboratory, or some potentially commanding weapon secreted illicitly in an orbiting space station or in the payload of a communication, weather, navigation, or other type of satellite. These possibilities, however statistically improbable, would pose anew the problem of deterrence in a different calculus, both for the general authority and for individual countries in making their own calculations.

If this sort of world ever comes into being, a threshold will have been crossed from one historical condition to another profoundly different one. However many stages it passes through, however tacit or explicit the labels, however gradual or violent the process, there is a Rubicon that divides the Tuscany of basically untrammeled national sovereignty from the Gaul of meaningful supranational authority. Nothing could be more dangerous to sound thinking and planning than to elide this fundamental truth. By whatever process and under whatever name, the agency that is to control world affairs effectively requires in the most important ways the design customarily associated with government. A central authority with effective powers in the realms of disarmament and the settlement of international disputes, and with the capacity to deal with breaches of the peace and acts of aggression, and above all in possession of the most vital attribute of government—a preponderance of military power—is a *government,* however limited. To grasp the profound difficulty in securing widespread acceptance of this sweeping rearrangement of things, one only needs to recall that ratification of the UN Charter by the United States Senate was conditioned on having the veto power. Today, even as nuclear weapons and technological change demand more multilateral cooperation, the nationalist movement in its purest form is only now sweeping the world south of the equator, and some if not all great powers argue vigorously against any form of explicit "supranationalism."

Even if Western acquiescence in the implications of its own proposals could be assumed, it is surely unsafe to make the further assumption that the ideological and power contests in the world will not continue in some form. This throws into question any program requiring that all powers subordinate themselves, their military strength, and their ambitions to a supranational authority. That is of course the central dilemma of world politics today, and it applies with ultimate force to the proposition of world government. The logical trap is completed with the familiar paradox: given an unabated continuation of international dynamism, the subordination of states to a true world government appears impossible; but if true stability developed under the present international system, the West might well lose whatever incentive it has for world government.

If, to test our hypothesis further, we assume that the West would favor a world under the effective control of the United Nations, the operative question is then how to bring it about. One way would be through a lengthy evolutionary process. The other would be through a crisis, a war, or a brink-of-war situation so grave or commonly menacing that deeply rooted attitudes and practices are sufficiently shaken to open up the possibility of a revolution in world political arrangements.

If we can for the sake of analysis make the further assumption that the preconditions exist, what kind of political environment could then be foreseen?

Remember, we are assuming a world in which relations between nations are characterized by significantly higher degrees of mutual trust, internationalist spirit, and unaggressiveness. But there is little in history to justify the belief that even without present threats the world political environment would be inherently stable. We have postulated by necessity a willing acceptance of limited world government by the great powers. We then have to postulate further either its acceptance by or imposition on all other nations.

This at once sets up future instabilities. Today the prime foci of instability are actually in third areas and center on economic disparities and nationalistic strivings for independence, factors which outside powers purposefully exploit. There is no reason to assume the disappearance under limited world government of the dynamic factors—the intergroup competitions, the racial and ethnic tensions, and the economic disparities—that permeate human history and create the conditions for political upheaval. History, short of catastrophe, is not discontinuous. To paraphrase von Clausewitz, limited world government may be regarded, at least in part, as a form of international conflict carried on under institutional arrangements other than unlimited state sovereignty. Thus as international stability is restored under benign forms of world order, detailed disputes of a chronic or secondary nature can be confidently expected to re-emerge. The new regime will then be faced with a continuous agenda of problems stemming from political ambition, inequalities, avarice, irrational behavior, the inhumanity of man to man, and the use or threat of violence to achieve political or social ends. This prospect can be ruled out only by the untenable assumption that history will have run its course and an end put to its dynamic, refractory, and otherwise troublesome qualities. Thus a world government, even if it could be created, would be subject to continuing pressures, the most exigent of which could lead to civil war on an international scale.

The crucial difficulty then is to ensure that no large-scale civil war can take place to test the "union," for war on a major scale would gravely threaten the system. It would revive the production and, given the instability of such a situation, the probable use of weapons of mass destruction. In any event such a war would be no more tolerable under a world government than it would be today, and for precisely the same humanitarian, social, and economic reasons.

But here the model runs into one of history's most vexing dilemmas. War is the traditional means for changing the international *status quo* in the absence of effective provisions for peaceful change. When war is not possible—and when no such provisions exist—the traditional consequence is injustice, which in turn breeds even more ungovernable instabilities and ensuing violence. Perhaps the most sobering consideration about world government is the nightmare prospect of world order at the price of world tyranny—a kind of global Holy Alliance to preserve the *status quo.* Flexibility and capacity to adapt to change in time and with foresight become absolute imperatives in view of the probable nuclear monopoly in the hands of the central authority.

To achieve the necessary viability and durability, then, the world authority must solve the problem that has pervaded all modern history, and accommodate the dynamic forces making for change without allowing them to lead to war. Specifically the system must, through its legislative action, its executive implementation, and its judicial interpretation, allow for changes in fact, in law, and in the system itself. Without a genuine breakthrough in this realm of peaceful change in which man has by and large so far failed, with persistently tragic results, nothing else about the world order has any meaning in terms of either the efficacy of the system or the values by which we would wish to continue to live.

Even allowing that such a breakthrough were possible, the chances of conflict over the one legitimate stock of decisive weapons that would remain make us think twice about centralizing such power. To do so would contradict everything we have learned since Montesquieu about diffusion and balance of power, plural centers of action, and multiple and diverse components of strength. It would make possible tyranny at the hands of a world force legitimately possessing a relative monopoly of the means of physical coercion. Such tyranny on a world scale could make local tyrannies look relatively desirable. One can only conclude that nuclear weapons are necessary to the very concept of world police power but too dangerous to entrust to an authority not characterized by diffused power, pluralism in the chief forces of society, and a multiple balancing of interests. For the single most vital decision about international forces in a disarming world would concern the location, management, control, accessibility, and manning of powerful weapons. NATO's chronic problems of "fifteen fingers on the trigger" pales into comparative insignificance alongside the prospect of 130 or so nations sharing control of a world force so equipped.

In directing a series of political-military simulations designed to illuminate some problems involving international forces[7] the author was struck by another problem of weapons technology that needs to be thought of in considering the relation between disarmament and peace forces. It is likely that the formulas proposed by the great powers for across-the-board disarmament will have the side effect of destroying certain local power balances, such as those involving Israel, South Korea, Pakistan, Turkey, or Iran, all of which today maintain armed forces high in proportion to population in order to balance far more populous hostile neighbors. To impose in such special situations a formula of "forces for internal security only," as present Western disarmament plans envisage in "Stage III," might tempt the country in question to seek "equalizers" in the form of unconventional biological, chemical—or nuclear—warfare capabilities.

Moreover, the logic applies equally to the broader picture. If a small Israel would feel the need of such "technological equalizers" to stand off far more populous neighbors, or others to hold back traditionally voracious abutters, what special problems would confront a modest-sized international constabulary faced with the manpower potential of teeming millions in every continent? At the least, planning for such a constabulary should consider novel technical means to keep the peace, in the form of techniques aimed at offsetting the danger of overwhelming hostile ground strength.

An international force in a disarmed world might well need exotic forms of protection against unfavorable numbers. Nerve gases, tranquillizer dart guns, psychochemicals, and other temporarily disabling or paralyzing agents all may be high in the armorarium of an international police, requiring possible exceptions to be made to the Geneva Conventions outlawing chemical warfare. They pose for the scientist and weapons designer a rather special set of requirements which he should begin to take seriously. For at least arguably such agents of persuasion and coercion would be likely to do the job in more appropriate and humane ways than more conventional military weapons whose efficient use depends upon the existence of the very kind of military targets that disarmament planners must assume will be outlawed.

[7]See Lincoln P. Bloomfield and Barton Whaley, "The Political-Military Exercise: A Progress Report," *Orbis,* Winter, 1965.

Three

INTERNATIONAL FORCE IN A DISARMING—BUT REVOLUTIONARY—WORLD

So far we have been discussing international force in its ultimate meaning—as the expression of coercive power in a world order characterized by total disarmament, the rule of law, and centralized political authority.

But general disarmament plans, like weapons of mass destruction, supply excessive solutions to problems, and, like those weapons, tend to leave unanswered many highly pertinent questions about lesser conflicts, low-level disorders, ambiguous enemies, and local policing jobs. By and large, strategic planners have come to recognize this weakness in military doctrines. But it is not certain that the planners of general and complete disarmament (GCD) recognized that a blueprint geared to the deliberate violation, the great war, superstates in hostile confrontation, may turn out to be quite irrelevant to the real problems of a disarmed or even semi-disarmed world. At best such a blueprint is bound to be deficient until it comes to grips with disorders other than classic open encounters of two states—that is, with the painfully familiar gamut ranging from civil war fomented in a great state by outside agents to the purely internal breakdown of law and order in a small state.

The point is not whether these problems are more numerous or more likely to occur than classic open interstate conflict. It should be enough to recognize the quality of the age we live in. It is revolutionary in two literal senses. One is the sense of ideological assault on the established order. The other sense is the continuing revolt of the emerging nations against foreign domination (real or imagined) before, during, and in many cases after independence. In a more figurative sense the future, like the present, will be revolutionary: virtually everything is likely to change—mortality, health, weapons, travel, communication, art, knowledge, the cosmos, and, *ex hypothesi,* political ideas. Specific revolutions may ebb and flow, but this systemic revolution is guaranteed to keep the political world dynamic through the foreseeable future. Disarmament planning which fails to take account of this dynamism does so at its peril. The instabilities we must plan to live with are bred of historical conflicts, racial discrimination, technology, economic disparity, and other deep-seated political and social factors, all of them producers of revolutionary situations with which any society, large or small, armed or disarmed, must cope.

I have dealt elsewhere with problems of limiting local conflicts through more far-sighted and progressive politics.[1] Here, we should be clear about the special problems of peacekeeping involved. Some of the changes we can foresee in both East-West and North-South conflicts are likely to be beneficial and ultimately favorable to a peaceful world. When the Portuguese African colonies, the sheikdoms in the Persian Gulf, and the island dependencies in the Pacific finally find their ultimate political status, the instability caused by at least Western colonial history will cease. Such present candidates for revolution and disorder in the form of pre-independence conflict as Angola may then become *status quo* powers. But one of the accompaniments of decolonization is the problem of internal disorder.

By the same token the Messianic quality may drain out of Soviet and, later, Chinese world policy as affluence and concern with mass consumption make the revolutionary doctrine increasingly inappropriate. Disarmament may accelerate this process. But while this is happening, new opportunities may open for peoples in Eastern Europe and minorities in Asia to assert their independence—a process that might be extraordinarily dangerous and bloody.

The third category of potential disorder is endemic and not likely to be affected by disarmament. There is nothing in the historical record to suggest that the incidence of civil wars and other local instabilities will significantly diminish merely because the great powers have agreed to restrict their strategic power. On the contrary, in such a situation the importance of local instabilities would doubtlessly increase until eventually it became the chief object of concern to the international community.

For these various reasons we can assume that local instability will be a crucial problem in a disarming world; that in that world only some aspects of the world situation will be affected by the agreement while others will remain unchanged. These two layers of reality are made vivid if we use the image of a world map overlaid with the kind of plastic

[1]See Lincoln P. Bloomfield and Amelia C. Leiss, *Controlling Small Wars—A Strategy for the 1970's* (New York: Alfred A. Knopf, 1969).

on which military planners chart their dispositions with a grease pencil. The underlying reality is that of the world map. It is the real world of geography, of national territory, of people, of states. All of these have their pasts, their ethnic characteristics and racial memories, minority relationships, national hopes and fears, geographic neighbors, and historical relationships with those neighbors and with other countries. This map remains essentially unchanged even if one assumes the signing of a treaty on GCD and, beyond that, the creation of an international military force to keep the peace.

The other layer—the transparent overlay, so to speak—represents those changes in the military and strategic situation created by an agreement on disarmament, along with the international order that accompanies it. The overlay does not and cannot replace the underlying map, as some utopian thinkers would have us believe. To some extent it imposes new conditions on the map, particularly in terms of the strategic "reach" of great powers. At a minimum, GCD implies alterations within the coalitions that now confront each other, in the relations between the United States and Europe, and in the relations within the Soviet bloc. Most importantly, whatever the political overlay when GCD is agreed to, it would itself undoubtedly alter in unforeseeable ways as the program goes successfully from one stage to another of disarmament.

For the vast majority of countries and peoples, however, in the first stages of GCD the overlay would remain essentially blank. For them reality would continue to be the land, the people, the racial memory, the boundary with the neighbor, rather than the shift in the military environment affecting the nuclear powers. For three out of four human beings the only change GCD will bring will be in the mathematical chances that their particular country would be involved in a great-power war, that they as individuals would be killed or maimed in such a war, or that their descendants would undergo genetic mutations as a consequence of atmospheric radioactivity. It can be persuasively argued that GCD would bring untold economic benefits to the peoples of underdeveloped countries as a result of savings, and it is to be devoutly hoped that the $220 billion or so spent today on the arms race[2] would be diverted in part at least to their crying needs. But one cannot automatically assume it, and if one did, it would not significantly alter all of the projections of political instability that concern us here.

[2]See *World Military Expenditures 1970,* U.S. Arms Control and Disarmament Agency, Washington, D.C., 1971.

GREAT-POWER ATTITUDES TOWARD LOCAL STABILITY

An analysis of the role of an international military force in a disarming world runs the risk of being too abstract. It helps to make it more concrete to examine elements of continuity in the policies of major powers.

If for the sake of brevity we sum up over-all American and Soviet strategies in oversimplified terms, they might run as follows: With respect to real or potential situations of local instability, the paramount American strategy has been one of seeking stability, at times regardless of the cost in image or ideology. But with time (and hopefully increasing wisdom) the United States may be prepared to run risks of short-term instability in order to achieve a more satisfactory long-term international community. Soviet strategy, in its essence, has been destabilizing, but over time it may be adjusting pragmatically to declining prospects, and compared to Chinese revolutionary *élan* it may seem increasingly "conservative." Above all, in its tactics the Soviet Union may be prepared to sacrifice important targets of opportunity if risks of general war appear too high.

What would be the effect of GCD on these strategies of the superpowers? What would it do to their present and historic approaches to stability and instability? If GCD were to be agreed upon in the foreseeable future, it is obvious that there would be no dearth of situations implying disorder, discomfort and turbulence. The crucial question is whether a lessened fear of war, specifically of local situations escalating into general nuclear war, would alter those basic strategies in significant ways. At least in theory the policy consequence of GCD might be a new U.S. willingness to encourage genuine independence for the nations of Eastern Europe. Similarly, the Soviet Union or China might adopt different policies if relieved of the fear that all is jeopardized by carrying a high-risk policy too far.

But this may not be the correct interpretation of the situation. It rests on the common assumption that in a situation of significant disarmament the United States, the Soviet Union and China would all be essentially relieved of their fear of war. But would the consequences of war really be less dreadful and unacceptable than at present?

In stage I, when there would remain up to 70 per cent of previous strategic nuclear delivery systems, obviously little would have been done to reduce to relaxed proportions the consequences of nuclear war between the superpowers. In stage II, when there would remain up to 30 per cent, the powers might still deter each other by adopting counter-city strategies, aiming their remaining weapons in such a way as to make a nuclear exchange in some ways even less tolerable than with a greater number of weapons aimed in accordance with a counterforce strategy. And in stage III, even though weapons of mass destruction were finally to be eliminated, a new situation might arise involving remarkable vulnerability of both sides to secretly hidden caches of rockets, or to the surprise introduction of new terror weapons (bombs in orbit, military lasers, secretly unfrozen bacteriological or psychochemical weapons previously dry-stored, etc.). In short, the new fear would be of secret or sudden rearmament.[3] In the modern world, as compared, say, with the 1920's, a rearmament race could be catastrophic. Certainly the marginal political and strategic effects of any surprise—military or technological— would be more drastic than in a highly-armed world. Perhaps then we cannot be so certain that GCD as presently envisaged would necessarily remove the constraints now limiting superpower policies. Perhaps it is not so obvious that they would drastically alter the policies they now follow.

What can now be said about the approach to instability on the part of the world organization that would come into existence under GCD? What sort of positions would the new international order be likely to take with respect to subversion, civil war, and breakdown of internal law and order? Would those positions and the constraints on them be very different from those taken by the same nations in the United Nations at present? Should we assume that with GCD there will have come into existence a genuine international community resting on a real consensus? What is the relation between that degree of consensus and the stake in stability which the international order will have? How would that order express a policy toward instability, particularly if its component parts differed about the merits of individual situations? Would it depend entirely on the great powers? Would it, *per contra,* depend far less on their will and wishes than it does today? These are the questions that go to the meaning of an international military force in a disarming world.

Before turning to the concrete application of that question we shall look briefly at the categories of relevant problems a future disarming world might face and see if the comparisons and contrasts with the past and present shed any light.

LOCAL CONFLICTS UNDER DISARMAMENT—SOME SCENARIOS

The start of a disarmament process implies many other alterations in the picture of world politics. Indeed, even without disarmament, changes

---

[3]This point was well made by Thomas C. Schelling in "The Role of Deterrence in Total Disarmament," *Foreign Affairs,* April 1962, pp. 392-406.

are taking place that affect prospects for international agreement on disarmament, arms control, or peacekeeping of a lesser variety, discussed in more detail in Chapter 6.

Many conflict situations in the present world are local in origin. At the same time, they are among the foremost issues of tension that keep the powers from agreement on fundamental reforms in the world system.

We cannot tell much about even the near future. But the past does offer some clues.

According to recent research at the Massachusetts Institute of Technology,[4] 60 or so "local conflicts" have taken place since World War II—small wars or near-wars involving no direct military confrontation between the United States and the Union of Soviet Socialist Republics. Some are still going on, such as the Arab-Israeli conflict and those in Kashmir and Cyprus. The rate is not necessarily high—an average of 1.5 new ones per year. Over 90 percent so far occurred in the developing areas. American military power was involved, directly and indirectly, in almost one-fourth of these small wars, and Soviet power and influence in approximately the same proportion (though not in all the same areas).

Already changes are discernible in the patterns of local conflict. It used to be that the easiest cases to predict were the inevitable decolonizations, some peaceful, some violent. But now only the Portuguese African territories, South West Africa, and pieces of the Persian Gulf remain pressure points, and even here history could arrange for Angola and Mozambique not to explode, i.e., for them to become happily biracial or perhaps to be protected for 25 years by white South African power—although this seems doubtful.

Neither is the old category of automatic Soviet activism, countered by automatic United States opposition, necessarily valid for the 1970's and 1980's. Not activism but serendipity accounts for the Soviet position in such places as Cuba, Egypt, Syria, Sudan, Algeria, Nigeria, and Somalia. Other people tend to make their own revolutions and then look around for outside support. (The United States did the same after *its* revolution and found it in Jacobin France, to the disgust of the conservative European powers.) An increasingly valid distinction can be made between local conflicts in which the Soviets involve themselves for relatively inexpensive influence, such as those now disturbing various parts of the Moslem world, and conflicts in which Communist regimes, established of, for, and by Communists, are at stake, such as Hungary in

---

[4]See Bloomfield and Leiss, *Controlling Small Wars.*

1956, the Democratic People's Republic of Korea (North Korea) in 1950-1953, Czechoslovakia in 1968, and the Democratic Republic of Vietnam (North Vietnam) throughout.

The sources of deliberate insurgency-fomenting will more likely be the People's Republic of China (Communist China), North Vietnam, Cuba, and possibly Algeria. Of these only China today possesses nuclear weapons and the others are unlikely to have them in the foreseeable future. Conflicts fomented by North Vietnam or Cuba have at least so far been unable to trigger direct Soviet or Chinese involvement and thus do not raise the same danger of escalation one fears in those threatening an American-Soviet collision. But whether or not touched off by ideological arsonists, "wars of liberation" will be in the forefront in the near future as colonial problems were previously. This leads to the second change in the local conflict picture.

This second change is an outgrowth of the virtual end of decolonization; the Congo collapse in 1960 was its harbinger. A second generation of leaders and ideas is already making its appearance in the less developed countries. The "morning-after" phenomenon is becoming institutionalized, with less and less hope that promised growth rates and modernization effects will soon be achieved. This "revolution of risen expectations" will be continuously fueled by growing literacy, radio, television, United Nations Conference on Trade and Development (UNCTAD) sessions, and technical assistance operations. It is ironic that a form of stability has manifested itself in inherently unstable situations such as that in the southern half of Africa or the eastern half of Germany. Paradoxically, the reverse may also be true. Inherently hopeful situations characterized by national independence, aid programs, growing school populations, and concerned citizens may well be the ones most likely to generate violence in the period ahead. In this sense West Africa, Southeast Asia, and the Persian Gulf are not much different from Detroit, the Chicago South Side, Bedford-Stuyvesant, or Roxbury: They all illustrate Peter Alexeivitch Kropotkin's aphorism that the hopeless do not revolt (but once hope is born, watch out!).

Anyone requiring persuasion that change and turmoil will be the order of the day should study the ages of men who rule important parts of the world, often where there is no tradition of peaceful transmission of power. The science of gerontology will not save them from a certain fate (and might give us important clues to their behavior in the meantime): Chiang Kai-shek is 85, Francisco Franco 79, Marshal Tito 79, Jomo Kenyatta 78, Mao Tsetung 78.

It seems inevitable that some years of turmoil, revolution, small wars, and attempted takeovers lies ahead. The failure of overnight modernization will create more fertile soil for "wars of liberation," and the latter, while often arising out of genuine revolutions, will also be fomented or egged on by Peking, Hanoi, or Havana and rather nervously supported by an increasingly stability-favoring Soviet Union (and nervously opposed by an increasingly neo-isolationist United States).

A third source of convulsions lies in the *developed* world. Possibly the most dangerous single situation for the future of mankind is a possible Sino-Soviet nuclear war (perhaps the best argument to reexamine the conventional wisdom that excludes UN involvement from great-power conflicts). Linguistic and religious clashes already bedevil Ulster, Belgium, and Canada. Greece and Portugal face inevitable change.

There may be still other sources. No great stretch of the imagination is needed to foresee a struggle between Hanoi and Peking given the lengthy history of tensions, particularly when the common interest in dealing with an external enemy disappears. Nuclear accidents may become more likely if additional countries get the bomb, and a whole new set of "reassurance" techniques may be needed of the kind developed for United States-Soviet strategic relations.

Local conflicts fall into three "operational" categories. Even in considering a disarming environment, history affords ample evidence that along with unpredictability is a fair amount of continuity in these.

These basic categories seem relevant for the near and middling future, drawn essentially from contemporary conditions.

Basically Internal

(a) The chief cause of internal disorders will doubtless continue to be the multiple and complex revolutions of the non-white peoples. The revolution in one of its aspects is against the dominant position of the white European West; in another it is against their own traditional past. From the history of past revolutions one can predict that this particular one may also eventually be at war with the very conditions that gave it birth and with the policies and people that carried the revolution through its perilous early stages.

(b) In the nation-building process we can anticipate that the simultaneous seemingly contradictory processes of fragmentation and unification will continue, with destabilizing results. Africa, with some 2,000 tribal and other local groupings, can be looked to as a continuous source of potential disorders as peoples within essentially artificial state borders search for their nationhood.

(c) Another potential source of internal disorder arises from the peculiar structures of internal rule with which many emerging countries have commenced their independent existence. Where the sinews of government are lacking only a rash man would predict a future of stability or even viability. When some of the one-party governments lose the momentum of their initial popular support, with no real provision for orderly transfer of power, trouble is certain, particularly if strong military figures emerge.

(d) In Communist-ruled countries the same issue of legitimacy makes for maximum instability in a succession crisis, with incalculable results if party discipline should ever fail to force together all contenders for power at that moment of maximum danger.

(e) There exists what can only be called neo-imperialism on the part of some of the new countries themselves. Examples are Indonesia's acquisition of West New Guinea, complete with Papuans, and under Sukarno its avaricious "confrontation policy" towards Malaysia; India's retention of Moslem-populated portions of Kashmir; and various forms of Pan-Africanism, Pan-Arabism, and Pan-Asianism.

(f) As indicated, some internal instability affects not the developing but the developed countries: ethnic, religious, and linguistic quarrels in Canada, Northern Ireland, and potentially Belgium, Italy, and the United States are examples.

(g) The seeds have already been sown for perhaps the most potentially explosive form of instability and disorder of all—that which may taken place in the multiracial societies of southern Africa. Without statesmanship, vision, and mutual tolerance of an order that seems totally lacking today, explosion in Southern Rhodesia and the Republic of South Africa is only a matter of time.

(h) Perhaps the chief lesson of history is the impossibility of foretelling in any significant detail the way present trends may unfold.

Internal Disorder with External Involvement

It is inconceivable that any GCD treaty in the foreseeable future could seriously dispose of the desire, the capacity, or the intention of some countries to undertake limited intervention, whether called "helping our friends," "assisting national liberation movements," or "answering a call for assistance." Even at the very lowest level of national armaments it will still be possible to lend a group of internal security police to help a neighbor restore local order, or to help police an election, or to rescue one's nationals who are besieged in the consulate. It will still be possible to broadcast messages of support and sympathy, if not downright calls to revolution, to other countries while technically staying within an injunction (which incidentally is now lacking in any draft disarmament plan) against hostile or inflammatory propaganda.

Thus, even if we rule out under GCD the possibility of unilateral intervention by a formal military establishment, there remains a great capacity for affecting situations of local instability even within the changed rules of political life under such a treaty; such intervention will doubtless appear to one state or another, and even to large majorities of states, as legitimate and consistent with disarmament.

Externally Created or Controlled Internal Instability

Will the obvious cases under this heading—deliberate, purposeful subversion and indirect aggression—continue under GCD? There are those who believe that GCD has to mean the end to such policies; that by the act of agreeing to a significant reversal of the arms race all powers will see the world differently and thenceforth refrain from pursuing the struggle by unacceptable means. Those who believe this tend to assume that any struggle which does go on will be pursued by means which *we* consider legitimate, in political and economic fields in which competition follows the ground rules we are used to, and in which we should be glad to compete. And indeed, inspection and enforcement procedures, peacekeeping machinery, and above all the increasing loss of freedom to manipulate threats of force (both because the force is diminishing and, more important, because relative military weakness becomes known publicly) would be costly politically, strategically, and ideologically to those who previously used secrecy to conceal weakness.

Nevertheless the burden of proof is upon those who believe GCD would signal a reversal in the political movements which hitherto have consistently spoken and acted as if their international aims were unlimited. My own belief is that if GCD should come about within a reasonable time span, i.e. within the next decade, we would not be entitled by any available evidence to assume the end of efforts at subversion and indirect—and perhaps also direct—aggression.

THE APPLICATION OF INTERNATIONAL FORCE

We have now set the stage for considering the actual application of international peacekeeping capacities to local instability problems in a disarming and disarmed world. By putting this range of problems in a disarmament setting we have introduced several constraints most of which have already been mentioned in passing—the lower level of strategic military power available to the largest nations; the changed atmosphere that will accompany, or at least follow, agreements to reduce weapons and military forces; the possibility that some nations' aims will remain unlimited, hostile to non-believers, and capable of using any remaining means of achieving those ends; and the threat of a rearmament race. (A related factor I have not mentioned is the substantial *arrière pensée* we can assume on the part of military leaders of all major nations in a disarmament agreement, wholly apart from ideology.)

A final constraint is the deterrent and possibly punitive power of an international military force in the face of threats to stability of the sort we have been discussing.[5]

Such planning as has been done has tended to start with a hypothesis that may be questionable. It is that since under GCD national armaments are to be replaced by international forces, it follows that, during and increasingly toward the close of the disarming process, international forces will be expected to cope with all military problems, including those caused by local instability. The only way to test this hypothesis is to pose the crucial questions and see what evidence may be adduced to help supply tentative answers.

From our point of view here the crucial questions are two: whether and how the proposed structure of international peacekeeping can cope with the problems involved in local instability; and how the process of actual decision-making—that is to say of political control of the use of military power, both at the international decision-making level and at the level of actual operations on the ground—might operate.

To examine the first question requires some still newer categories. To find out whether and how an augmented international organization can cope with problems of local instability, we look to the political processes of the institution itself. The key to these processes in any future institution we can foresee at this time is the position of the principal states. Unless one envisages some future political Lilliput in which the midgets dance freely over the bound bodies of those possessing significant national power, the great powers will largely dominate the strategic scene. Until late in stage III of GCD this seems the only prudent hypothesis.

The categories of great-power involvement in the relatively low levels of local violence we are here considering are three:

Great-Power Agreement

The easy category of disputes in the modern world is that in which the United States and the Soviet Union are in agreement. The Suez episode of 1956 illustrated dramatically the force of such agreement. The two superpowers, once in accord, can endow the United Nations with all the powers it requires to subdue a small-scale conflict.[6] This,

---

[5]Hans J. Morgenthau develops in his essay in Part Two a theoretical approach to the relation between police power and maintenance of the status quo.

[6]See the reasoning employed in *Controlling Conflict in the 1970's*, Panel Report of the United Nations Association of the USA, New York, 1969.

the dream of Chapter VII of the present Charter, would apply equally well in a disarming world in which both powers concurred on the need to dispatch an international force to deal with a given situation of local instability. The decision-making process in the organization would be operating under its most favorable conditions, at least in our recent experience. The force in the field, if it ran into difficulties, would presumably be backed up with the overwhelming power of the two.

However, this picture has some darker tones to it. First, it will be recalled that when Soviet enthusiasm for exploiting the disarray of the West in Suez further inspired it to make the obviously mocking proposal of a joint Soviet-American force, the United States instantly drew back and reaffirmed the underlying strength of its attachment to Britain and France; the "aggressors" were our friends, and the matter was not to be carried to the point of humiliating, degrading, or otherwise punishing them. Also, as shown in the Congo, a joint decision to apply an international force to a local situation can quickly evaporate if in practice it comes into conflict with the larger strategic aims of a great power. The Soviet vote in favor of the Congo force did not stop it from castigating the operation within weeks and proceeding to a long-term campaign of attempting to sabotage not only the UN operation in the Congo but also the United Nations itself.

It is possible and even likely that because of its special nature a local disorder involving highly complex internal politics, racial enmities, or shifting international coalitions (the Congo model) could remain intractable to easy settlement even if an international force were introduced with full agreement among the principal powers. Even when the Soviet Union and the United States pursued the same policy in 1947 toward the creation of Israel and in favor of the Israeli side in the first Palestine war, this had little or no effect on the long-term prospects for settlement of the basic dispute. (Agreement between the two did, however, partition the land, create cease-fire machinery, and in 1956 produce the first real UN force.) Similarly, when the United States and the Soviet Union took essentially parallel positions in the late 1940's in favor of a Kashmir settlement, and in 1965 in ending renewed hostilities between India and Pakistan, it had little visible effect on the underlying tensions growing out of deep-seated causes such as communal conflict. (But the UN observer groups did have an effect on the continued cessation of hostilities.)

The two superpowers can be in harmony under GCD—indeed, by customary reasoning, ought to be in greater harmony in view of their attachment to an arrangement whose overturn would mean renewal of a dangerous arms race—but what if other "great powers" demur?

Finally, and perhaps most ironically, if the Charter dream of great-power unanimity were to become a reality in view of the high stakes the principal powers believed they had in preservation of the new order, the countervailing sentiment of the smaller powers might well reassert itself as they watched their 1945 nightmare of solid great-power hegemony come to life.

With full appreciation of these complications, United States-Soviet cooperation in a disarming world could well provide the basic political precondition for an international decision to intervene with force in a situation of local instability, particularly a situation of such universal concern that other great-power opposition would not appreciably deflect the decision.

Easiest of all would be a decision to intervene in the Portuguese colonies of Angola and Mozambique if indigenous forces succeeded in creating ungovernable turmoil for the Portuguese, or if the Portuguese pulled out, or if in either case an Algerian-style situation arose between the Africans and the growing number of *colonos* (who appear determined to hold out regardless of what Lisbon might do). South West Africa might also be an overwhelmingly agreed-upon case if the South African control slipped.

A conflict in Rhodesia in which the outnumbered whites ever lost control over the situation would pose exquisitely difficult problems for the international community. Appeals from the whites would undoubtedly be met by South Africa and would confront the United Kingdom with painful choices. Appeals from the blacks would be met enthusiastically by others. But such an explosive situation would clearly require an international military presence as a *force majeure* to end bloodshed and restore a semblance of order, and the dangers of the situation would undoubtedly result in widespread political support for the force.

Some Great-Power Disagreement

One can imagine cases in which it might be considerably more difficult to form an effective constitutional majority for an international force to deal with a locally unstable situation even if a majority of small countries favored it. If the United States or the Soviet Union objected mildly, a force might still be created and used, as it has been in Cyprus since 1964. But until some later stage of disarmament the force would not be a standing one and would therefore have to be raised. The attendant difficulties of finance and logistical support, particularly airlift and sealift, would give the great powers an effective veto even if the latter is not written into the procedures.

Violent objections by secondary powers to the point of also jeopardizing the agreement could make it difficult, if not impossible, to go through with an international action. Even with Algeria out of the way, France has indicated hostility to international forces for peacekeeping. China, even if somehow persuaded into a GCD agreement, is unlikely to support "bourgeois" political-military actions, at least some of which would deal with situations termed "wars of national liberation" in its lexicon.

The British may be forced into cruel dilemmas by the possibility of international military action. And the United States might for the first time face the prospect of a UN force introduced into this hemisphere, even though it prefers an OAS force (as it did—successfully—to give multilateral coloration to its unilateral landing in the Dominican Republic in 1965). But another time it might not care enough to insist on frustration of or opposition to the international political system.

Violent Great-Power Disagreement

I have suggested that the crucial factor in GCD would be the feelings with which the major powers regarded the prospects of renewal of the arms race, and the ways in which they construed their security in the light of that prospect. It was all very well in the past for the Soviet bluffs to be called in Korea (1950) and Cuba (1962) and for the Soviets to cut their losses with fair grace.

The world may have watched impotently as Soviet tanks crushed the Hungarian uprising of 1956, and as Warsaw Pact forces occupied Czechoslovakia in 1968. But another uprising could find the world community favoring UN intervention in a collapsed East Germany or a strife-torn Albania. The Soviets would have to measure the consequences of a repressive unilateral intervention against multilateral action with its equally unpredictable consequences.

We are thus reminded of the difficulty peacekeeping machinery has in coping with internal collapse or subversion in which a great power believes it has an overwhelmingly important stake. One can imagine a "war of national liberation" in Latin America opening to Moscow—or Peking—new prospects; local disorders in Outer Mongolia or Sinkiang as a result of the deep-seated power struggle between China and Russia, with one power favoring international intervention for "policing" purposes and the other bitterly opposed; or a situation in the Middle East, Africa, or Asia that two or more powers believed involved their "vital interests." If a majority decided over the opposition of a superpower to introduce international forces, any of these might strain the peacekeeping machinery to the point of collapsing the system itself. The decision-making process establishing and politically controlling the means of peacekeeping might not work here until some distant stage when the international community possessed such force as to be able to coerce any offender however large or obstinate.

The case of a South African eruption has deliberately not been placed within any of the three categories. The South African situation, with its predominantly racial flavor and the problems for some European peoples if the question of international intervention arises, might present the most difficult challenge of all to an international peacekeeping system. If the situation deteriorated to the point of a total collapse of law and order and uncontrolled bloodshed, perhaps both white and non-white sectors of the international community would join in applying the only available remedy. If things were not quite that bad, the white government might go a long way in maintaining control, perhaps with the help of white volunteers and mercenaries, while the Africans and other colored peoples appealed to the non-white races—and to Moscow and Peking—on grounds of human rights and racial solidarity. These circumstances could be corrosive for the international decision-making process.

CONCLUSION

Some of the factors give promise that within limits the international community can use an international force to deal with certain instances of local instability where in an earlier age the great powers once sent in troops to fill the vacuum and restore law and order. But I have suggested that the job cannot always be done by an international force. Vacuums will always exist, and the need for stability requires that they be filled in acceptable ways. But it is a long road historically from the Boxer Rebellion to Luanda or Johannesburg—or Berlin. The road becomes tortuous at those points where the great powers, singly or in pairs, are themselves the creators, controllers, or abettors of the particular disorder, or if they are divided on quasi-religious grounds about its desired outcome.

It is evident that the first category—the major powers in essential agreement—is the one in which political control is the least complicated or difficult. The decision to use a force, the definition of its mission, and the instructions to the Secretary General about its deployment are all well within the range of the possible. Political control is thus established, and it remains only to make the operation a success in fulfilling its mission. (As the Congo showed, this may not be so easy.)

The second category—the great powers in some disagreement, but not necessarily willing to risk all, particularly if we postulate their increasing dependence on international security mechanisms in a disarming world—

is not very different except in detail. When the chips are down, it is likely that the required political consensus will develop, particularly if the convenient escape hatch of abstention is still available (as in Cyprus). The involved great power will find it expedient to turn back, disassociating itself from its protege or proxy. At the least, while continuing its grand strategy it will adjust its tactics in order not to run risks so high as to break up the system. This sort of situation will complicate tremendously the problem of political control at the administrative level of the Secretary-General, who will be given the task of carrying out what is likely to be an ambiguous directive, accompanied by contradictory instructions and under conditions of sporadic and uncertain support by members. (The Congo came to involve all these qualities.)

The final category—one or more great powers irrevocably in opposition to international action because of their stake in the local situation—is the most difficult for the system to master. Action taken in the face of it will at the worst destroy the system, at best supply highly controversial political directives to a force. The exact degree of difficulty depends on multiple factors: the exact stage of disarmament, the evolution of international machinery able to coerce great powers, the growth and use of adjudicatory organs and attendant enforcement measures, the existence of provisions for genuine peaceful change, the actual mechanics of decision-making under the proposed system (whether in terms of weighted voting, qualified [three-quarters, four-fifths, etc.] majorities, or other special features), and whether there exists a fall-back arrangement comparable to Article 51 or the "Uniting for Peace" procedure which even under disarming conditions might ensure that the law-abiding faction of the community could assert its will for peace and order.[7]

---

[7]For some proposals both on majorities and on voting, see Lincoln Bloomfield "To Resurrect the United Nations," *New York Times,* July 21, 1971.

Four

THE SOVIET VIEW OF INTERNATIONAL FORCE

The Soviet Union's conduct in the United Nations has consistently reflected its persistent suspicion of "supra-national" armies.[1] All attempts to endow international institutions with any real power, such as the negotiations for Article 43 forces to be put at the disposal of the Security Council, as well as the Uniting for Peace Resolution in 1950 and subsequent efforts to field UN troops, have invariably met with Soviet insistence on the right to veto so long as the Soviet Union is in a minority position. The Congo experience brought to a head the tendencies which had already long since been evident.

In dealing with specific decisions to mount UN field operations during the postwar years the Soviets have always—or almost always—tied their position to their broader insistence on using the Security Council, where the minority position of a great power can be protected. Alternatively, they have proposed arrangements for the operation of international agencies, such as the so-called Troika Principle, which even without the power of veto in the Security Council would serve to protect Soviet interests against the feared coalition of the non-Communist powers. The Soviet Union abstained in the vote establishing the UN Emergency Force in Egypt in November 1956 on the ground that only the Security Council could approve the creation of any UN armed forces. The Soviets also abstained on the resolution setting up the UN Observation Group in Lebanon in the summer of 1958, and in the same period they opposed the advanced planning tentatively proposed by the Secretary General with a view to making contingents more readily available.

---

[1]Alexander Dallin, *The Soviet Union at the United Nations* (New York: Praeger, 1962).

The Soviet Union did vote in the Security Council in favor of ONUC in July 1960, but doubtless, as with its temporary absence from the Security Council when the Council put the United Nations into the Korean fight ten years before, it soon came to regret its impetuousness. In June 1963, with regard to the decision to send a 200-man observer corps to Yemen, the Soviets insisted that it should be dealt with by the Security Council and not by the Secretary General.

The next year when the UN Security Council created UNFICYP Moscow, after abstaining on a paragraph empowering the Secretary General, joined in making the resolution unanimous. In 1965 it voted to strengthen UNMOGIP, although later complaining about excessive Secretariat discretion over UNIPOM. After the June war of 1967 an enlargement of UN observer operations along the Suez Canal was achieved without formal objection.

Behind the superficial manifestations of this policy lies a profound cleavage between Communist and Western views about the very nature of international organization.

By any authentic interpretation of Communist doctrine a powerful non-Communist supranational organization at this stage of history can only mean a plot by the capitalist powers to check Communism's forward momentum and destroy its hard-won gains. By this interpretation existing international organizations such as the United Nations must be checked when they go beyond a purely servicing function. If they cannot be checked, the Communists prefer that they be eliminated. Moreover, even more explicitly than the West, the Soviets reject any implied relationship between disarmament and world government. Thus, whether or not the Soviets really want some significant disarmament, they tend to view with profound suspicion any attempt to impose a new and, by definition, anti-Communist international order which under the guise of disarmament controls would frustrate their movement. It is not even a question of degree. At the level of minimum arms control the issue is still that of penetration into Soviet society by a necessarily hostile power. And when one goes up the scale of disarmament measures toward truly comprehensive programs, the conflict sharpens acutely; the Soviets determinedly oppose both the Western assertion that supranational institutions are required and the equally conventional Western thesis that the necessary amount of inspection, political authority, and the like increases with the degree of disarmament.

When it comes to the notion of world peace forces to take the place of national armies under general and complete disarmament, the Soviet position has been a curious one, apparently shifting in the course of the late 1950's and early 1960's, but perhaps not really shifting at all in any fundamental sense of the political relationships at stake.

In October 1959 Premier Khrushchev addressed the Supreme Soviet on the subject of disarmament, making it clear that the international forces gambit on the part of the West was doubtless a ruse as to which right-thinking Communists should be highly suspicious:

> The discussions on disarmament have hardly begun, and the skeptics have raised the question of what international forces should be created in place of the national forces. . . . When all countries disarm and all armies have no arms, then nobody will be able to start a war. The question arises: For what purpose, then, are supranational armed forces necessary?[2]

Secretary of State Herter's February 18, 1960 speech to the National Press Club, quoted earlier, which set the tone for the Western official line regarding international forces and disarmament, set in motion a series of Soviet responses. The first one came in the form of relatively lengthy analysis of the problem by S. Vladimirov in the Soviet journal *International Affairs* in April of that spring. In that article Mr. Vladimirov laid out with clarity the underlying Communist view of the Western line. His first point was that disarmament and international armed forces were incompatible concepts since disarmament would remove the need for any such peacekeeping activities:

> Disarmament will remove mutual suspicion, mistrust and fear of cataclysmic war; these feelings will give way to trust, mutual understanding, and businesslike co-operation. The only sensible policy, the policy of peaceful co-existence and economic competition between the two social and political systems, will reign supreme in international relations.

Heaping scorn on the notion that international armies would have anything to do, Mr. Vladimirov took a look at the potential threat from such national forces as would remain:

> The "possible threat" to peace on the part of the national police or militia is likewise a poor argument. Even with a runaway imagination it is hard to picture that these contingents will be a threat to other countries in a disarmed world with all-embracing international controls and an atmosphere of mutual trust, considering that they will be small numerically, equipped only with light arms, and dispersed over the home territory.

And in the event of some state "complicating the international situation by its actions," even though this should not happen, given the pitiful

[2]*Pravda,* November 1, 1959, p. 3.

capabilities of remaining national forces, "there will always remain the possibility of applying moral pressure as well as economic and political sanctions provided for in international agreements."

If this unexpected faith in moral pressure did not suffice as an argument, there was the further reassuring belief in the inevitability of ideological progress:

> It should be specifically emphasized that the forces of peace, already a powerful deterrent to imperialist war moves, will multiply immeasurably in a world completely disarmed. Their impact on the development of international relations, which is growing from day to day, will become even more pronounced when, in a disarmed world, the bellicose imperialist circles are deprived of the material means of starting war. The forces of peace will not allow anyone to return to the old practices of the arms race and international gambles.

As a result of all these factors, "a disarmed world does not need an international police force."

Having thus disposed of the logic of the problem, Vladimirov then turned to the real issue: the villainous hidden purposes of those who were making such preposterous suggestions. The real motive in setting up an international gendarmerie corps, he said, was "to turn it into an instrument of a certain group of Western Powers . . . the West as before is striving for an international military instrument which, officially an organ of the United Nations, would in practice be at the beck and call of a certain group of powers. And the purpose? What the Western powers want most is to use the UN flag to secure privileges to promote their selfish interests."

Specifically the Western powers were seen by Mr. Vladimirov as planning to use international forces for the following purposes:

> First, to fight the national-liberation movement in the colonies and dependencies.
>
> Second, to crush any action by the democratic forces within the capitalist countries.
>
> Third, the plans for such a police force are spearheaded against the peoples of the small countries.
>
> Fourth, some people in the West plan to use the international police force to exert military and political pressure on the disarmed Socialist countries.
>
> In other words, the present campaign in the West for an international police force sets itself tasks which are not merely foreign to peace and universal security but clash with them.

That fall Mr. Khrushchev again spoke before the UN General Assembly. At some time in the interval preceding this speech the Soviet Union apparently decided to accept, at least verbally, the principle that some kind of international military force should be a concomitant of disarmament. For according to Premier Khrushchev the Soviet Union had prepared a position for the disarmament discussions in June 1960 along these lines:

> After our proposals were submitted in September last year, the question was raised of how to ensure the maintenance of international law and order under conditions of general and complete disarmament.... We carefully studied these considerations and drew the conclusion that the only realistic possibility in present conditions would be, in accordance with the United Nations Charter, to place, when necessary, police (militia) detachments at the disposal of the Security Council to ensure keeping the peace.[3]

As Alexander Dallin wrote, "the change was significant if one contemplates that it required overcoming a deeply ingrained hostility and ceasing the intense campaign just waged in opposition to such a plan. Once reached, the decision became part of the Soviet disarmament scheme."[4] Thus in his several addresses to the General Assembly in September and early October 1960 Premier Khrushchev said the Soviets agreed in principle to the idea of international forces:

> An identical point of view has materialized in our proposals, as well as in those of the countries making up the NATO military alignment, regarding the necessity to follow up agreement on disarmament with the creation of armed forces of all countries under international control, to be used by the United Nations as decided by the Security Council.

But he insisted on linking agreement in principle with the Troika solution, ridiculing the idea that such forces could be under the command of the Secretary General.[5] The Soviet delegation tabled a draft disarmament resolution calling upon states "to make available to the Security Council, where necessary, units from the contingents of police (militia) retained by states for maintaining internal order."[6]

The die appeared cast for a policy of public acceptance of the Western world government corollary, but this was illusory. The notion

[3]*New York Times*, June 4, 1960.
[4]*Op. cit.*, p. 139.
[5]*Documents on Disarmament, 1960*, Department of State Publication 7172, p. 276.
[6]UN Document A/C.1/L 249, October 13, 1960.

of a world force at the disposal of a majority appeared to the Soviets—as it probably also appears to the US Senate, the French and British governments, and many others when they are being fairly honest with themselves—to be full of potential dangers and injustices. The ambivalence of the Soviet attitude was revealed by Y. Korovin in an article in February 1961, in which the logic of the Soviet line seemingly conceded the need for international forces after general and complete disarmament, but for rhetorical and polemical purposes only. The existence of an international force after disarmament was completed was, according to Korovin, quite unnecessary. But for such a force to be constructed *before* the world was totally disarmed would compound the dangers that make the same proposal in a disarmed world dangerous and unnecessary too. Thus the circle was closed.

> The formation of an international army before general and complete disarmament is effected would lead in practice either to the rise of unprecedented "supermilitarism," if the international armed forces were stronger than the armies of the Soviet Union and the United States, or to the perpetuation of extreme inequality in international relations if the international force were employed only against small and weak countries.[7]

If the Soviet planners believe as deeply as they have appeared to in the potential dangers for the Soviet Union in a world in which the Red Army was demobilized and Moscow's rockets destroyed, and in which justice would be administered by a majority still susceptible to Western control, they nonetheless somehow have been able to continue publicly to swallow their profound doubts in order to accept formulae for a negotiated agreement with the West. The most striking of the formulae is that of the Joint Statement of Agreed Principles for Disarmament Negotiations agreed to between the United States and the Soviet Union on September 20, 1961, quoted earlier.

The Soviet draft treaty for general and complete disarmament was originally submitted by the Soviets to the General Assembly on September 23, 1960, was circulated at the request of the Soviet delegation to the United Nations on November 8, 1961, and has been reiterated at intervals since. In it there is no provision for an international military force in the first or second stage of the proposed treaty arrangements except for the following:

> In the second stage joint studies will be undertaken of the following measures to be implemented in the third stage: (a)

[7]Y. Korovin, "Disarmament and Security," *International Affairs* (USSR) February, 1961, p. 57.

measures to ensure observance of the treaty on general and complete disarmament after the implementation of all the measures provided for by that treaty; (b) measures to maintain peace and security in accordance with the United Nations Charter under conditions of general and complete disarmament.

But in the third stage, in the very last numbered item in the Soviet draft treaty we have the following:

Measures for preserving peace and security in accordance with the Charter of the United Nations will be put into effect. States will undertake, where necessary, to place at the disposal of the Security Council units from the contingents of the police (militia) remaining at their disposal.[8]

The most explicit Soviet statement on peacekeeping guidelines in recent years was in 1964.[9] The Security Council's paramount role was reaffirmed; UN forces should be drawn from Western, neutral, and communist states—an echo of the post-Congo "troika" concept that came close to wrecking the Secretariat; and in an oblique acceptance of Dag Hammarskjöld's Suez guidelines, permanent members of the Security Council—the Big Five—should not be among the troop contributors. The Military Staff Committee would be the Council's source of military advice and assistance. "Supplier" countries would have a voice in peacekeeping decisions. (In 1970 great power participation in a Mideast peacekeeping force was hinted at.)

There had been nothing to indicate that peacekeeping under disarmament would operate on any very different principles. One is forced to conclude, on the evidence before us at the present time in history, that the Soviet Union has no intention of voluntarily relinquishing to a majority of non-Communist states the effective control of power in the world, specifically the capacity to enforce on the Soviet Union the will of that non-Communist majority. At the same time, the Soviet Union for its own reasons has accepted Western insistence on the international forces corollary, but it has been careful at all times to keep this explicitly within the framework of the great-power veto. In the Soviet draft treaty the reference to the Security Council is in truth a reference back to the world of 1945 in which under Article 43 such forces were to be placed at the disposal of the Security Council, where the great-power veto obtains.

One might even conclude that the Soviet leadership is more aware of

[8]UN Document A/4505, September 23, 1960.
[9]GAOR, 19th Session, Annex 21 (1964-1965), pp. 2-4.

the power implications of the general and complete disarmament program and its world government corollary than the planners in the West seemed to be. For there is consistency between the Soviet view of power relationships in the present world and its view of such relationships under disarmament. Since this consistency takes a form which is in important ways destructive of progress in the attainment of a more satisfactory world order, Western policy must do all in its power to substitute for the Soviet vision of the future one which reflects real harmony and trust among nations organized efficiently to keep the peace.

There is one conceivable change in the arrangements for organizing international forces that could have a serious effect on the present Communist view of their utility and propriety. That would be the acceptance of units from Communist states in international military forces in the present world, or indeed any other kind of world. One can envisage certain future circumstances in which forces from the Soviet bloc would find their way into an international UN expedition—as in the Middle East crises of the early 1970's.

Against this stark but indispensable backdrop of political and ideological opposition, matched by an as yet unplumbed reluctance of others including ourselves to accept the full implications of the "world government corollary" of present disarmament plans, what conclusions can we draw?

Five

DISARMAMENT AND FORCE—SOME CONCLUSIONS

There are two fundamental questions. One is that of reality—will any of this come about? Does it belong within any rational time span as we look ahead? The other is—if the prospects are poor for achieving present disarmament goals, what can be done to improve these prospects, including if necessary revising the goals themselves?

For both comprehensive disarmament and its corollary—limited world government—two difficulties stand out from our analysis as paramount. One is the historic quantum jump implied in centralization of military and political power in the world, a revolutionary concept that we ourselves may not have grasped or accepted any more than have others. The other is the presently insurmountable difficulty of bringing into any unified, democratic, world-wide system the still very conflictual relationship between the Soviet Union, the People's Republic of China, and the "NATO West." The very notion of a politico-military framework superior to all three, plus the Third World, today seems remote.

Alongside these dilemmas the details of structure are almost trivial. Defects in those details can hardly account for the likelihood that general and complete disarmament is stalled for present purposes and, barring wholly unforeseen changes in the political and strategic situation, is likely to remain so in its present all-out form.

If a genuine world authority *were* to become politically feasible, there is no dearth of applicable blueprints for its inner detail. There is no theoretical reason, for example, why the present United Nations could not be transformed by Charter amendment into an instrument of effective global power. Alternatively, the process could be a completely new start, in the way the Articles of Confederation were scrapped to write the United States Constitution. But it is not terribly important which method is used. The paramount issue is not, as some suppose, the difficulty of amending the Charter. It is to reach a political consensus about ground rules in the world. If this came to pass, it would be a secondary question whether to incorporate the changes in the present Charter or to write a new one. The overwhelming central fact would be the loss of control of their military power by individual nations. If this became achievable, the details would surely not be insurmountable.

If on the evidence the Communist powers are unlikely to go this route in the present era, it then becomes easy to blame the stalemate on them.

At the same time there is increasing evidence that the Soviets, like Americans, sense a deep interest in somehow moderating the strategic arms race. So to stop with the conclusion that the Soviets are blocking the presently charted road to disarmament has the fatal defect that, while emotionally satisfying, it does not advance the world toward the urgent security goal, and in fact may be concealing such real opportunities as exist.

On the assumption that the national interests of the states concerned and the common good of mankind require that ways be found to significantly moderate the arms race, it is possible that the superpowers have painted themselves into a corner with present GCD plans, which have become the enemy not only of the good but also of the possible. Some people may be content with the predicament; those who have a commitment to military solutions will no longer support—as some on both sides do now—a disarmament policy when it begins to look even slightly realistic. But if the goal of significantly moderating the arms race has a high priority, political risks must be taken for it.

The most urgent charge on disarmament planners is thus not technical but political. To escape from the present policy prison requires serious and urgent rethinking of the political corollaries to disarmament, freed of stereotypes. If serious national interests in realistic arms control and disarmament measures are to be made to converge even moderately, policy must be both believable and attainable. The present proposals for GCD have neither of these qualities. Total disarmament has impressed few responsible people as desirable, or credible.

What disables GCD planning at root is its "world government corollary," by which significant reductions in armaments can be brought about and controlled only at the price of greatly increased international political authority and military power, to the point where the state system as we know it would be radically transformed. Under present and foreseeable political conditions it is likely that this corollary and therefore the plan as a whole can be implemented only by war, or in some unspecified way persuading everyone, including ourselves, to agree to live with political concomitants that today are safely in the realm of propaganda.

It is here that the question of timing becomes crucial. One perceives two means of achieving the necessary motivation for all-out disarmament.

The path to which a statistician might attach the highest probability on the basis of historic evidence is that of long-term evolution. Under this process it is difficult to foresee a limited world government[1] within twenty-five years at the earliest, fifty years more conservatively. Only this path would be likely to embrace the indispensable process of community-building, involving a series of organic stages of consensus, value formation, and the experiences of common enterprise, which must underlie a true international polity.

A second path can be envisaged leading to "crash disarmament." This would involve a grave crisis or limited nuclear exchange sufficient to bring about a sudden transformation in national attitudes through a series of traumatic shocks. Such a set of unnerving trips to or over the brink might happen. Yet it is this contingency that least supports present policies. It is this one that offers least chance of overcoming ingrained political habits. It is this one that least supplies the vital underpinnings of community that give life and durability to a political society.

I conclude that disarmament planning, in order to become more realistic and thus more likely to be feasible, must reduce the connection with a centrally armed world government that the world may not be ready, able, or willing to accept. For many of the same reasons, planning should modify its presently grandiose and politically unimaginable goals that envisage total disarmament down to levels of internal security needs. A more realistic plan for serious reduction of existing military forces to more moderate levels, under suitable—but not excessive—verification, would then carry a corollary that would be not only realistic but also urgently desirable. Existing international institutions for peacekeeping should be strengthened, but not asked to take on impossible and even self-destructive burdens. The pooling of existing military forces to resist major armed aggression would remain for the foreseeable future the function of a constitutional majority at whatever level of delegated sovereignty and reserved powers the political traffic will bear.

What might be labeled "Significant Arms Control Plus a Responsible Capability" must for the foreseeable future connote the ability to carry out the most important national commitments, which means some usable national power. However, it also connotes the ability to deal with

---

[1]By far the most widely cited disarmament plan involving limited world government is the so-called Clark-Sohn plan. See Grenville Clark, and Louis B. Sohn, *World Peace Through World Law*, 2nd Ed. (rev.) (Cambridge: Harvard University Press, 1960).

what may be the most pervasive problems of a disarming world—local conflicts. The ultimate goal should be a strategic and political world all nations have at least a chance of accepting as credible. It could take the form of a new three-stage plan which ends short of general and complete disarmament; it could mean elimination of the present Stage III; or it could be a new "non-stage" plan.

The peacekeeping arm of world organization can develop from the modest proposal outlined later on and eventually provide a stand-by or even standing constabulary-type force, probably of well under 100,000 men, capable of the lower-level actions ranging from observation and patrol to repelling clear cases of aggression across borders by minor states, and even by middle powers, so long as the significant powers agree to intervention. But a form of veto remains as ultimate protection for the great powers and those most closely related to them. However qualified the majority in the Assembly, there can be no pretense in plans made at this stage of history that nations such as the United States and the Soviet Union could be physically coerced by military power in the hands of a numerical majority of states.

My own research strongly suggests that there may be a significant threshold, possibly somewhere in Stage II of disarmament as it is now envisaged, which represents a dividing line between the capacity of nations to act responsibly, and that nether bank of "the undiscover'd country" of a UN monopoly of military power to whose bourn no traveler may in fact ever go, let alone return. It is possible that the fundamental requirements of minimum deterrence, significant disarmament, and the ensuring of equilibrium in the international system may not have to depend on going all the way to a totally disarmed world, or on having to contemplate living with an unacceptable international political structure.

Six

THE PROSPECTS FOR PEACEKEEPING

When the United Nations Charter was drafted in 1945 the provisions for keeping the peace had to be drawn up in the abstract. There was no tangible enemy, crises were in the future, and commitments were made in a vacuum. It was only when it became clear what the world was really like that "peacekeeping" was invented. It turned out that in most conflict situations there was no definable aggressor or victim, that the danger was uncontrolled escalation of local conflicts into the nuclear realm, and that the real enemy was a fantastically complex set of instabilities, inequities, and passions to which 1945 international ground rules were inadequately related.

In the 1970's the need for international peacekeeping must be related to the real situations one can foresee. The capacity of the international system for peacekeeping must be calculated in terms of the real political environment.

The postwar years can be divided into four periods of peacekeeping. In the first period, 1945 to 1956, "peacekeeping," in the sense of noncoercive military forces under the banner of the UN, was unknown. In the second period, 1956 to 1965, following the invention of just such forces for Palestine and the Congo, peacekeeping seemed full of promise as the answer to the question of law and order in the "ghettos," so to speak, of the world. In the third period, 1965 to the early 1970's, it became dubious, contentious, and subject to the disabilities and suspicions of all efforts to tackle turbulence in the developing areas as problems of "law and order," intelligence, and, as it were, urban renewal. What of period four?

"Peacekeeping" can come to mean some new and different things demanded by changing times. Indeed, until now peacekeeping has meant something very different to the chief parties thereto. In the logic the United States has recently followed, it has among other things meant an agency for "stability" and thus the prevention of the spread of Communism. To the Soviet Union it has meant a convenient agency for pacification of situations that become uncontrollable and thus dangerous to Soviet interests as long as peacekeeping operations themselves remain controllable.

To actual peacekeepers—the Scandinavians, Canadians, Indians, Pakistanis, Brazilians, and others who have sent the troops—it has been a contribution to an improved world order. And to many of the actual and potential "peacekeepees" it connotes something entirely different: the means to achieve one side's objectives of power, justice, or retribution against its enemy—or, a great-power imposed limit on their freedom of action.

It takes all four of these factions to peacekeep, and inevitably different interests will be at stake. But great-power relations remain central to the prior question of how important and dangerous local conflicts become to the world, and the ideological element has been in fact crucial in putting the Big Two at odds on peacekeeping. A crude symmetry seems to have been developing between American and Soviet desires, at least in some areas, to restrain third world states from generating international violence (though not internal violence). However imperfect, this is the central possibility on which to construct a peacekeeping and conflict-minimizing strategy for the future.

If a limited common interest has developed between the United States and the Soviet Union to limit local conflicts, it has surely grown out of the acknowledgment that unilateral intervention is not very profitable and may on occasion entail costs that far outweigh the presumed benefits. In the United States few secrets are kept, and it is clear that there is a growing indisposition at all levels to see this country become directly involved at the present time with its own military forces in new local conflicts. It may be that only a clear and present danger will override these fears of getting "involved" in another such situation, at least in the immediate future. As an American one can welcome this shift as a healthy and overdue corrective for over-involvement around the world based on the assumption that the United States had a stake in the provisional outcome of virtually every local situation or that a temporary victory for anti-United States elements anywhere constituted a prima facie threat to United States security.

We do not really know anything about the internal debates which may be taking place within Soviet leading circles that lie behind the modest evidence of Soviet concern for improved means of controlling and limiting local conflict. One can only hope that Moscow has also learned about the limits to local "victory," the costs of being, in effect, controlled by a local faction one supports, or the evanescence of even a billion dollars worth of investment in arms (as in Indonesia—though that could change too).

Having rejected unilateral intervention, the tendency may be to retreat into hand-wringing rather than a search for constructive alternatives. An important alternative would be for the superpowers to carve out spheres, not of influence, but of abstention (or restraint, as former Undersecretary of State Elliot Richardson chose to call them). If the United States, for one, is not willing to use its military power directly to intervene in some local conflict situations that may upset a local or regional balance, a wider peace may be threatened, requiring urgent measures of pacification; or longer-term stability may require that the roots of the conflict be dealt with through peaceful change procedures of peacemaking. In other words action may still be needed.[1]

Put differently, a decision not to intervene, whatever its other merits, may sometimes leave a dangerous vacuum. This defines a broad interest in *conflict-prevention* and lends urgency to improving two elements that are traditionally weak: 1) a *conflict-minimizing or controlling approach* and 2) *multilateral substitutes for American or Soviet power in local conflict situations.* A decision not to intervene unilaterally needs to be accompanied by nonmilitary or peacekeeping measures that are likely to deal effectively with conflict-generating pressures. The inexorable logic of this gives new pertinence to the availability of agencies of action aimed at tranquilizing local conflict or at least furnishing substitutes for superpower unilateral military intervention in order to prevent, contain, or terminate conflicts—what I have called a "strategy of conflict control."

In other words, far from being the ultimate decision, the decision against unilateral military intervention ought to be regarded as only the preliminary to *other* equally—or more—important decisions in the political, economic, social, psychological, and multilateral spheres. There is an undiminished need for treatment of acute symptoms, i.e., actions toward deescalation, separation of combatants, peacekeeping devices, aid to regimes enjoying popular support, control of arms shipments, and the like. There is an even greater unfilled need for longer-range remedies that are addressed to causes.

In the face of predicted conflicts accompanied by United States retrenchment the "multilateral option" is clearly a most important means for achieving the needed precrisis conflict-prevention and the later conflict-limiting functions. Long relegated to the realm of political

[1]See Lincoln P. Bloomfield, "After Neo-Isolationism, What?" *Bulletin of the Atomic Scientist,* April, 1971.

theology—except at times of great need—it is called for now by the logic of the times. At the same time it remains elusive and by no means as promising as it was a decade ago.

There has been some movement toward revival of peacekeeping. The UN Special Committee on Peacekeeping Operations (committee of 33) has made a good, if modest, start in its "Model I" which spells out the elements of *observer* missions, i.e., those missions short of UNEF-type peacekeeping but extraordinarily useful for preconflict prophylaxis. The Soviet Union said some forward-sounding things about peacekeeping in 1964 and has expressed interest recently in moving forward, though how much remains to be seen. In the United States, while President Richard Nixon's failure to even mention the subject in his maiden UN appearance in 1969 was discouraging, new interest is being shown by work such as the United Nations Association of the United States of America panel report on peacekeeping whose recommendations were subsequently urged on the president by 80 members of the Senate and the House of Representatives.[2] In the spring of 1971 a 50-member Commission submitted to President Nixon a report which called for new attitudes, new initiatives, and new procedures to make peacekeeping a more effective option.[3]

Still, the prospects are no better than fair for some very serious reasons. In examining those reasons it is important to distinguish between the gut issues and the nuts-and-bolts questions. Details of earmarking, financing, logistics, staff work, and the like are all relevant to making peacekeeping more effective. Indeed, improved capabilities might help create the much needed climate of *expectation* that multilateral peacekeeping is a realistic option—an expectation that has been declining in recent years. But the basic obstacles lie deeper.

One grave defect of the whole concept (including both observer missions and peacekeeping forces) is that it involves two things that seem to be the hardest for any government to do—taking preventive steps in advance of a calamity, and resting its confidence in an organization over which it has only minimum control. The latter preoccupied the Soviet Union during the ten to fifteen years in which it was a small and distrusted minority, itself profoundly distrusting any "uncontrollable" organization. Today the United States also distrusts the UN's "swirling majorities," given the latter's frequent anti-American attitudes,

[2]*Controlling Conflict in the 1970's* (A report of a national policy panel established by the United Nations Association of the United States of America, 1969).

[3]*Report of President's Commission for the Observance of the Twenty-Fifth Anniversary of the United Nations* (Washington: GPO, 1971), pp. 4-7.

to carry out a peacekeeping operation either efficiently or in ways that conform to United States estimates of its own national interest. Among the "gut" issues of multilateral peacekeeping and peacemaking, then, is the growing superpower distrust of a majoritarian organization. This distrust is even likely to increase, not diminish, to the extent that the Big Two compromise some of their remaining differences and agree on improved multilateral capabilities. But the time has not yet come when the Big Two are once again, as in 1945, lined up against the rest on the issue of who controls UN operations. The Soviet Union suffers contradictory impulses; it is torn between the desire of a Great Power with internal problems to keep the rest of the world relatively stable and the dynamics of a world outlook that entails a struggle for allies within the Socialist world plus the traditional czarist policy of expansion south into the Persian Gulf, all flavored by remnants of messianic and doctrinaire Communism.

The Soviet Union, in contrast to Communist China, supports bourgeois nationalist leadership and movements in the less developed countries, in many places scorning the local Communists who are often outlawed and/or in jail. The Soviets are believed to disapprove of Castro's militant and violence-provoking tactics in fomenting Latin American revolution. Premier Alexei Kosygin in fact spoke of a conflict control strategy to the UN General Assembly in 1967:

> A seemingly small event, or so-called "local war," may grow into big military conflicts. This means that every state and government should not only refrain from bringing about new complications by its actions—it must undertake every effort to prevent any aggravation of the situation and, moreover, the emergence of hotbeds of war, that should be quenched whenever they appear.[4]

But the signs remain contradictory. In recent times Moscow has both reaffirmed its worldwide commitment to the "national liberation movement" (see, e.g., commentator V. Mayevsky in *Pravda,* June 19, 1968) and its opposition to armed uprising by Communists to seize power in underdeveloped countries (*Pravda,* September 15, 1968). Soviet amphibious and airlift capabilities have improved; landing forces are being trained; Soviet naval activity and military assistance in the Mediterranean has increased substantially since the Middle East war of 1967 as an accompaniment of an activist Soviet influence-seeking policy

---

[4]*New York Times,* June 19, 1967. See also the speech reported in *Izvestia,* November 26, 1969:

"The raging flames of these fires together with other hot spots in the world present an extremely serious threat to the interests of universal peace."

in the Arab Mediterranean and the Persian Gulf. We seem, as a Yugoslav commentator recently wrote, to be witnessing

> the increasingly obvious effort of the USSR to break out of the bounds of the continental Eurasian geostrategic shell without relying directly on nuclear missiles of intercontinental calibre.[5]

But as others, notably Marshall Shulman, have warned us in recent years, the Soviet shift may also be a result of Moscow's calculations that the *United States* had adopted a basic strategy of intervention in any and all "small wars" in the developing regions to enhance American influence and control. "This," says the Yugoslav writer,

> also makes it clear why the Soviet Union is endeavoring to develop naval power, certain branches of the air force, etc. Unless all the logical assumptions deceive, *this is an effort to counter the imperialist strategy of local and restricted wars with its own weapons, the weapons of that selfsame local and restricted war.*[6]

Precisely the same set of questions must be addressed to this development as to, say, the recent Soviet buildup in strategic weaponry. Does it represent a new and malevolent thrust toward victory in the Cold War, a catching-up with American military doctrines after the usual three-to-five year lag, an effort to stem the "mad" Americans in *their* drive for "world domination," or a bureaucratic victory for one or another organizational unit in the Soviet internal power struggle?

There is some evidence to support the belief that, while all four questions could be answered affirmatively, the dominant argument lies in the second and third. The Soviets will probably bring more influence to bear in local conflicts where their power is available. On the same evidence they will not invariably use their power to help the Syrians or Algerians or Cubans or Vietnamese to escalate local fighting to the potentially thermonuclear level. On the contrary, they are likely to use their power as they habitually use power—to accomplish desired political results. In the case of the Middle East this probably includes deterring the Israelis, giving the Arabs highly tangible—and thus dangerous—expressions of Soviet support, deterring the United States from seeming to threaten the Arabs, and, we can hope, aiding deescalatory policies when things get too threatening for comfort. Still, the presence of Soviet vessels, transport aircraft, fliers, and, above all, paratroopers would give an entirely new and portentous dimension to any local conflict, and this development must be watched closely.

[5]Andro Gabelić, "New Accent in Soviet Strategy," *Review of International Affairs,* reprinted in *Survival,* February 1968 (Vol. 10, No. 2), pp. 45-46.
[6]*Ibid. (Emphasis added.)*

When it comes to internal struggles, "wars of liberation" will retain their sacred place in the Soviet litany—as long as nuclear escalation does not threaten and preferably under terms with which increasingly pragmatic Soviet trade and aid policies can continue to live comfortably. It remains to be pointed out that the so-called "Brezhnev Doctrine" implies the right of the Soviet Union to intervene militarily with no sanction from any external agency in any country it defines unilaterally as within the "Socialist" camp, to quell what it interprets as threats to the continued purity of Moscow-defined socialism and the orientation of policy toward Moscow. It can be assumed that this covers the Eastern European states including Romania, and possibly Yugoslavia, and undoubtedly North Vietnam, North Korea, and Cuba. (China and Albania are dubious, Algeria and other "bourgeois socialist" clients even more so.)

It is necessary to be equally frank about the United States. The latter's policy, whether because more idealistic, more sensible, or more certain of the UN's political compatibility with American interests, has historically been far more supportive of the UN's multilateral mechanisms than has Moscow's policy.

But despite the official rhetoric (*and* frantic efforts to get international peacekeepers onto the scene in specific crises) there is no doubt of the very low priority the multilateral capability has in fact enjoyed at the highest levels of United States policy. This may seem a harsh indictment, particularly of the special parts of the American government where positive efforts have been persistent. But in terms of larger United States strategic perceptions one must conclude that, over and above Soviet rigidity, the United States has itself never really assigned a significant *priority* to genuine improvements in multilateral peacekeeping capacity.

The inner reason for this may lie in the highly selective nature of United States interests in such a capability. The United States has a demonstrable interest in multilateral peacekeeping for Africa and the Middle East, an interest that at times verges on the desperate. But the United States has also traditionally rejected this approach for much of Southeast Asia as well as for Latin America and the Caribbean. Washington's total failure in the Cambodian "incursion" of 1970 to pay even lip service to the UN Charter or to UN peacekeeping and peacemaking possibilities merely dramatized the low estate into which the UN approach had fallen.

There is thus an inner tension in United States policy growing out of partial and selective acceptance of an international potential. This in turn stems from a central ideological component no less real than

Moscow's. Those critical of the United States assert that it uses the UN and the Organization of American States (OAS) to support the status quo against change, even legitimate change. The charge is of course a distortion. (Moreover, stability is not a totally meaningless goal for any nation.) But in order to take full advantage of multilateral diplomatic and other international machinery the United States needs to persuade others that its resort to multilateral agencies is neither a cover for planned unilateral military intervention nor a tool aimed at shoring up repressive and unpopular military dictatorships. It must persuade other members of international political organizations that the United States is sincere in its desire to minimize conflict *while accepting and even encouraging legitimate internal and external changes in the status quo.*

In this connection one principle of international peacekeeping that seems increasingly persuasive is that of *using multilateral machinery to insulate, i.e., "neutralize," a conflict area from external interference* while processes of change work themselves out internally. A motto for the approach might be "change without escalation." A more relaxed United States stance toward the process of change is far more feasible—and potentially constructive—if in the meantime significant external interference is coped with (as it never could be in Vietnam). Harassed officials argue, with some justice, that the OAS (or UN or whatever) is weak, refractory, unsympathetic, inefficient, etc. But it may also be that the process is a circular one.

More generally stated, any conflict-control policy is futile if genuine popular aspirations are suppressed in the name of antiviolence; some turbulence in the short run may be the only assurance of longer-term stability in today's world. Thus to "control" a conflict, far from suppressing it, may imply allowing certain things to take place that the United States might earlier have considered unacceptable as a threat to its interests or an open invitation to extremists to meddle in or take over.

This prescription calls for a more objective judgment, in the longer lens of United States history, about the proper attitude of this country toward revolutionary movements that have demonstrable popular support. Its concomitant is a Soviet policy that learns to trust multilateral action as not automatically working toward United States—or at a minimum anti-Soviet—ends. Clearly this is the price of any durable and meaningful understanding between the Big Two about multilateral alternatives to unilateral intervention.

At a more concrete level there are two other hang-ups that impede American-Soviet collaboration in using the multilateral option. One, both substantive and procedural, grows directly out of the ideological attitudes discussed above. It has to do with how the operation is to be *controlled.* The symbol around which the argument evolves is the UN Secretary-General. There is a profound difference in the ways in which the two sides see that figure. To the Soviets, particularly since the days of "Secretary-Generalissimo" Dag Hammarskjöld in the Congo, the Secretary-General's office is viewed precisely as are all other institutional forms—in terms of the reality of political power. The Secretary-General, if he is to have authority to act, must by definition be part of a system in which the Soviet Union has a veto over actions it disapproves.

The United States, on the other hand (perhaps because the UN Secretary-General has always been relatively friendly and politically trustworthy), typically sees the problem as one of *efficiency:* How, once a political decision is made to launch an operation, can it be most efficaciously handled? It positively offends the American sense of managerial competence to contemplate a Secretary-General hamstrung in his day-to-day execution of a political mandate by a presidium of voting state representatives breathing heavily over his shoulder.

Other problems arise outside the realm of superpower relations. The middle powers referred to above—in a way the most important element of all—have remained faithful, with the (Scandinavian) Nordic peace-keeping force continuing to be trained and made available and with ten countries (Austria, Canada, Denmark, Finland, Iran, Italy, the Netherlands, New Zealand, Norway, and Sweden) earmarking standby troops.

But the wave of enthusiasm in Canada in the mid-'60's for peace-keeping as a new métier of the newly unified Canadian armed forces suffered a serious setback when the United Nations Emergency Force (UNEF) was unceremoniously withdrawn from the Gaza strip in May 1967. Japan has now spoken publicly of such a métier,[7] and the peace-keeping "fire brigade" of old is probably still faithful. But the great irony of contemporary politics is that the much-hoped-for American-Soviet cooperation has the effect of making lesser powers suspicious.

The countries most likely to be peacekept, so to speak, represent another obstacle to advance agreement on a reliable and functioning peacekeeping system in the period ahead. There exists in the Afro-Asian nations, and in Latin America as well, suspicion of "neocolonialism"; opposition to international pacification and tranquilizing efforts that obscure what are conceived as just causes; and a preference for home-grown or indigenous peacekeepers in the form, for example, of the Organization for African Unity (OAU) but without many signs yet of either efficacy or capability for serious operations in the field. (Others such as Guinea have, however, called for a UN force in recent years.)

---

[7]See, e.g., Kei Wakaizumi, "Japan Beyond 1970," *Foreign Affairs,* April 1969 (Vol. 47, No. 3), p. 514.

Another international "structural" difficulty is that the UN has yet to find an answer to the question of how the international community can and should relate to *internal* conflicts in which there is an international interest. Virtually the whole array of "third-party" mechanisms that have been developed seem to be almost useless when it comes to the most intractable conflicts of all—those *not* involving a clearcut invasion of one country by another. This calls for a major effort to apply international law to the new situation in ways that will command the respect of the majority of nations while adapting to dynamic change; the "peaceful change" field remains in urgent need of serious rethinking (see below).

In addition, by its very nature the UN is a blunt instrument, exposing countries to large numbers of conflicts, generating publicity, and mixing any new item with other quarrels nations bring into the UN with them. Diplomats typically prefer not to go that route if they believe they can deal with a situation *in camera* or in their vest pockets—what one might call the "John Foster Dulles syndrome." There is invariably someone who does not wish UN machinery to be invoked, usually someone from a country with a "special position" in the area. In the 1950's it was France in both Indochina and North Africa (a France that, in Dean Acheson's retrospective words, "blackmailed" the United States into supporting its position).[8] In the Suez preinvasion summer of 1956 the barrier was Secretary of State Dulles's overweening diplomatic egotism (my own retrospective words).[9]

All these reasons were, in the light of later history, poor ones, entailing political and human costs (wars in many cases) outweighing any conceivable political embarrassment or messiness so feared by the cautious diplomat. If the United States had followed its deeper instincts in all these cases and had not put first its European allies' aberrant and self-defeating colonial policies, the outcome for all would have been better. To the extent that in the thermonuclear age UN action *does nothing but isolate a conflict from great-power involvement,* to that extent it is a uniquely valuable instrument of conflict control.

Another "structural" point has to do with timing. As with nonmilitary policy options in general, delaying until a full-blown crisis the use of such machinery is likely to rule out a wide spectrum of possibly constructive policies.[10] Beyond this, the very existence of a crisis is

[8]Quoted in *New York Times Book Review,* October 12, 1969.
[9]Elaborated on in Lincoln P. Bloomfield, "The U.N. and National Security," *Foreign Affairs,* July 1958 (Vol. 36, No. 4), pp. 597-610.
[10]My associates and I have documented the "reverse curves" of, on the one hand, multiple options available for conflict-prevention in early stages of conflict when great-power leadership is uninterested, and, on the other hand, the dramatically shrunken options that are by then available when those leaders do finally notice an explosive situation. See *Controlling Small Wars: A Strategy for the 1970's.*

likely to render the utilization of effective multilateral machinery either impossible or unpersuasive because the direct interests of external powers may have already become so apparent.

Some final issues go to the nature of the international "community" itself. The international system has in fact retrogressed since the early 1960's when Dag Hammarskjöld refused to withdraw the UN operation in the Congo (ONUC) every time Patrice Lumumba or Joseph Kasavubu alternatively announced its ejection. As long as the rule persists of un-limited power to the "host government" to refuse admission and to eject UN observers at will, this vital capacity can remain at the mercy of one side to a quarrel who in a real-life situation could be the least responsible and the most "guilty" of the parties involved.

There have recently been indications that the Soviet Union may be reconsidering this absolute veto by a host government. If there were no such veto, it would be of central concern whether multilateral peace-keeping is to be entirely of the "consent" variety or whether it may be coercive. Chapter VII of the UN Charter on Security Council enforce-ment, particularly articles 42 and 43 about military forces, was con-sidered to be a dead letter until three things happened in recent years. ONUC wound up fighting (and defeating) the Katangese forces of the refractory Moishe Tshombe, thus in effect "winning the war"—not what most supporters of the operation had been told was intended. The second thing that has happened is a new interest in the West in meeting the Soviet Union halfway on peacekeeping, perhaps by the route of article 43 (but really as a way to reassure Moscow that normally the Charter—Security Council—Military Staff Committee—veto route can be followed and without evidently implying any serious intention to revive the emphasis on *coercive enforcement* that article 43 had originally implied). The third thing that happened was Security Council Resolution 255 of June 19, 1968 providing guarantees in connection with the Treaty on the Nonproliferation of Nuclear Weapons, guarantees that may one day lead the way to collective enforcement not because of any abstract theory of collective security but because the Soviets and Ameri-cans wish a legal framework for countering a Chinese (or other) nuclear threat.

Sometimes referred to as chapter "6½," the new peacekeeping approach could, under some circumstances, turn into coercive enforce-ment despite the rhetorical disclaimers. This is not because any particu-lar precedent has been set; the UN "police action" in Korea was not really peacekeeping and in any event was not *formally* taken under chapter VII; and Katanga is deemed an unlikely-to-be-permitted-again freak. But, as noted earlier, peacekeeping to some African states means a UN-backed coercive assault on the white supremacy bastions of

Southern Rhodesia and South Africa. This purpose stands in stark contrast to the accepted peacekeeping pattern of observing alleged infiltration, enforcing standstill agreements and truces, and conciliating between potentially reconcilable differences. It should be recalled that if the International Court of Justice (ICJ) had changed its balance by one vote in its ruling of 1966 regarding South West Africa, the possibility would have been open for the Security Council to call for enforcement of the court's judgment under article 94 of the Charter, with evidence that some Western powers were willing to follow this legal road to multilateral coercion.

The point is that in some cases (though by no means in all) there *is* a commitment by the UN to a specific political end—in the case of southern Africa the end of apartheid and the principle of one-man-one-vote. Thus a UN peacekeeping operation might go to the scene of violence there with an a priori commitment for one particular outcome rather than impartially and in a conciliating mood, as in Kashmir, Cyprus, the Middle East, Yemen, and indeed all the observer missions. Or such a purpose could develop out of an initially more limited purpose. (An instructive analogy might be Korea where an expanded aim of reunification of Korea became in the fall of 1950 the rationale for expanding the "police action" into a march across the 38th parallel and up the peninsula toward the Yalu River.) We may really be speaking of chapter "6¾" when we speak of peacekeeping via article 43, and we ought to know what we are getting into.

This expansion of peacekeeping toward enforcement is all entirely speculative, though sobering. In fact equal significance may attach to the other end of the spectrum where the efforts of the committee of 33 have concentrated so far—*observer missions.* Often loosely spoken of together with the UNEF-type force as "peacekeeping," these missions ought to be distinguished from the latter because of their special qualities. The UN committee of 33's "Model I" referred to earlier on small observation fact-finding and reporting operations looks modest alongside the spectre of UN "peace-enforcing," so to speak, in southern Africa or Ulster or wherever. But the political early warning and even deterrence function of "the man with the binoculars" has been consistently underrated.

Consider how modern history might have differed had the French defeat in Vietnam in 1954 been followed by a UN conciliation and observation mission and UN observation of elections (as spoken of at the Geneva convention of 1954) rather than by the United States of America. Consider how, when the first complaints were made of infiltration and indirect aggression from outside the Republic of Vietnam (South Vietnam), a functioning multilateral observation operation might have then been mounted to observe and report. If one really wishes to stretch one's mind, consider a billion-dollar "McNamara electronic line" that really worked, manned by 20,000 UN observers—and consider that the former was, in fact, finally constructed but never really used and that the latter represents the size of ONUC. The combined costs would have been trivial by contrast to the bloodshed and treasure ultimately expended. And virtually any outcome of such a political/peacekeeping approach would have been better for everyone concerned than what resulted from an insistence on unilateralism. The Soviet Union may also come to reckon the calculus of costs of its unilateral intervention and control policy in more enlightened terms as those costs mount with declining benefits.

It is time to apply these lessons to new situations where new tragedies threaten. Serious consideration should be given to multilateral neutral observation of complained-of infiltration and external subversion; at the same time care should be taken not to interfere with processes of internal social, economic, and political change that may take place within a country. The portentous implications of a Sino-Soviet war are sufficient to warrant suggesting international observation of the disputed borders while proposing multiple techniques of "third-party" resolution of the issues. Neither excessive delicacy, legalism, nor "realism" seem valid reasons for missing a step that might help to avert worldwide disaster.

What can and should be done? Action seems possible under three headings.

Partiality

"Partial" great-power interests have tended to make UN peacekeeping a continuation of great-power policy rather than a substitute for it, with the Congo perhaps the most egregious case. But Cyprus illustrates the possibility of common sense and a "higher realism" that in this case ultimately overrode the initial impulses of the United States to keep the matter within the North Atlantic Treaty Organization (NATO) (thus getting on NATO'S agenda a country that considers itself in a different region, with predictably polarizing results in the area). It also overrode the initial impulse of the Soviet Union to gain a new foothold by a quick arms supply deal (thus widening further the area of potential great-power conflict). In West New Guinea American interests, at least on paper, would have favored its NATO ally, the Netherlands; instead, given the realities of the situation, the United States became "neutral."

In other places where narrow national advantage is being sought, the mounting dangers of war may be contained through the means of augmented third-party presences and mechanisms. In the Middle East it is not too late to reintroduce a serious peacekeeping and peacemaking capability. The preconditions are Soviet willingness to apply more restraint both to themselves and to Cairo and Damascus; and United States willingness to demand from its de facto ally Israel greater compliance with Security Council Resolution 242 of November 22, 1967, if necessary, in exchange for the American protective alliance. In the Persian Gulf the Soviets are historically on record as aspiring to a physical presence in the centers of oil.[11] Even if they did not, change would still be inevitable in the feudal societies of that region. Indeed, conflict in one or another form is also inevitable there, given the potent oil and strategic interests including those of Japan (which depends on the Middle East for 91 percent of its crude oil).

The prescription is not for utopian panaceas on the part of either human nature or the international community. What is needed is a more explicit mutual recognition that conflict should be regulated and potentially violent power-plays kept within tolerable limits—an improvement, in other words, over the game of chicken now being played in the Middle East between both clients and suppliers. Two other prescriptions suggested above are, first, that it is possible to harmonize concern with "popular" social forces and concern with "external aggression" by means of an observation capability that concerns itself only with charges of *external* interference. A second suggestion involved the Sino-Soviet conflict, where the stakes are much too high to follow the rule book about UN impotence and where Moscow might be brought to see the value for itself, as a "status quo power" in the region, of neutral third-party observation. Needless to say, the utility of the third-party mechanism in such cases would be greatly enhanced if UN membership were universal (the nonmembership of three parties to the Vietnam war created a prima facie handicap to any possibility of UN peacekeeping).

Peacemaking

What some have called peacemaking in connection with peacekeeping is really our old friend *peaceful change*, about which much has been said and little done, at least voluntarily and purposively, in the period of history in which change is the swiftest and most inexorable. The realms

---

[11]I refer to the well-known proposal by V. Molotov to Hitler in 1940 that Germany recognize as the focal point of the aspirations of the Soviet Union "[the area] south of Batum and Baku in the general direction of the Persian Gulf." Reprinted in Raymond James Sontag and James Stuart Beddie (ed.), *Nazi-Soviet Relations 1939-1941: Documents from the Archives of the German Foreign Office* (Washington: Department of State, 1948), p. 259.

of change are social, economic, political, and territorial, and in all cases of interest they involve the very centerpiece of politics—the distribution of power. Power is not usually surrendered without a fight by those who have it; wars, local conflicts, and the cries of justice and equity all arise out of the human failure to regulate this process more intelligently.

The UN Charter was an improvement over the League of Nations Covenant in this respect. But the machinery is still defective, as is the ability of those holding power to comprehend both the virtue and the long-term wisdom of magnanimity. This is true whether the issue is United States investment policy in Latin America, Arab refusal to accept the permanence of Israel, Israeli intransigence toward Arab refugees, South African inhumanity toward blacks, Indian retention of Moslem-majority Kashmir, Chinese suppression of Tibetans, or Soviet control of Eastern Europe.

Assuming a human inclination always to emulate the Bourbons with regard to voluntary change, machinery is obviously needed to enhance the process of peaceful change. The present General Assembly is incapable of coherent policies in detail, being often committed to extreme and extravagant outcomes with little regard to the rights of minorities. The Security Council is more efficacious, but its majority is entirely *parti pris* in the Middle East, for example, and thus incapable of presiding over statesmanlike changes. The ICJ in the South West Africa case in 1966 showed itself as unsound and politically motivated as was its predecessor in the comparable Interhandel case of 1931 that wrote its earlier epitaph. In short, the system itself seems to favor either no change or violent change.

This is, of course, an exaggeration. But the extreme caution of chapter VI about recommending terms of settlement in disputes ought to be increasingly ignored in cases where commitment to a particular outcome will be more beneficial than the necessarily impartial fire-fighting activities. As long urged by Louis B. Sohn and others, an equity tribunal should be established. Some new uses of the ICJ might be found via implementation of article 50 of the court's statute concerning fact-finding missions. Today, taking a case or a piece of a case to court may be a good face-saving device at a crucial moment in some dangerous or deadlocked instances that look—and are—profoundly political[12] (for instance, at some point the future status of Taiwan, Indonesia-Philippine claims to disputed lands, even Sino-Indian and Sino-Soviet border claims, and Near East water rights). Until the UN is made universal, impartial arbitration ought to be revived from its moribund condition. Mediators ought routinely to accompany observation and peacekeeping forces.

---

[12]I have changed my mind about this since writing "Law, Politics, and International Disputes," *International Conciliation*, January 1958 (No. 516).

Alternative proposals for dangerous deadlocks ought to be put forward by others rather than permitting the argument to continue between intolerable extremes (as in South Africa and Rhodesia).

Improved Capabilities

It is in this deeply political context that one can support with enthusiasm proposals to improve the peacekeeping mechanism.

Modified article 43 modalities for peacekeeping should be thoroughly explored with a view to finding a new synthesis that conforms to Soviet concern for constitutionalism and American concern for maximum efficiency. Standby forces would encourage and facilitate peacekeeping when the need arises. The United States Military Assistance Program should implement its unused provisions for helping nations build up peacekeeping forces. A peace fund of $60 million should also give peacekeeping a shot in the arm, though Moscow and Paris must cooperate by contributing. Double-earmarking to both the regional and UN levels is constructive. Support should be given to the peacekeeping training under the new International Peace Academy centered in Vienna.[13]

All of these "nuts and bolts" improvements have the dual virtue of making peacekeeping more effective while helping generate a new climate of *expectation* that peacekeeping is real and can realistically be turned to. Finally, proposals along these and other lines might best be advanced by middle or smaller powers, which are themselves in default for standing on the sidelines and waiting to see what the superpowers would say or do instead of filling the vacuum with imaginative and compelling proposals of their own.

In conclusion, the prospects for a workable system of multilateral peacekeeping remain fragile. But what the Communists call "objective factors" make them somewhat more favorable as we go into period 4 of the age of peacekeeping. It remains futile and even destructive of progress to insist upon a sweeping transformation of either human nature or the international system. It remains imperative to work mightily, and in tangible ways, toward a broader interpretation of national interest. The dramatic failures and high costs of unilateralism, combined with forecasts of a planet that continues to be convulsive and conflict-ridden, generate an iron logic that *ought* to make multilateral peacekeeping and peacemaking less a meaningless political litany, and more an accepted instrument of conflict prevention and limitation. But until national leaders at the highest level look to that alternative first instead of last and until a climate of genuine expectation about multilateral peacekeeping exists, the circuit between iron logic and a system of purposeful conflict control cannot be closed.

[13]See Appendix 7 for a report by IPAC.

Seven

A PROPOSAL

Let me advance a concrete proposal which will synthesize the points I have been making and which is geared to the conclusions reached as to what the traffic today might bear—but only might.

THE GOAL

It helps first to state the goal. The goal is to improve the capabilities of the United Nations for peacekeeping action within the limits of political reality but beyond the confines of excessive inertia, caution, or timidity. In order to meet this standard a proposal should address itself to the present and immediate future rather than to the long-range or even middle-range future. It should build on the lessons of UNEF, ONUC, and UNFICYP. It should pay appropriate—but not hypnotized—attention to the political obstacles. It should be sobered—but not paralyzed—by the financial crisis produced by peacekeeping of the 1960's. These constraints favor something other than a *standing* military body, the need for which is in any event not proven. They also rule out that other form of international police force—the *individually recruited* UN constabulary whose members lose their national uniform and identity as national soldiers. But a proposal bounded by these restraints would nonetheless go beyond the existing situation.

I see no reason to alter in any substantial way my earlier proposal for the creation of a modest *stand-by* force of the proper sort, trained and equipped for the proper jobs, and in an appropriate condition of readiness and availability when needed. The ultimate size of the stand-by reserve force would be 25,000 men plus several specialized units. It would be built up to full strength over a five-year period, after which the annual training of new contingents would offset attrition. It would be subject to the appropriate organs of the United Nations, following precisely the same constitutional procedures as at present and with the same authority and safeguards *against* authority. Thus for the first time one could count on the availability and readiness of a reasonable number of trained personnel for peacekeeping assignments at a modest level, on as good a geographic distribution basis as the UN membership itself, and able to get to trouble spots in the necessary strength in the necessary time and with logistical support for a suitable period. The trained units would constitute a cadre which could be supplemented as needed.

ORGANIZATION

My proposal is based on the assumption that battalion-strength units represent probably the most appropriate basis today for contributions. The battalion is a unit of a size likely to be maintained by smaller countries. It ensures some homogeneity in terms of morale, customary diet, religious practices, and the rest. At the same time it permits relatively low-level integration of units within regiments, different-sized task groups, brigade groups, even divisions. From the standpoint of simple arithmetic an eventual stand-by force of 25,000 can be made up of single understrength battalions of approximately 500 men each from 50 countries, or of overstrength battalions of 1,000 men from 25 countries, without the participation of the great powers or of the predictable number of smaller powers which would not take part because they have no armed forces, disapprove of the policies a substantial UN majority is likely to favor, or object to UN police forces in principle. The total adds up to a modest stand-by force which is potentially organizable into five brigades or two small divisions; it is more likely that battalions would be made up into a tailored force, such as UNEF and ONUC, not necessarily corresponding to any conventional military formation.

The image of the proposed stand-by UN force should be that of police rather than army, and preferably that of constabulary rather than police. Whatever label is used should denote primarily the roles of observation, patrol, and civil-pacifying functions rather than enforcement, punitive, or typically combat functions. At the same time the force should be equipped—as UNEF and ONUC were in fact—to defend itself and to hold off equivalent-sized military formations until it could be reinforced.

It is here that the experiences so far go a long way to supply the details of this proposal. The experience in the Congo and Cyprus showed the special need for training in sophisticated riot control and civil government, in troop and vehicle movement control, in helicopter operations, and in signals (communications). These are of course the skills likely to be in the shortest supply in the very countries most suitable politically to do the job. It therefore seems as sensible today as it did when first proposed that the United Nations vote to organize a modest UN training program at reasonable cost, rotating battalion-size units in and out for special peacekeeping training purposes, and, when they are trained, returning them to their home forces, where they would be kept in special and hopefully honorific reserve status until called on by appropriate vote of the Security Council or Assembly.[1]

As was suggested then, the force could be trained at a facility made available by a neutral country such as India. Approximately 2,500 men would train at any given time, that is to say five 500-man battalions for a period of 6 months. This would result in training 5,000 men a year, or a total of 25,000 in 5 years, about the maximum time for ensuring that at least a substantial cadre of trainees would be available at the end of the cycle. The men would be regulars, or at any rate volunteers and not short-term draftees. For one thing, the former are demonstrably far more successful in the difficult assignments involved; for another, they will stay in the service and remain available longer.

THE TRAINING PROGRAM

The personnel requirements for such a training facility might vary within certain broad limits, depending on the extent to which the trainee units might bring their own support personnel, the extensiveness of the training, the condition of base facilities, and so on. A careful analysis of probable needs to accomplish the precise mission envisaged here suggests that the training facility would have a permanent base unit of 802 men organized as indicated in the following table, with an alternative column based on a reduced strength of 3,000 trainees annually.[2] The instructing staff could well be drawn from the military officers and non-coms in more than 30 countries that have now served in UN operations. If the UN Institute for Training and Research ever grew to its full potential, perhaps it could be in overall charge.

The curriculum for a six-month intensive training course would be pointed to those skills and functions that are unique to the sort of

---

[1]See Lincoln P. Bloomfield, "The UN and National Security," *Foreign Affairs,* July 1958, and *The United Nations and U.S. Foreign Policy,* (Boston: Little, Brown and Company, 1960, and revised edition 1967). A most valuable early analysis with recommendations is *A United Nations Peace Force* by William R. Frye (New York: Oceana, 1957).

[2]For the staffing out of this proposal, as well as other helpful advice, I am most indebted to Colonel David L. Evans, USAF, who at the time of this writing was Air Force Research Associate at the MIT Center for International Studies.

Estimated Personnel Requirements for a UN Training Base

	Facility Operation and Maintenance	Training Function (for 5000 Trainees per Year)	(Alternate Figures for 3000 Trainees per Year)
Personnel and Administration	20	20	10
Intelligence and Security	20*	20	10
Operations	10	80	60
Supply and Maintenance	50**	50	30
Food Service and Rations	40***	5	5
Plans	20	20	15
Construction and Engineering	100**	50	20
Accounting and Finance	10	--	--
Communications	100**	60	30
Public Information	5	20	10
Chaplain	2	5	5
Inspector General (Safety and Standardization)	--	10	10
Surgeon	40	30	20
Judge Advocate	5	10	8
	422	380	233
TOTAL		802 (655)	

*Base security only; i.e. military police.

**Initial preparation or modification of the facility will require additional personnel. Figures listed would be required to replenish consumables; repair vehicles; maintain light aircraft; maintain grounds, buildings, and training areas; maintain communications facilities and training equipment; etc.

***If units being trained do not bring their own field-messing facilities and food service personnel, this figure will have to be increased proportionately. More unification and *esprit,* as well as better health, probably would be attained by having the base supply all food service.

police or constabulary job actually needed. A major part of the course would be elementary grounding in language. A basic familiarity with English or French as a second language would be most important in terms of obeying military orders and acknowledging communications. Second would be a standard signals procedure for communication between units and up and down the chain of command. Third would be observation and patrol duties, including special military and civil-police type of training, crowd handling, maintenance of law and order in small units in isolation, enforcing discipline, observing ceasefires and the violations thereof, making accurate vehicle and head counts at checkpoints, surveillance and reporting techniques, and so on. There should be a training unit in intelligence functions that, under whatever name, are indispensable to any UN field operation.

It should be possible to experiment with a minimum common diet for mixed troops in the field. It might be desirable to experiment with mixing the units below the battalion level, possibly building on the "buddy" system successfully developed in Korea between American and Republic of Korea forces.

The curriculum should include at least one actual field exercise, in which, for example, one battalion would simulate a mob, or a disaffected populace, or refugees. Such "police games" could build profitably on both the experience in political-military simulation developed in the past few years and the more traditional war-gaming employed in military training the world over.

It may be argued that the financial problem implied by the proposal I have outlined is so overwhelming that this sort of training should be limited to commissioned and non-commissioned officers. Certainly that would be better than what we have now. But training of actual troops has important values that go well beyond those of the more modest proposal for training officers. The principal reason lies in the small resources that even at best would be available to perform police or constabulary tasks of the sort in mind here. The more ready a group of men is to take on the responsibilities and duties which at best cannot be precisely anticipated, in an alien area that cannot be predicted, and under conditions foreign to their normal military environment, the more efficient a job the United Nations can do with small resources. Five-hundred trained men can do the job of 5,000 untrained men, as was demonstrated positively by the unique abilities of the Nigerian military police in the Congo, and negatively by the difficulties that arose there with relatively untrained and unsophisticated units.

Another reason for preferring the training of enlisted men as well as officers is that, as an incidental benefit, the program could begin to produce from neutral nations some manpower trained in at least some of the special skills that will be required to verify compliance with arms-control and disarmament agreements that may be reached. One of the political-military simulations mentioned earlier unexpectedly brought out the potential usefulness of disarmament inspectors as a source of ready-trained observers in a crisis. It could work quite the other way around, with great potential benefit, if and when an arms-limitation agreement is reached that suddenly imposes a demand for appropriately trained neutrals. In fact, an "elective" subject for those men already possessing the required language skill could well be training in disarmament and arms-control verification techniques.

Another secondary value would be to train and have readily available international units for disaster relief, a need tragically underscored by such events in recent years as the earthquakes in Peru and Chile, and the tidal wave in East Pakistan.

Experience indicates that it is equally important to have a suitable advance plan for the logistical movement and support of any UN force that is to be moved unpredictably to some unforeseeable location. I can only repeat recommendations for advance and highly specific earmarking of airlift and sealift facilities so that improvisation will not be quite so frantic next time, so that they can be called on virtually automatically by those charged with moving a force almost overnight, and so that, in the absence of other alternatives, it would not be necessary to accept offers of transport—from states which wish to introduce national personnel for reasons of their own.

The United States has furnished important logistical support, but now the capabilities of others are growing, particularly given distribution of jet transport craft. From a political standpoint it will be highly desirable to have on earmarked reserve transport craft not belonging to the great powers as soon as it is possible to integrate these efficiently into a planning system.

In addition to the basic constabulary type of training described above, there should also be a technical assistance program aimed at preparing specialized units from the underdeveloped countries for service along the lines we have indicated. At present it is virtually impossible on short notice to recruit a signals unit from any but the most advanced Western countries. This may be true for a period of time, but technical assistance can shorten the wait for the various specialties such as transportation units, troop and vehicle movement control units, and helicopter service personnel that proved to be in such short supply in past UN operations. The technical capabilities of some of the middle-tier countries are advancing sufficiently so that they should be able to contribute specialized units of this sort if additional training of a uniform nature can be furnished.

I proposed several years ago that the United States take a fresh look at its Military Assistance Programs with a view to their far more pointed utilization to develop units for UN police purposes—a purpose clearly spelled out in the original MAP legislation but ignored in practice. The retrograde succession of military coups in Latin America, doubtless to be emulated elsewhere, gives special point to the suggestion. As a bonus, troops could be trained at least in part for "civic action."

FINANCING

To return to resources, the issue of financing, often said to be the dominant difficulty in seeking to improve the United Nations' readiness for peacekeeping operations, discourages any really major advance planning for the future despite our intuition that there are bound to be new situations where a UN force may become the best available option. In another perspective the financial opposition merely symbolizes the political opposition. For in any relative terms the costs involved are so small in proportion to the defense expenditures or gross national product of the advanced countries as to make UN forces a bargain by any reasonable standard.

Yet, there remains the practical problem of financing the force proposed here. Some other studies indicate the range we are seeking. For example, the Clark-Sohn Plan for a World Peace Force calls for the annual expenditure of $9 billion.[3] William Frye's more modest proposal in 1957 for a standing peace force of 7,000 men was estimated then to cost $65 million for the base, $1 million a year to maintain it, and $25 million a year to operate and sustain the force on the most economical basis.[4]

I am going to assume here that a training base can be secured for the purpose without a major capital outlay, as a contribution in kind by, for example, India, Sweden, Pakistan, or the Philippines. (If it had to be financed, the cost of the base, including permanent barracks, classroom facilities, hospital, warehouses, runways, vehicle repair facilities, electric power, roadways, water and sewage, senior staff quarters, recreation facilities, training and maneuver areas, etc. would total at least $50,000,000—an unacceptably high figure.)

Even the $26 million figure of Frye exceeds the perspective we are limiting ourselves to here. The projected operating costs for the training command proposed here would be in the neighborhood of $10 million annually, wholly apart from the training facility itself, the base pay and allowances for the trainees, and their transportation to and from their home country. This is less than the cost of supporting ONUC for one month during the Congo operation.

The figure of $10 million is arrived at as shown on page 73, with alternative figures showing the estimated cost if the annual intake of trainees were 3,000 instead of 5,000.[5]

This figure may be compared with a total of $8.3 million arrived at on the basis of an earlier formula of $8 to $10 per day per man for such a training facility—$7.3 million for 2500 men at a time on the lower rate—plus $1 million for base maintenance.[6] To both these would

[3] *World Peace Through World Law,* 2nd ed. (Cambridge: Harvard University, 1960), p. 320.

[4] Frye, *op. cit.,* pp. 75-78.

[5] I am indebted to Colonel David L. Evans, USAF, for this table and the subsequent one on headquarters staff. The figures used for personnel costs assume officers at the average rank of major, and a preponderance of non-coms among the enlisted personnel. It would be important to be able to select and pay superior personnel as instructors.

[6] "Military Aspects of a Permanent UN Force" by Lt. Cols. Charles A. Cannon, Jr., and A. A. Jordan, in Frye, *op. cit.,* p. 167.

be added the approximately $1.5 million for the augmented head-quarters planning staff discussed below. Both total approximately $10 million.

Annual Base Operating Costs	$1,000,000
Cost of Base Support and Training Personnel	
350 @ $6,000 plus 452 @ $4,000	3,908,000
(300 @ $6,000 plus 335 @ $4,000)	(3,220,000)
Rations for Trainees	
2500 @ 1.07 per day	946,400
(1500 @ 1.07 per day)	(585,800)
Cost of Training per Trainee	
2500 @ 2.50 per day	2,281,250
(1500 @ 2.50 per day)	(1,386,750)
Total Yearly Training Costs	
for 2500 men	8,165,650
(for 1500 men)	(6,174,550)

The alternative figures are based on reducing the program to an ultimate total of 15,000 men trained over a five-year period, 3,000 per year, 1,500 at any one time. The base and training staff would be reduced proportionately. (The ratio of trainees to instructing staff under the larger scheme is 6.57 to 1, and under the more modest one, 6.43 to 1; this compares with approximately 10 to 1 in United States military training, but it is justified by the special circumstances.) The over-all annual cost would be somewhere around $7.5 million. It would seem that the larger program would be considerably more economical.

The total annual cost of $10 million depends on cutting the costs in every way possible. One means suggested earlier that would reduce the budgeted assessed costs of the operation would be a maximum of contributions in kind. As indicated, the training facility could be a contribution without cost to the UN; the instructors could be loaned from the advanced military powers on a similarly credited basis; the troops could be lifted for training on planes or ships of powers, including ourselves, who might consider it a useful training exercise in transport of non-American forces in an emergency. (It would also represent the start of the earmarking arrangement.) The rations could be contributed on the same basis. All these, as suggested, would stand as credits against future assessments for UN field operations.

It may well be that some who oppose the strengthening of international institutions would refuse to pay their share of this item in the regular budget, along the line pioneered by the Soviet Union when it announced in May 1963 its intention to deduct selectively from its regular contribution the Soviet share of those detailed items to which the Soviets object. Here too the debts of the defaulters should be carried on the books. The United Nations should continue to dun them. But their failure to pay should not be permitted to erode and eventually destroy programs the world needs.

For the longer run, it has become increasingly clear that the present method of financing the United Nations is an imperfect one, and may be no longer suitable or adequate to the needs. The bond issue has been a stop-gap, not a permanent solution. Suggestions have been made for increasing the sources of independent revenue for the organization, and one that may be promising is for the United Nations to receive a share of the revenues from exploitation of the sub-sea bed, as proposed by the United States.[7]

But the financial problem is political in its roots. There is no dearth of money to do the job if states are willing to supply it. Indeed, the United States could handily do it all, except that it would probably be fatal to the health of the organization and to American support for it. The fundamental issue of sovereignty in all its contemporary ambiguity underlies the financial problem; the latter cannot be solved by somehow assuming a solution to the former.

The practical problem is not just paying back debts. The problem is what to do about the next crisis requiring that the United Nations mount a field operation, and the next. Suggestions have been made to buy time in which such vital operations can be fielded, by establishing a security or peace fund.[8] But this remedy is only a temporary one. Moreover, it still requires payment by the very countries now refusing to pay.

The United Nations is simply going to have to have resources of its own to enable it to do a job which is in the interest even of those who are seeking to sabotage it by withholding their financial support. My own suggestion has been for an Endowment: a capital fund sufficient to provide annual income that will enable the United Nations to carry out at least a significant part of the task the nations charge it to do but without always following up with the financial wherewithal. No increase in international powers is involved; simply the knowledge that means exist to back up a decision made by exactly the same political process as today.

No one can foretell the reaction to such a proposal. It may be wildly optimistic to guess that a world-wide appeal for, say, a one-billion dollar

---

[7]Statement by President Richard M. Nixon May 23, 1970 (White House Press Release).

[8]See UNA-USA reports referred to above, and Report of President's Commission.

endowment fund for the United Nations would be oversubscribed by individuals, foundations, governments, and private corporations. Already there have been a number of efforts on the part of American citizens to supply private funds to the United Nations. Some Quaker groups in the United States have made a practice of "tithing the tithe" for the United Nations as for a church. Some communities in this country sent to the United Nations money which they would have spent on fall-out shelters. These gestures are idealistic, and, because of their small size, quixotic, although well meant.

What is needed is an effort on a world-wide scale to supply funds by tapping a wellspring of good will, hope, idealism, and the urge to make a personal contribution to a meaningful cause; who can say how deep this spring runs? I can envisage a general fund-raising drive that might give the whole enterprise the shot in the arm it so badly needs. Contributions should of course be tax-exempt. With a growing reserve of funds, the organization can go ahead and do its job without depending either on its enemies to pay their share—an unrealistic hope—or putting the US government in the position of appearing wholly to subsidize it.[9]

The various proposals outlined above should not be taken as a quantum jump from the existing realities to some novel kind of world force. They should be presented as a modest series of measures that build on past experience in the light of anticipated needs of the future. Those who oppose the growth of constructive and stabilizing peacekeeping capacities for the United Nations will predictably continue to oppose even these modest steps—although in some likely circumstances they will once again find it to be in their own interest. Above all, the proposal should not be tied to the utopian vision of peace forces, international armies, or world police under general and complete disarmament. The degree to which any of the great powers see it as a potential major threat to their security would thus be minimized. The proposed force would be employed under the same constitutional majorities in the Security Council and General Assembly as today in terms of actually fielding an operation. The substantial difference would be in readiness and efficiency.

The general philosophy adopted here in the matter of UN forces is, then, to strike out in modest ways to enhance essential peacekeeping capabilities while keeping well within the *de facto* ground rules of the nationalistic age, taking the most extraordinary care to preserve the

[9]Lincoln P. Bloomfield, "The United Nations in Crisis," *Daedalus,* Fall, 1962. See Norman J. Padelford, "Financial Crisis and the Future of the United Nations," *World Politics,* July, 1963. For a comprehensive analysis of the whole financing problem see John G. Stoessinger, *Financing the United Nations System* (Washington: Brookings Institution, 1964).

fiction of the sovereign equality of states. Proposals for a standing UN force, for taxing powers to support the force, for direct individual recruitment into a common uniform, or for weighted voting in the assembly are not necessary or relevant to the present system, even reinforced by a modest standby force (although they would all be relevant if and when the General Assembly were ever endowed with genuine legislative powers rather than only the power to recommend). For now, the problem in its essence is to stay within the boundaries of political reality but to get the job done. The most that can be hoped for—and that will be a great deal—is a modest step toward regularizing this international capability so that it does not have to be invented anew and the world organization undergo a political revolution each time the need arises.

One of the cardinal errors of the contemporary peace movement is the notion that steps toward a world community, toward peaceful settlement of disputes, and toward greater tolerance between nations are necessarily habit-forming in the face of overriding ideological, political, or territorial conflict. The inevitability of historic progress toward world order has simply not been proven, however high our persistent hopes and visions. One thing that has been proven to be relatively habit-forming the world over, however, is the "police function." Let us admit at once that anything approaching a genuine police function in the hands of the United Nations is anomalous and even legally inexplicable in the absence of a genuine international political consensus of basic political values that must underlie community and its police powers. But an approach to the problem that is pragmatic and empirical demonstrates both a need and a possibility for an international function that, while neither police nor military, is more the former than the latter.

One might say that this is a case where it is desirable to rise above logic and even legal principle in the name of the higher principle of surviving a period of the world's history when formal institutions are inadequate to the need, when political warfare stands in the way of real consensus, and when only a second-order agreement—not to destroy the world—is the current basis of cooperation among the superpowers.

An earlier genius like Dag Hammarskjöld could perform with virtuosity his political pirouetting along the knife edges of ideological conflict in the name of getting the job done, all without any sound institutional, political, or financial basis. The task that faces the responsible powers is to institutionalize the best of Dag Hammarskjöld's genius so that it does not depend on the presence or availability of such genius. It is to meet as best one can, imaginatively, creatively, but with realism, the day-to-day requirements of a world whose management rests in the hands of simple men with complex problems.

PART II

A Symposium

on

International Forces

of the Future

Hans J. Morgenthau

POLITICAL CONDITIONS FOR A FORCE

I

A police force, domestic or international, must meet two requirements: it must be reliable, and it must be effective. While obviously it cannot be effective if it is not reliable, it can be reliable without being effective, and it is for this reason that the two prerequisites must be distinguished. A police force, in order to be reliable, must be loyal to the political authorities and share their conceptions of law and justice. A police force, in order to be effective, must stand in a certain relation of power to that fraction of the population which is likely to call forth police action by breaking the law.

The police within the state are the instrument of a central authority which is supposed to be endowed with a will culminating in decisions, and it is these decisions that the police are called upon to put into practice. In legal terms the police have the function of enforcing the laws; in political terms they have the function of upholding the authority of the government; in social terms they have the function of protecting a status quo as defined by the laws and expressed in the government's policies. In a well-ordered society the police are but rarely called upon to enforce a change in the status quo; the enforcement of new race relations against groups committed to an outlawed status quo is a case in point in our society. In revolutionary societies, on the other hand, the police force is the main weapon with which a revolutionary minority imposes its will upon a recalcitrant population.

It follows that the police force will be reliable in the performance of its functions only if it has either been forged into so disciplined an instrument of the government's will that it will execute whatever orders it is given regardless of content, or else if its convictions and interests are at the very least not openly at odds with those of the government.

Thus the police force, knowingly or without knowing it, is bound to be deeply involved in the political controversies of the society in which it operates.

Lenin maintained correctly against his opponents within the Marxist camp that the dictatorship of the proletariat could not afford to take over the enforcement agencies of its bourgeois predecessor and use them for its own purposes; forged for the purpose of maintaining the rule of an exploiting minority over the exploited majority, they could not be so used. Instead the proletariat had to create its own police, open and secret, appropriate to the special tasks of a new society. During certain periods of violent labor struggles in our society, the police force, regardless of the legal merits of the case, tended to transform itself into a protective guard for the employers, reinforced at times by the latter's private police. The police have at times refused to enforce the law for the protection of members of racial minorities. In certain regions of the United States they have habitually used their power to deprive such members of their rights through positive action. During the crisis at the University of Mississippi in 1962, state and federal police tried to enforce incompatible legal rules and conceptions of justice. Wherever a society is rent by deeply felt controversies, even though they do not lead to open violence, the political preferences of the police are likely to color the performance of its function.

On a lower level of motivation the police, frequently individually and sometimes collectively, have yielded to the temptation of private gain and neglected to enforce the law against certain types of violations, of which traffic, gambling, vice, and housing code violations are outstanding. If this corruption occurs on a massive scale, the police may transfer their loyalty altogether from the legal government to another, private one in the form of a crime syndicate. The police in our society remain a reliable instrument of law enforcement because normally no more than an insignificant number of them will be opposed to the legal order they are called upon to enforce.

The reliable performance of its functions by the police force within the state is thus not a simple technical matter to be expected with mechanical precision. Quite the contrary, it depends upon political, social, and moral conditions which may or may not be present in individual members of the police or the police force as a whole. These conditions must be created and maintained through a continuous effort of the political authorities. In other words, the functioning of a police force depends not only upon its internal technical qualities, but also upon the political, social, and moral climate within which it operates. If the latter is not favorable, the former will avail little.

The effectiveness of a police force is determined, aside from its reliability, by the power relation that exists between itself and the recalcitrant fraction of the population. For the police to be effective, that power relation must meet three prerequisites.

Of all the citizens of a particular society only a very small fraction must be engaged at any one time in breaking the law. If large numbers of citizens simultaneously break the law, as they did with regard to prohibition and rationing and as they are still doing with regard to gambling, the police force, although it meets the standards of reliability, ceases to be an effective agency of law enforcement. Second, however great the differences in power are within a given society, the combined power of law-abiding citizens must be distinctly superior to any combination of even the most powerful lawbreakers. If it is otherwise, as in the case of the medieval feudal lord and his modern counterpart in the form of private concentrations of economic power, the police are bound to be almost as impotent as the citizenry at large. Finally, the police force must be manifestly capable of coping effectively with all foreseeable threats to the legal order. This obvious capability serves to deter attacks upon the legal order that go beyond the piecemeal violations of individual legal rules. In other words, its visible readiness for effective action makes its actual employment in good measure unnecessary.

This quality of unchallengeable superiority, aside from being the result of the reputation for reliability, is a function of the two other prerequisites. In consequence the government is able to rely upon a numerically small and lightly armed police force to maintain law and order. In the absence of these prerequisites the state would need a numerous and heavily armed police force in order to meet frontal attacks upon the legal order itself. That is to say, the state would need an army rather than a police force, and the relations between government and people would be tantamount either to civil war or a military dictatorship.

II

It follows from what has been said thus far that the problems with which an international police force must come to terms are posed by the peculiar character of the international society since that character affects both the reliability and effectiveness of the force.

First of all, an international police force by definition cannot be at the service of a single government to which it gives allegiance and whose orders it executes unquestionably because of that allegiance. An international police force can only be the instrument of an international organization, such as the United Nations. It is this relationship that makes its reliability a continuous problem. In a society of nation-states it is possible for some outstanding individuals to transfer their loyalty from their respective nation-state to an international organization either on a particular issue or even in general. But it is too much to expect that large masses of individual members of different nations could so transfer their loyalties that they would execute reliably and without question whatever orders the international organization might give them. The reliability of an international police force cannot be taken for granted by virtue of the morale and discipline which we have come to expect from the domestic police.

The reliability of an international police force is a function of the legal order and the political status quo it is called upon to uphold. Yet the enforcement of an international legal order and the protection of an international status quo present a police force with problems quite different from those the national police has to solve. Great international conflicts which lead to the violation of international law and conjure up the danger of war and therefore call for the intervention of an international police force are typically the ones in which the survival of the existing legal order and of the political status quo is at stake. The task which the international police force must here perform is not the defense of the legal order and of the political status quo against piecemeal violations, but against an all-out attack. What is at stake here is not the enforcement of a particular legal rule, but the survival of the legal order itself.

One nation or group of nations will be committed to the legal order as it is and to the existing status quo; another nation or group of nations will be opposed to them; a third will be indifferent. The members of the international police force belong to all of these three types of nations, and their sympathies concerning the issues at stake are bound to vary with the preferences of their respective nations. The members of an international police force will be a reliable instrument of an international organization only in the measure that their legal preferences and political sympathies happen to coincide with the policies of the international organization they are called upon to support.

In consequence the international organization commanding a police force will have to cope with three different contingencies with which national political authorities do not have to deal under normal circumstances. If the challenge to the legal order and the political status quo emanates from or is supported by a great power, the police action reverts to the traditional pattern of a coalition war. That is to say, an army composed of contingents of the nations supporting the legal order and the political status quo will be opposed by contingents of the nation or nations opposed to the legal and political status quo, with the contingents of neutral nations tending to one or the other side. This was the pattern of the Korean War. That this war was called a police action by the supporters of the status quo did not affect the nature of the operation. At best it made it easier for certain nations, which otherwise might have been inclined toward neutrality or a half-hearted effort, to join the defense of the status quo or to commit themselves more fully to it.

If the status quo is challenged by a nation of the second or third rank which has a vital stake in changing it, the sympathies and interests of many other nations are likely to be actively engaged on one or the other side. This contingency will confront an international police force with choices that are bound to be detrimental to its reliability or efficiency or both. If the international police force is composed of national contingents assembled in advance of and without regard to this particular conflict, those of its national contingents which are out of sympathy with the status quo may not be relied upon to defend it. If the international police force is being assembled *ad hoc* in view of this particular conflict and hence is being composed only of reliable national contingents, it faces the risk of being too small to provide an effective defense of the status quo against the forces opposing it.

Even if an international police force appears at the beginning of a conflict to be a reliable and effective instrument of an international organization, it is still faced with an ever present threat to its reliability and effectiveness. An international police force may be politically cohesive at the beginning of a conflict on the basis of a community of sympathy and interests on the part of the nations to which its individual members belong. Yet it is a moot question whether and to what extent such a community of sympathy and interests can survive the initial stages of the conflict. New interests may replace or modify the initial ones; new opportunities may present themselves for the pursuit of old ones. As the interests of the nations concerned change, so will the reliability of the respective contingents of the international police force to defend a status quo which may run counter to those interests. A multinational military force, be it called an international police force or an army, is thus always threatened with partial or total disintegration. Its survival as a reliable and effective force depends upon the persistence of the national interests on which it rests.

What distinguishes an international police force from a national one is, then, the lack of an automatic commitment to a particular legal order and political status quo. Such a commitment can be taken for granted, at least normally and except for piecemeal or marginal deviations, in a national police force. It cannot be taken for granted in an international one, but must there be created and re-created and maintained for each issue. The task an international organization faces in fashioning a police force for a particular issue parallels that of a group of nations seeking political and military support for a particular status quo. The international police forces which have been organized by the United Nations have reflected both the composition and the political and military character of the two-thirds majorities of the General Assembly to which they owed their existence. That is to say, no nation which did not support the police action by its vote in the Security Council or General Assembly supplied contingents for the police force, and of those who so supported it only a small minority supplied contingents. The contributions of these nations were a manifestation of their political interests and military capabilities.

Thus, of the then sixty members of the United Nations only sixteen provided in 1950 armed forces of any kind against North Korea, and of these only the United States, Canada, Great Britain, and Turkey can be said to have contributed more than token forces. South Korea and the United States provided about 90 percent of the armed forces that fought in Korea on the side of the United Nations. For the United Nations Emergency Force stationed along the Egypt-Israel armistice demarcation line, the international frontier south of the Gaza Strip, and at the Gulf of Aqaba the following nations provided troops: Brazil, Canada, Colombia, Denmark, Finland, India, Indonesia, Norway, Sweden, and Yugoslavia. The United Nations force in the Congo was originally composed of contingents from Ethiopia, Ghana, Guinea, Morocco, Tunisia, Sweden, and Ireland. The composition of that force subsequently changed according to changes in the policies of some of the participating nations. However, what remained as the distinctive feature of the United Nations force in the Congo was the numerical predominance of contingents from African nations, which had a special interest in the pacification of the Congo without the intervention of non-African nations. What this United Nations force had in common with that of the Middle East was the absence of great-power contingents, pointing to the policy of the United Nations to use its armed forces for the purpose of isolating the territorial issues from great-power intervention.

The tenuous character of an international police force reflects the tenuous character of the commitment of a number of sovereign nations to a particular legal order and political status quo. The deficiencies of an international police force are the deficiencies of the international order revealed in the perspective of a particular task. In a world of sovereign nations the idea of a reliable and effective international police force, after the model of the national police, is a contradiction in terms. An international police force, by dint of being international rather than national or supranational, cannot be more reliable and efficient than the political interests and military capabilities of the nations supporting it allow it to be.

This situation would not be materially affected by arms control or limited disarmament. At best the control and limitation of national armaments might increase the effectiveness of an international police force in conflicts among major powers, provided that the stabilization and decrease of national armed forces were to go hand in hand with a corresponding increase in the strength of the international police force. Without the latter proviso, arms control and disarmament might well have an adverse effect upon the effectiveness of an international police force; for they might adversely affect the ability and willingness of national governments to put armed forces at the disposal of an international organization. The best that can be expected from arms control and limited disarmament is a change in the distribution of armed strength between national forces and the international police force in favor of the latter. But the basic political issue bearing upon the reliability of an international police force will continue to make itself felt even in a partially disarmed world; for such a world would still be a world of sovereign nations.

The situation would be radically different in a totally disarmed world. Total disarmament can no more be envisaged in isolation from the over-all structure of international relations than can an international police force. Total disarmament requires as its corollary the existence of a supranational authority capable of committing organized force to the defense of the legal order and the political status quo. In other words, total disarmament and world government go hand in hand; they complement each other. In a totally disarmed world the problem of an international police force ceases to exist and reappears in the form—new in its dimensions and old in its substance—of the police of a world government.

III

A historic example will serve to illustrate the dependence of an international police force upon the political purposes which it is intended to support. The illustration is provided by the armed action of the Holy Roman Empire against Frederick II of Prussia during the Seven Years' War. It is surprising that to the best of my knowledge nobody has analyzed the Holy Roman Empire as it existed from the Peace of Westphalia of 1648 to its dissolution in 1806 as the prototype of an international organization which shows revealing similarities with its 20th century successors—the League of Nations and the United Nations.

The medieval emperor of the Holy Roman Empire was supposed to perform the peace-preserving and law-enforcing functions for the sake of which modern international organization has also been established. In the words of James Bryce:

> He was therefore above all things, claiming indeed to be upon earth the representative of the Prince of Peace, bound to listen to complaints, and to redress the injuries inflicted by sovereigns or peoples upon each other; to punish offenders against the public order of Christendom; to maintain through the world, looking down as from a serene height upon the schemes and quarrels of meaner potentates, that supreme good without which neither arts nor letters, nor the gentler virtues of life can rise and flourish. The mediaeval Empire was in its essence what its modern imitators have sometimes professed themselves: the Empire was Peace: the oldest and noblest title of its head was "Imperator pacificus." And that he might be the peacemaker, he must be the expounder of justice and the author of its concrete embodiment, positive law. . . .[1]

Originally the emperor was supposed to perform these functions as the head of a universal empire, that is, as the highest secular authority within the Empire's territory. The Treaty of Westphalia reduced these functions to international ones by recognizing the territorial sovereignty of the princes and cities subject to the emperor. The emperor was in consequence precluded from interfering directly with the administration of any territory belonging to the Empire. All major political decisions concerning the Empire, such as the making of war and peace, levying contributions, raising troops, building fortresses, passing or interpreting laws, were the exclusive competence of the imperial Diet. Yet the Diet, in the words of James Bryce,

> originally an assembly of the whole people, and thereafter of the feudal tenants-in-chief, meeting from time to time like our early English Parliaments, became in A.D. 1654 a permanent body, at which the electors, princes, and cities were represented by their envoys. In other words, it was not so much a national Parliament as an international congress of diplomatists.[2]

The Diet had the authority to protect the legal order and the political status quo of 1648 by summoning the members of the Empire to collective military action. In addition France and Sweden, which were

---

[1]James Bryce, *The Holy Roman Empire* (New York: The Macmillan Company, 1923), p. 259.
[2]*Ibid.*, p. 396.

not members of the Empire, had in 1648 been made guarantors of the order of 1648 and hence had received the right to intervene in the affairs of the Empire on behalf of that order. But the Diet, similar to the United Nations, could only request member states to put money and armed contingents at the disposal of the Empire, taking what the member states were willing to give; it could no longer, as it once did, enforce the "matricula" specifying the quota of contingents each state was obligated to furnish to the imperial army.[3] Thus the Holy Roman Empire developed in a way which is the reverse of the development many expect the United Nations to take: starting as a supranational organization, it ended as a federation of sovereign states.

After Frederick II of Prussia invaded Saxony in August 1756, the Elector of Saxony appealed against this breach of the peace to the Emperor and the imperial Diet. After the Emperor had exhausted the peace-preserving and law-enforcing measures with which the imperial constitution empowered him (the so-called *Dehortatoria,* addressed to the King of Prussia; the *Avocatoria,* ordering the Prussian armed forces to leave the seditious service of their king; and the *Monitoria,* the *Excitatoria,* and the *Inhibitoria,* addressed to the imperial territories in order to prevent Prussian enlistments) the council of princes of the Diet decided on January 17, 1757, by a vote of 60 to 26 to declare in the name of the Empire war against Prussia and to employ the military resources of the Empire for the purpose of restoring the Elector of Saxony to his throne. Pursuant to this resolution a special tax was levied on all the states of the Empire, and an imperial army was raised.[4] The composition of that army, the factors determining its composition, and its fate shed a significant light upon the problems facing an international police force.

The states of the Empire split according to their religious and political preferences. All the Catholic states took the side of Austria; the majority of the Protestant ones, that of Prussia. The Protestant princes of Hanover, Brunswick, Lippe, Waldeck, Hesse, and Gotha protested against the resolution of the Diet; they were allied with Great Britain, which in turn supported Prussia. On the other hand, the King of France as guarantor of the Treaty of Westphalia—which guaranty had originally been aimed at Austria—declared his support for Austria in its struggle with Prussia, and it was especially due to his efforts that the imperial army was assembled. In other words, it was not so much the resolution

---

[3]*Ibid.,* p. 394.
[4]F. C. Schlosser, *Geschichte des Achtzehnten Iahrhunderts* (Heidelberg: J. C. B. Mohr, 1837), Vol. II, p. 319; Reinhold Koser, *König Friedrich der Grosse* (Stuttgart and Berlin: J. G. Cotta, 1903), Vol. II, p. 47 ff.

of the Diet but special political relations between France and individual German states which induced the latter to provide contingents for the imperial army. Thus the King of France requested the electors of Cologne and the Palatinate to provide the number of troops promised him in previous treaties. He concluded new treaties with the Elector of Bavaria and the Duke of Wurtemberg in which he promised them subsidies as compensation for a number of regiments to be provided. He made similar agreements with a great number of minor German princes. As a result of these effots an imperial army numbering 32,000 men was assembled. They marched into Thuringia in September 1757 to join a French army numbering 24,000 men.

When 9,500 of this "Combined Army," as it was officially called, encountered 1,900 Prussians on a reconnoitering expedition, they were put to flight. As the *Cambridge Modern History* put it:

> Here the extraordinary deficiencies from which the combined army suffered for the first time made themselves evident. . . . The army of the Empire was composed in motley fashion of contingents supplied by numerous small dynasts. This had not hindered Marlborough and Eugene from winning partly by means of the army of the Empire the battle of Höchstädt; but in their day English and Dutch subsidies had helped to establish that army on a satisfactory footing. At present, in consequence of lack of money, such intolerable conditions prevailed among the Imperial troops that Hildburghausen [the commanding general] despaired of being able to keep his forces together for long, and therefore impatiently sought a decision by battle.[5]

On November 5, 1757, the day of the battle of Rossbach, the imperial army had shrunk to 11,000 men. Of these, 7,000 were disbanded at the beginning of the battle. Those who remained were put to flight. The Bavarian and Franconian infantry threw their rifles away while the Prussians were still in the distance. The precipitous and disorderly retreat of the run-away army at the beginning of the battle became in the eighteenth century a by-word for cowardice and disorganization.[6]

The battle of Rossbach signified the end of the imperial army. According to Ranke, the very name disappeared.[7] The reasons for this catastrophe must be sought in the unreliability of the imperial army,

---

[5]*Cambridge Modern History*, Vol. VI: *The Eighteenth Century* (New York: The Macmillan Company, 1909), pp. 265, 267.

[6]Koser, *op. cit.*, pp. 132, 135.

[7]Leopold von Ranke, *Sammtliche Werke*, Vol. XXX: *Zur Geschichte von Österreich und Preussen zwischen den Friedensschlüssen zu Aachen und Hubertusberg* (Leipzig: Duncker and Humboldt, 1875), p. 312.

which was the result both of religious and political factors. The appearance of France in Germany as the ally of Austria against Prussia could not fail to be considered as a Catholic alliance against the foremost Protestant power in Germany. Thus the Protestant elements of the imperial army quite openly sympathized with Frederick II. The disintegrating effects of the religious preference were reinforced by divergent political sympathies. This became obvious at the battle of Leuthen, following the battle of Rossbach by a month. The Austrian commanders could not trust ten Bavarian battalions because of the political conflicts which then existed between Bavaria and Austria; the same was true of fourteen battalions of Wurtembergers who hated their tyrannical ruler and admired the victor of Rossbach as the champion of German Protestantism. The Austrian commander placed those contingents on the left wing where he did not expect the Prussian attack. Frederick attacked exactly at this point with the result that eleven out of the fourteen battalions of Wurtembergers fled immediately, leaving behind only a few killed and wounded.[8]

[8]Schlosser, *op. cit.*, p. 335; *Cambridge Modern History, op. cit.*, p. 275.

Stanley Hoffmann

Erewhon or Lilliput?

A Critical View of the Problem

The predictive power of the social sciences is poor. That of the science of international relations is particularly mediocre, since it deals with a type of social action—the conduct of foreign policy—that is pervaded by uncertainty and in which even the most carefully calculated actions partake of gambling. Therefore, to try to forecast the chances of "international military force" in general during the years to come would be an exercise in futility. There are, however, two tasks which a political scientist can begin to perform. One consists of making the necessary distinctions; they may appear tiresome to the general reader and trifling to the impatient reformer, but both those gentlemen ought to remember that the opposite of distinctions is confusion. The second task consists of examining what kinds of international forces appear to be compatible with the international system in which we live.

I.

Our experiences with international forces begin to be impressive. In addition to the United Nations experiments, discussed elsewhere in this volume, we should keep in mind not only such precedents as the Boxer expedition and the temporary international administration of Crete after 1897 but also those military alliances that have, in war or in peacetime, united a very large number of states against their enemies. Attempts at devising other international forces either through negotiations or in the literature of international reform provide us with more types. Consequently, even if we limit our discussion to armed forces that are supposed to intervene (violently or not) in order to prevent, to restrain, or to repress the use of force by nations in conflict, and thus do not consider here the kinds of surveillance forces or inspection systems that arms control or disarmament agreements may entail,[1] we discover that the expression "international force" covers a large number of possibilities. I would like to list the main questions which ought to be asked apropos of each such force.

1. A first group of questions deals with the *political context.*

A. What is the situation of national forces, i.e., what might be called the *arms context?* Does international force operate in a world in which each nation remains fully armed and free to arm, or does it play its role in a disarmed world, or in a disarming world—and in the latter case, at what stage of the process? Carrying out any of the missions that will be listed below would present different problems in each of these cases. We are familiar with the conflicts to be expected in an armed world; the circumstances may be full of surprises, but the types of clashes are quite well classified. A totally disarmed world is something we know nothing about, since it is difficult to imagine an international system without a hierarchy of nations, or to think of a hierarchy in which the scale of military might would play no part. Furthermore, such a world may well be an impossibility (for national police or constabulary force might play the same role after "disarmament" as the previous armies). A disarming world may combine the disadvantages and the dangers of an armed system and of a disarmed one—i.e., suffer from all the traditional conflicts as well as from the incidents and suspicions of the disarmament process.

It is interesting to note how the statesmen's ideas about the relation of international force to the arms context have fluctuated. In the days of Versailles and the League Covenant, it was deemed essential for collective security to operate in a world in which national armaments would have been reduced to a minimum. After World War II the Charter of the UN reversed the order of precedence: the machinery of Chapter VII was to be put into effect first, and the Charter is remarkably discreet about disarmament. The dangers of the arms race and the failure of collective security in an armed world have brought the super powers back to schemes that would seem depressingly familiar to Léon Bourgeois; this is especially true of the recent United States "Outline of Basic Provisions of a Treaty on General and Complete Disarmament in a Peaceful World." Whether this cyclical turn of recent history is a vicious circle or not remains to be seen. But in the late 1960's, disenchantment with collective security and de facto renunciation of disarmament seem

---

[1]The United States proposals for general and complete disarmament of 1962 distinguish also between the functions of the International Disarmament Organization and those of the UN peace force.

to have converged on schemes for arms control which, in effect, leave the world well armed while avoiding the issue of an international force.

B. What is the *basic structure* of the international system? Does the force operate in a system of competing units, or as the secular arm of a world state? All known international systems are variations on one or the other of those models. Obviously, each one can appear in a variety of forms. A federal world state would differ from an imposed empire, and the medieval *Civitas Christiana* was something else again. World arrangements in which sovereign units are the essential actors include balance of power systems and revolutionary ones; systems in which the units compete without institutionalized efforts at cooperation and systems in which international organizations try to regulate and mitigate the competition; and systems in which the autonomy of the sovereign unit is real and systems in which military, economic, and ideological developments have resulted in a considerable amount of "integration," i.e., a devaluation of national borders unaccompanied by anything like a world state.

Despite those variations, and despite intermediate situations (Empires with networks of dependents and vassals amidst a system of competing units), I would maintain that there are essential differences between the two models. Any scheme which aims not at abolishing national armies but at moderating the amount of violence to which states can resort is based explicitly or implicitly on the assumption that there can be no sudden mutation in world politics and that the state, despite academic indictments or burials, is here to stay. Any scheme which aims at disarming states and at setting up an international authority (political and military) that would settle disputes and maintain order establishes in fact, if not in words or in intention, the beginning of a world government.

C. What is the nature of the relationship (or relationships) of *major tension* in the system? Let us assume that we are still in a world of competing units, fully or partially armed. As long as there is no world government, even if the units have only "police forces" at their disposal, and even if some international forces exist to prevent the units from resorting to violence, the risk of interstate war—the distinguishing mark of international relations—will persist. Consequently, two questions are important, both concerning the relations between the big powers. Are we dealing with a bipolar or with a multipolar world? (Despite all the analyses that stress, quite correctly, the changes from the simpler calculations of power and balance in the past to the "multiple equilibrium" and the multiple levels of power of the present,[2] the traditional distinc-

---

[2]As an example of these analyses, see George Liska, *International Equilibrium* (Cambridge: Harvard University Press, 1957) and Glenn H. Snyder, *Deterrence and*

tion, which takes military might as the chief criterion of the great power, remains valid for several purposes at least, especially what might be called the power of life and death—i.e., of settling major disputes and of plunging the world into global war.)[3] In the case of a multipolar system, are the tensions between the major powers of a shifting or of a more permanent character? In other words, what is the degree of rigidity of the alignments in the system?

It is difficult to describe what effect the existence and spread of nuclear weapons will have on the traditional dynamics of world politics —and consequently on the chances of an international force. Some of the prophets of a world government endowed with a world police display what Raymond Aron, when discussing Marx, termed catastrophic optimism. According to these prophets, only if the nations of the world have reached the very brink of thermonuclear war or have already gotten a taste of doomsday will they be wise enough to put an end to a game they keep playing out of habit and mutual distrust, even though it has become insane since it is now capable of annihilating the players; and the more nuclear players there are, the more this tragic moment of truth becomes likely.[4] If one believes on the contrary that statesmen will succeed in the effort to have their cake and eat it too—i.e., stick to the game but play it with enough self-restraint to avoid the catastrophe of nuclear war and the cure of a world leviathan—then the lessons of the recent past become more applicable. A serious crisis between the major powers will bring about not the leviathan but the kind of turbulence with which Berlin and Cuba have acquainted us, and in which international force seems to have the choice between no role at all and a modest one when the confrontation between the chief contenders is not a head-on collision. In addition, there are those who believe that the spread of nuclear weapons makes a continuation of the game more, rather than less, probable.[5] Only future events and coming tests will show which one of these concepts is closest to the truth.

Defense (Princeton: Princeton University Press, 1961), who distinguishes a strategic balance of terror and a tactical balance of power.

[3]Military might itself depends, of course, on industrial potential, population, space, etc., and the use of this might, now that it includes nuclear weapons, poses problems and suffers limits that will be mentioned below. See the author's *Gulliver's Troubles* (New York: McGraw-Hill, 1968), Part I.

[4]This seems to be the case of Herman Kahn. See *Thinking about the Unthinkable* (New York: Horizon, 1962), Chapter 7.

[5]This is the case of General Pierre Gallois; see his *Balance of Terror* (Boston: Houghton Mifflin, 1961). The author's own views, which are gloomier, have been expressed in his contribution to: Alastair Buchan (ed.), *A World of Nuclear Powers?* (Englewood Cliffs: Prentice-Hall, 1966).

2. A second group of questions concerns the *mission* of the force.

A. A first question is one that remains academic at present: will the international force be a permanent one ready to be used whenever a central political authority decides that the conditions for the force's employment are met; will it be an *ad hoc* force set up in and for an emergency; or will it be the kind of stand-by force to which Chapter VII of the Charter referred, i.e., a force to be mobilized whenever a political decision to this effect would be made, but whose constitution would have been carefully prepared in advance and in detail? A subsidiary question in the case of a permanent force concerns its location in between conflicts—where would it be stationed?

B. In a world of states the relationship between the force and the parties involved in a dispute or crisis is of fundamental importance. The issue, to put it broadly, is that of consent.

(1) Does the force intervene with the consent of those parties, or against the will of one (or even all) of them? In the former case, even if the consent is a grudging one and has been wrested only by diplomatic pressure of a stringent sort, and even if one of the purposes of the force is actually to expel a state or a group of states from a position or an area (as in Suez with respect to England, France, and Israel, or in the Congo with respect to Belgian troops) the mission of the force can be termed interposition or neutralization. If at the outset or in the course of the operation the relation becomes an adversary one, the force's symbol is no longer the fireman. Depending on the point of view, it is either the policeman-in-action-against-a-delinquent or the pyromaniac: we are in the hypothesis of collective security (a military operation against a state and on behalf of a victim) or of collective action (a military operation either against a domestic trouble-maker or—a somewhat less easily imaginable hypothesis—against a group of feuding states that forcibly resist international intervention). The term "police," which is often used with reference to international forces, is both ambiguous and misleading. It is ambiguous because there is a great difference between police activities which are peaceful and police operations which involve the use of force. Domestically as well as in the international milieu, it is misleading because in either case the relation of the "policeman" to the "citizen" (whether law-abiding or delinquent) has nothing in common with the relation of an international force to a state or even a rebel group.[6]

[6]As I. L. Claude has pointed out, the relation between even a world government and a rebel group would be more like that between a national government and a minority, than like that of a government to an individual trouble-maker. (*Power and International Relations* [New York: Random House, 1962].)

(2) In the case of a non-adversary relationship, the issue of consent appears again at the other end of the operation. Can the host state determine freely the termination of the force's mission (cf. Egypt vs. UNEF in May 1967), does the force's withdrawal have to be negotiated with the political authority that controls the force, or can the operation continue even after the host state has withdrawn its consent?

C. The next set of questions concerns the *specific functions* of an international force.

(1) Preliminary questions refer to the nature of the conflict. If the role of the force is an adversary one, there are two key questions. First, who is the enemy (or who are the enemies): a major power, an ally of a major power, a small state? Second, is the conflict an international one (and in this case, does the force have a mandate as the rescuer of one side) or a domestic one (insurrection, secession, civil war) in which the force carries out a mandate against one of the factions? Or is it a mixture of domestic and international strife? The distinction between domestic and international conflicts and the nature of the contenders are also important if the force's role is a peaceful one.

(2) The scope and content of the mission may vary considerably. In the case of collective security or collective action, what are the military and the political objectives assigned to the force, and does it have to observe certain restraints either in the choice of arms, or in the selection of targets, or in the geographical scope of its operations? In the case of a peace force an important aspect of its mission is the stage at which it intervenes. Its function may be to insulate a local conflict from outside intervention (Middle East, Congo); to separate warring nations or factions (Cyprus); to supervise a truce and to prevent the parties from coming to blows again; to carry out or supervise the implementation of a specific solution.

(3) It is also important to ask in each case whether the role of the force is an essentially negative or a positive one: does the mission consist of repelling an invasion, insulating an area or a problem, preventing or stopping an outbreak of violence, or does it consist of carrying out a substantive solution of the underlying dispute either by force (cf. the reunification of Korea under the resolution of October 7, 1950) or by the mere pressure of the force's presence? The experiences of the UN have demonstrated both the frustration of purely negative definitions whenever the parties were still locked in battle and the political difficulty of positive definitions in a divided and explosive world. In Korea after 1951, when there was no more talk of unifying the country by force, the problem of how to put an end to the war after the military status quo had been approximately restored plagued the operation, just as the assignment of negative missions to the UN Congo operation

(ONUC) complicated the Congo force's task in the midst of a civil war. On the other hand, the resolution of October 7, 1950, brought about an escalation of the Korean War which weakened political support for the operation in the General Assembly, and ONUC's use of the right of self-defense so as to carry out the positive task of reunifying the Congo under Mr. Adoula's government has been highly controversial.[7] Mr. Hammarskjöld's interpretation of the limits and possibilities of the UN made him prefer not only non-adversary interventions to adversary ones but negative tasks to positive ones.

3. A third group of questions concerns the *operations* of the force.

A. The problem of political support is obviously essential. Even in the case of a force at the service of a world government, national differences will certainly not vanish right away, and it will not be possible to discuss "one world" as if it were merely a state writ large. *A fortiori* an international system of separate states would have to be examined pretty much in the way in which students of the UN have analyzed the postwar world, no matter how strong the powers of the international authority in charge of controlling the force. The most important questions that have to be asked are:

(1) What states approved the resort to the force and the definition of its mission; what states opposed it; what states abstained?

(2) How have support, opposition, and abstention evolved during the operations?

(3) What is the nature and extent of financial support? The scrutiny of political support is not enough; there may be a discrepancy between political and financial backing, and the financing of the force must be studied separately.

B. The *composition* of the force raises another set of important questions.

(1) Professor Schelling's essay[8] discusses the size of the force. It may be rash to assume that the size and the mission will always fit together perfectly. Like all measurements of power in world politics, the notion of size is a relative one: the impact of the force depends on the ratio between its own size and that of the forces it has to tame, separate, or

---

[7]The fact that even in the resolution of November 14, 1961, the use of force was explicitly authorized only for the negative purpose of expelling mercenaries from Katanga has of course added fuel to the controversy. But the very caution of the document indicates the political difficulty of obtaining support for more positive definitions, as well as the practical difficulty of remaining on the cautious side of the line.

[8]See pp. 112-132.

deter. One of the main troubles of ONUC was the disproportion between a force that was large by UN "peace force" standards on the one
hand and the size of the former Belgian colony and the complexity of
the force's mission on the other. Conversely, the larger the force, the
more its sponsors may be tempted to make it play a major "positive"
task—a temptation that may account in part for the Soviets' insistence
on limiting the size of the world force in the negotiations on Article 43
of the UN Charter.

(2) The political composition of the force is equally important. One
may ask first who provides its members. At San Francisco it was assumed that peace would be maintained primarily by the "big policemen"; in recent years it has been necessary to keep the big powers out
and to ask the small states to provide emergency forces.[9] A choice
between a force supplied by states geographically distant from the
trouble spot and a force composed of neighbors would also be full of
consequences. So would the choice between a force made of contingents
from states that have been scrupulously neutral in or indifferent to the
dispute in question, and a force provided by states sympathetic to one
or the other party, hence open to pressure from it. (Unfortunately,
sympathies develop, change and switch.) Appearance and reality do not
always coincide: a force whose men and commanders are drawn from
small states but whose equipment, means of transportation, and weapons
are provided by a major power has, within the international competition, a meaning quite different from that which the champions of international neutralization and "vacuum filling" would like to reserve to
international force. Secondly, one should ask who determines the political composition of the force, and in particular how much of a veto does
the host state have (if the relationship is a non-adversary one), and how
free are the participants to withdraw from the operation when they see
fit.

C. This brings us to a last set of problems, which can be summed up
by the oldest question of political science and the ultimate question of
political strategy: *who commands?*

(1) Since a force is always at the service of a policy, the question
means, in the first place, what is the authority that decides to resort to
the force, defines its mission and its composition? Three possibilities
appear. The authority may be a coalition of states which go through a
process of bargaining comparable to the process of coalition-building in
national multiparty systems.[10] On the other hand, it may be one major

---

[9]See I. L. Claude, "The UN and the Use of Force," *International Conciliation*,
March 1961 (No. 532).

[10]The relevent precedents would be the Boxer expedition and the discussions
among the Allies on strategy and on a unified command during World Wars I and
II.

state that obtains a mandate to serve as the political brain of the operation or takes the initiative and succeeds in getting the main lines of its policy approved by the necessary majorities (Korea serves as a precedent here). Or the political command may be shared between a body of state delegates—in which either one of the two formulas just described operates—and an international executive distinct from state delegates. This last solution evokes the UN Emergency Force (UNEF), the UN Observer Group in Lebanon of 1958 (UNOGIL), and ONUC; but in its first stages at least a world government would probably have to conform to that model also, just as the European Communities actually divide political authority between the supranational organs and the councils of ministers. Obviously the respective powers of the international executive and of the body of state agents may vary enormously. The relations between the two institutions, however, are of decisive importance since there is a definite connection between the nature of this relation and the kind of international force that is likely to emerge or to operate. The more the international executive depends on the states for political and financial support, i.e., the less freedom of action it enjoys, the more reluctant the state may be to create large and permanent forces under the third formula, out of fear that the executive would use the men and money made available to him in order to emancipate himself or, should large forces become necessary at some point, the more likely may be resort to one of the other two formulas of control.

(2) The question of military command and of civilian-military relations is also important. Is the military commander an international civil servant, or a national officer who wears an international hat for the duration of the enterprise? Appearance and reality may be at odds once again: if the political control of the operation is of the second type, the degree of international autonomy of the commander may be very low or purely fictitious. In all cases other than that of a permanent army, the division of authority between the international commander and the various national commanders of the contingents involved must also be studied closely.

II.

So many combinations between the hypotheses distinguished above are possible that they defeat the attempt to set up a few models of international forces. True, most of the factors I have lised are interdependent; but because there are so many factors, the number of possible outcomes is just as high as that of the combinations of the different and interrelated causes of potential conflicts.

Nevertheless, all proposals for international force, whether modestly presented as efforts at preventive interposition of the sort described in Mr. Hammarskjöld's last annual reports, or advocated by heralds of collective security, or advanced by champions of world government, are based on one belief and pointed in one direction. It is the belief that "international anarchy" carries increasingly intolerable risks due to the dangers of traditional self-help in a thermonuclear world. It is in the direction of greater centralization of power, for even the dispatch of a small military observer corps to supervise a truce between minor states is an advance over either uncontrolled violence or pure and simple diplomatic intervention by third parties.

Some may argue that the proponents of an international order less dangerous than the present one rush in the wrong direction—that centralization of power means a more rather than a less bitter contest for control, and more rather than less of the scourge of intervention. There is indeed some truth in the argument. However, we shall assume that neither the isolation of each from all, envisaged by Rousseau,[11] nor the antithesis between peace and enforcement developed by Mr. John Burton[12] make much sense: the former is ruled out by history and technology, the latter rests on a truncated conception of the causes of conflicts. Consequently, the question that must be examined is this: how much centralization of power can realistically be introduced into the present international system? Since one cannot forecast the impact of cataclysms, let us assume that thermonuclear war will not break out in the near future. Let us assume also that even if nuclear weapons continue to spread, the distance between the super powers and the nuclear *parvenus* will remain considerable for quite a while; and let us remember that even if steps are taken toward explicit arms control or disarmament agreements,[13] we would still be dealing with a world of armed nations, competing ideologies, heterogeneity in state structures, regimes and levels of developments; consequently none of the sources of conflict described by Professor Bloomfield[14] would dry up.

1. The present international system makes extremely unlikely the setting up of a permanent international force or of a stand-by force of the kind envisaged in Chapter VII of the Charter.

[11]See Stanley Hoffmann, "Rousseau on War and Peace," in *The State of War* (New York: Praeger, 1965).

[12]See his *Peace Theory* (New York: Knopf, 1962).

[13]For reasons that will be discussed more fully below, I do not believe in the possibility or success of ambitious explicit agreements of that sort until *after* a radical transformation of the present system (to be defined below) has already begun.

[14]See pp. 22-37.

A. There are important reasons which militate against both those types of forces.

(1) The most fundamental reason is not, perhaps, what I. L. Claude calls the essence of sovereignty: the state's right to be unpredictable.[15] In the present competition, which is of a revolutionary nature, a state may be quite willing to mortgage this right and to combine its forces with others—but only to the extent to which it feels gravely threatened by an enemy that is concretely identified. The more lasting this enmity is thought to be, the more sacrifices to the common defense—or to common deterrence—are likely to be accepted. The existence of a clear-cut common enemy may dictate a joint policy, to be served by a combined or integrated military force; but the nations' common interest in avoiding all-out war is too abstract and too vague to dictate a sufficiently precise common policy that a permanent or stand-by force could uphold. A world force that would be above and beyond the very real lines of enmity that crisscross the world is inconceivable. A world force that would protect effectively all those who feel threatened against all their potential enemies is a contradiction in terms. A world force that would give a seal of approval to one particular set of states against another, while disregarding other patterns of hostility, would not be a world force. The circumstances which doomed Chapter VII have not been transcended. In the present international system (and in any other system of competing states) the establishment of a permanent or stand-by force requires either the consent of the major powers or the willingness of many of the lesser ones to side with some of the major states against the other camp.

(2) A permanent or stand-by force established by consent of the major powers could only be the expression of those common interests in survival, moderation of conflicts, and mitigation of the arms race that commentators never tire of describing as the "real" interests of the contenders. Unfortunately, reality—as shown by the nations' behavior—is more complex. The common interest in peace and prosperity is one thing, the creation of a common force quite another. When the competition entails a risk of world destruction, each super power may well give up the use of force at those levels and in those places where the danger of escalation is too formidable; but this is not to be confused either with giving up the threat to use force nor—even less—with the establishment of a world force to repress and replace the nations' resort to arms.

It is not easy to support, say, NATO and a common force at the same time. As long as the competition between the major powers lasts, each one can hardly act as if its allies were more dangerous than their

[15]Claude, *Power and International Relations*, p. 121.

common enemy, and the pressure that those allies put on the major ally when they suspect it of becoming flabby in the defense of the alliance's joint interests makes any explicit recognition of the super powers' common interests more rather than less difficult. A mutual desire for a *détente* is thus more likely to take the form of unilateral, parallel (and easily reversible) measures of restraint, or joint, limited measures not affecting allies directly, rather than the setting up of joint forces or of a "third force" explicitly and permanently backed by the first two. As long as the major powers are engaged in a contest that may hopefully remain peaceful but is nevertheless total in the sense of being an ideological competition as well as a power struggle, they are unlikely to set up a force which none of them could be sure to control and which could be used against the interests of one of them—or even against their common ones. For if it is true that the possession of a nuclear arsenal tends to inhibit the super powers' freedom of action and to upset the traditional hierarchy in some respects,[16] and as it is true that the expenses of a world force would fall heavily on the super powers, the desire of each one of them to be protected both against its chief rival and against small power irresponsibility would definitely weigh against the creation of a permanent or stand-by force.

(3) As for such a force established by a coalition composed of one major power, its allies, and the bulk of the "nonaligned" states, it would be a kind of NATO force writ large (and probably made small). The aims of such diverse nations and interests converge openly at times and may perhaps be said to coincide in the long run and in a very general way, but such a convergence is not guaranteed in advance for all concrete cases. Many of the non-communist nations either would refuse to support a scheme that would consecrate the East-West conflict as the dominant one, even though their own sympathies may be on the Western side, or in any event would wish to continue the neutralist game whose essence is to preserve a nation's freedom to flirt with both sides and be courted by both. Thus, a coalition force of this type would all too easily be denounced as a recipe for world war.

Nor is it clear that powers of the middle rank, even if they are allied to a super power against a common enemy, would support a scheme that would enshrine—in fact if not in words—a duopoly in the sense of a permanent division of the world, each half being led by one major state. De Gaulle's objections to what he called America's monopoly in the

---

16Recent developments after the Cuban crisis confirm this analysis. There is one additional advantage of informal restraints over explicit agreements: violations are less likely to produce crises. For law operates as a plate glass window: breaking it makes noise and brings out the police, whereas throwing a rock across an open field draws less attention.

Western camp remain a warning. In a multipolar system a lesser unit can become a major player if it plays the game well enough; in a bipolar one a lesser state, in order to become a big contender, must try to change the rules of the game. A permanent or stand-by force risks being an instrument at the service of the status quo, and the middle rank powers (without whose consent no such force could be created in the absence of big power agreement) would probably object on three counts: their fear of strings imposed by their chief partner; their fear of being deprived of the freedom of choice that they need in order to raise themselves to the top level (and that may entail some military blackmailing ability); and the concrete grievances (territorial, economic, etc.) which they would be afraid of having to give up in the event of a world force they do not control.

B. More specific arguments can be used against each of the two kinds of "non-improvised" forces that could be envisaged.

(1) An international standing army is out of the picture. Problems of composition and stationing would be insoluble, and the question of loyalty would arise in its most acute form. For an army must be at the service not merely of an ideal but also of institutions that give some flesh to the ideal. If such an authority could be established in a way that would not make it a major stake in the nations' contests, our troubles would by definition be ended. We have not reached Erewhon yet. It is impossible to see how today's contenders would agree on creating such a monster. It is impossible to see how, should they have agreed on it in a fit of cosmic absent-mindedness or in a state of shock, the army would meet Professor Morgenthau's two tests.[17] What would be the reliability of a force in which totalitarians and non-totalitarians may be juxtaposed, or, if it were drawn exclusively from the reservoir of small, nonaligned states, in which an insidious battle for control would be just as permanent as the army? What would be the effectiveness of a force whose mission would stagger from the Scylla of terms so vague that its functions would appear too nebulous to the Charybdis of terms concrete and pointed enough to give the force a sense of purpose, but at the price of militant partiality? The precedent of mercenaries is a very dubious one. Not only were they hardly instruments of world order, but they predated the age of national loyalty. A permanent standing army may be conceivable in a post-nationalist age when world politics would be much more moderate than in the past century. The way the world looks now brings to mind President Kennedy's rueful remark that things are likely to get worse before they get better.

(2) A world force composed of national contingents earmarked by

[17]See pp. 79-89.

the states and kept ready for international use, by making less impossible demands, would make the problems of political authority and loyalty appear less formidable. A European community which was still in the making and which did not have precise and positive common foreign and military policies was not able to give birth to a European army. But the degree of cooperation created in NATO by the common, well-defined military threat has been sufficient to permit NATO to be satisfied with much more limited military integration than had been envisaged for EDC, and consequently, NATO's decision-making procedures can be much shakier than those which EDC would have required.

However, the very spectacle of NATO—especially since the early 1960's—provides us with two warnings: first, at the level of the world as a whole (or even of the non-communist world) the sense of a common, concrete threat vanishes. Secondly, even within NATO a joint negative interest does not erase the important disagreements in political and military strategy due to divergent assessments of the means to the common end, to conflicting geo-strategic priorities, and to the members' different positive purposes, which correspond to differing visions of the world *after* the final success of the common enterprise; hence, a complex inter-allied battle for control.

The establishment of an international stand-by force would run into the bog in which the negotiators of 1946-1947 sunk along with Chapter VII and, should a disarmament agreement be in the making, the insistence on the need for such a force as the corollary of a gradual elimination of arms race, arms threats, and armed attacks is likely further to complicate matters. For, in the first place, the establishment of a force of this kind presupposes one of two things: either there has to be a decision by the relevant states to let an international organ, such as the UN Security Council, decide in each case whether to mobilize the force and for what reason; or else there has to be a fully worked-out agreement defining in advance and in detail the kinds of circumstances in which the force could be used and the kinds of missions it could perform in each case. In the former case it is hard to imagine that nations whose enthusiasm for compulsory jurisdiction is on the whole well checked would let an international organ play what might be Russian roulette with their interests without "adequate guarantees" which, being incompatible, would be pretty hard to define to everyone's satisfaction. In other words, there would be a pre-emptive battle for control of the decision-making organ, of which postwar debates about the veto (when the Security Council was that organ), contests for two-thirds majorities (when the General Assembly became the battlefield), and discussions about a troika (when the Secretary-General's role increased) have given us a foretaste. But in the second possibility it is easy to predict that either the states would fail to agree on a meaningful definition, both exhaustive and precise enough (just as they have failed to define agression), or else the agreement on a document would not really settle anything, and in case after case a battle royal would break out around the issue as to whether or not the events fell into one of the slots of the agreement.

Let us, however, assume secondly that a stand-by force has been created under one of those formulas. Permanence would still risk being either a facade or a farce. The effectiveness of the force would be rather unpredictable because, although a stand-by force would seem much preferable to an improvised one, no two conflicts are really alike. For a stand-by force to be well prepared in every possible case it would need contingents as numerous and an arsenal as rich and diversified as those of the only states that can presently afford to devise omnibus strategies —the super powers.

As for the force's reliability, it would also be dubious. Should a conflict break out between the major states or between a major state and a close ally of the other one, a political choice would still have to be made between the risks of a collective security operation and a mere attempt at neutralization. It is all too likely that a world force could move in to "insulate" the area only if the major powers had first decided to let the force come in as a face-saving device, i.e., if the test of strength has not ended either in a war or in a humiliating capitulation of one of the contenders. The availability of the device makes resort to it easier; however, it is hard to imagine the major powers agreeing in advance either *never* to test their strength or nerves again, or to settle ritually *any* such test in so suave a fashion.

Should a conflict break out in an area in which the major powers are not directly and militarily involved, they might well agree to let a peace force of the UNEF or ONUC type intervene, but again the decision would have to be made at the time of the emergency. It is hard to imagine them agreeing in advance *always* to let a third party—say, the Secretary-General—make the determination, or agreeing in advance *never* to send contingents of their own nationals into an area. It is of the essence of international uncertainty that one cannot predict whether a conflict will remain of a certain type, compatible with great power abstention, or whether it may not pose such risks for a major state that its direct intervention will become the lesser peril. (The evolution of the Middle East conflict since 1956 is most instructive.) It is hard to imagine the major states drawing up in advance a list of "non-competing" countries—the permanent Procrustean bed of world order— for it is of the essence of the international competition that a list of this sort must be either dramatically short (with bad consequences for efficiency) or thoroughly unreliable. On the other hand, it is hard to imagine the major powers agreeing in advance *always* to include their nationals in the force; for it is also of the essence of the contest that each major power will try to keep its adversary out of a certain area, or to prevent it from consolidating whatever foothold it may already have.

Nor is it easy to imagine the smaller powers committing themselves in advance to well-defined patterns of action. The failure of big-power talks on Article 43 may have spared the super states the embarrassment of endless discussions with the smaller ones over Chapter VII, and the experience of the "Uniting for Peace" resolution has confirmed that solemn generalities do not determine concrete cases. Since the resort to international neutralization is most likely in crises affecting immediately the smaller states, few are likely to sign or to support a blank check for a procedure that, however neutral in intent and well devised to keep the over-all balance of force intact, may nevertheless affect quite unevenly the parties locally involved.

Thus the idea of the stand-by force runs into two sets of obstacles. The larger powers, because they have a preponderance of military strength, are unlikely to erect any institution capable of interfering with their own conflicting attempts at shaping the world they want. The smaller states, because they do not have enough power to shape their own future, are unlikely to accept any institution that may at worst condemn them even more to the role of pawns and at best remain indifferent to and independent from attempts at resolving fairly their substantive difficulties and disputes; nor, for that matter, are the big powers united enough to impose permanently such a scheme.

2. None of this means that within the present international system states will not be able to agree on the occasional establishment of international forces. The lessons of past years are more complex. On the one hand, even so mild a "stand-by" authority as the Peace Observation Commission has been reduced to a slumber much like death; on the other, the Members of the UN have set up forces of various sizes and missions. The political circumstances that have made them necessary may be with us for a long time to come.

A. The nature of the system seems to rule out one kind of force: the collective security force. If there is a genuine international community, collective security operates through a reflex of solidarity, expressing a common interpretation of common interests, which triggers the reaction against a violator of the common law, who is clearly seen as a delinquent. In a world less certain of the ultimate common good but still capable of agreeing on procedures and rules of the game, collective security becomes the modern version of the mechanism of imbalance that kept down the ambitions and the gains of trouble-makers (large or small) in balance of power systems—the mechanism by which an alliance of states tries to suppress attempts to upset the balance, undertaken by states that are seen as temporary adversaries, but not as necessarily evil or permanent enemies.

Today's international milieu is very far removed from the harmonious but theoretical model of a community. Alliance situations are realized, but three factors tend to dissociate alliances from collective security. The existence and the diffusion of nuclear weapons, along with the resulting danger of escalation, have made a resort to conventional force in inter-bloc relations less likely. The enlargement of the UN has made the one exception to this statement, Korea, quite definitely unique, for it is probable that no majority could now be found to give a seal of UN legitimacy to the military operations of one alliance. The increasing fragmentation of the two chief rivals' alliances, which limits, in effect, alliance solidarity to the European theater, makes the availability of recruits for collective security at the call of a super power most dubious. Collective security against a major power or its close allies is just about as impossible as the drafters of the Charter calculated: the risks are too high, the likelihood of majority support is too small, the dilemma of preparation is too insoluble. For it is impossible either to prepare in advance an operation against one of the major members of the organization or to improvise in an emergency an effective operation against a super power. Against it or its allies the only international forces that may perform military functions (at an obvious risk) are the coalesced forces of an alliance.

Outbreaks of violence among or within smaller nations, or in the last colonial or quasi-colonial areas, may well provide a majority of UN Members with the temptation of resorting to collective security or collective action, especially if the crusading spirit of anticolonialism can be enlisted. However, the twin dangers of competitive great power intervention and of politically and financially destructive great power opposition[18] would rise in such a way that peace forces for interposition and neutralization, inspired by the UNEF and ONUC precedents, with missions defined perhaps in more positive terms but stopping nevertheless short of the collective use of force, remain the most likely prospect. For in the present world the nature of the delinquency is often not clear-cut enough, and even when there is sufficient agreement

---

[18]One can envisage that the United States would support interposition forces in case of serious troubles in Angola or, say, South Africa; it is hard to imagine the United States backing a collective security expedition against an ally or a close partner of an important ally. In the case of Rhodesia, the UN attempt at sanction has been a failure, and the call for acts of force has not been heeded.

against the delinquent or the trouble-maker, a collective-intervention force runs the risk of disturbing even more the precarious balance of terror or power.

B. The kinds of international forces that remain possible are thus *ad hoc* forces of interposition which could be established and dispatched whenever:

(1) The major powers explicitly agree on measures in an area in which they are not militarily involved to prevent a conflict from escalating or to prevent some of their respective allies from dragging the world into disaster.

(2) One major power succeeds in convincing a majority of states to intervene in a conflict of the type described under (1) despite the opposition of the other major power. This opposition may complicate the undertaking, but if the area of the conflict is not one in which the opposing power is deeply committed and involved, the majority is less likely to be intimidated—especially if the other major state is skillful in presenting the operation as an effort to shut out bloc competition. An enterprise of this sort becomes an exercise in ambiguity. The lesser states hope that this insulation from the main contest will take place; the major state which encourages that hope wishes nevertheless to consolidate its own position by posing as the champion of the small; its antagonist hopes that there will be enough difficulties to thwart the ambitions of its rival—while wishing perhaps also that the operation would succeed just enough to prevent a dangerously direct confrontation. The volatile character of this brew of expectations explains why configurations of such a sort may reproduce themselves from time to time but can hardly be codified.

(3) The major powers agree to entrust an international force with a task of supervision after an agreement on a problem affecting their immediate and essential interests in areas of direct involvement. So far, despite suggestions concerning Berlin or the Middle East, there have been no such cases.

C. Forces of interposition remain however subject to some serious limitations.

(1) The forces' efficiency and reliability continue to depend on the nature and the size of the tempests they will have to master. As the Congo has shown, even a sizable force may be in trouble if the problem it deals with keeps getting more formidable, like the Sphynx's questions. And the disintegration of UNEF has exposed the fragility of small forces caught between the armies of incensed adversaries, as well as that of the Secretary-General in a world of conflicting states. Paradoxically, insofar as collective security operations are ruled out, large scale inter-nation wars might not be the worst kind of tempests that forces of inter-

position would have to face, since those forces would intervene only after the belligerents had agreed to suspend hostilities. But major internal or colonial upheavals are both more unmanageable and more to be expected. The idea of organizing a UN force for Algeria at any point during the seven-year rebellion staggers the imagination; no such force was seriously suggested in the cases of Biafra, East Pakistan—or Vietnam. In case of serious trouble in east and south Africa, the prospects for UN forces are hardly rosier. Whenever the force is asked to intervene in a situation in which the major contenders have not agreed on the force's principle and mission, the operation will be in danger even if the host state—legally the sole authority but politically one among several contenders—has formally assented. The force, already too small for its mission, will constantly risk gliding from interposition to an adversary relationship; on the other hand, increasing its size will raise the stake in controlling and defining its mission.

The consequences for the force's morale are obvious. Even if the formal definition of its task remains, in Dr. Dicks' words,[19] simple and unpolitical, the realities would be complex and controversial. For, as the Congo has again shown, simplicity is a function of the situation rather than of the drafting of the basic resolutions, and the genuine alternatives are not political versus unpolitical, but generally accepted versus hotly contested. Large domestic upheavals and ferocious colonial battles may still have to be resolved through the gruesome, time-honored process of the violent confrontation of the parties, as Proudhon had warned a century ago. And any step beyond insulation from the outside world might suck the force into the maelstrom.

(2) A second limitation is the financial one. The bigger the expedition, the more the force may have to depend for its material and financial support on the super powers or on one of them. The political consequences are obvious. At present and in the foreseeable future the super powers seem unwilling to support jointly undertakings designed to keep them out of an area or capable of favoring one camp against the other. Operations that depend on the financial good will of one of the super powers can pretend to be efforts at interposition rather than expressions of an alliance only as long as they are kept small; past a certain threshold, the major power tends to be worried lest the degree of political control it has over the operation not match the expenses it incurs,[20] and the smaller states tend to get fearful about the political slant of the enterprise. The financial troubles of ONUC have made the

[19]See pp. 133-151.
[20]The same is true in UN economic development institutions.

states more aware of the importance of financial security for international forces but not more capable of agreeing on the means of providing it. Consequently, although the circumstances enumerated under B. are likely to recur, the Members of the UN may become more hesitant than in the past to plunge into political waters with no financial bottom.

3. None of these reservations suggests that a passage to a more moderate international system will not improve the prospects of international force.

A. However, in this gradual shift to moderation, the contribution of international force, while far from negligible, may well remain modest. The primary condition, to put it simply, is the end of the Cold War as the all-pervading tension. Such a change implies both a progressive decline of ideology, i.e., an end to the proselytism of communist dogma (or other dogmas), and a return to a multipolar situation. As long as there is a clash of radically antagonistic philosophies of domestic and world order, the fear of nuclear war will be the main source of wisdom, the only firm common standard in the game. Should a multipolar world emerge, the chief contenders of today would be forced to recognize the limits of their ambitions and prospects, and such felt restraints might corrode their ideological ardor. Obviously, whatever consolidates those parts of the world that lie outside the main camps and keeps the military competition of those camps away from such areas favors moderation in the long run. Here international forces of the kinds I have described as possible have a role to play. However, aid to underdeveloped countries and the stalemating of forcible communist expansion across borders through the maintenance of the "balance of terror" and through military alliances are likely to contribute even more to the appearance of new poles of power outside (and also within) each camp, and to the erosion of ideology.

Moreover, the period of change will also be one of tension: a risk of disintegration for one camp, the frustrations of a loss of control for the leader of the other (although the general direction would be the one it had desired), the trials and errors of nuclear diffusion, the continuing heterogeneity in levels of development, and the hazards of the population explosion are among the forces of trouble. Even if all those are under control, the gap between the advanced nuclear powers and the others will not be closed soon, and a decline of ideological fervor in one part of the communist ex-camp cannot be equated with the end of ideology throughout.

B. A more moderate system will probably find more ways of using an international force. A world which technology is shrinking, in which the fear of nuclear war or nuclear rearmament would still be a common concern, but which would no longer be torn by conflicts as revolutionary as the present ones, would not only be guided by a more generally accepted set of rules of the game, it would also need a higher degree of centralization of power.

(1) Two tendencies would thus converge to favor international forces. First, explicit agreements on arms control or disarmament would have become possible. As long as the political competition has an intensity and a scope as great as today, faith in large scale arms control requires a belief in the capacity of the duopolists to agree explicitly against their respective allies, or a belief in their willingness to coerce those allies, a belief in the possibility of divorcing arms from politics, and a belief in the transcendence of ideological and geographical asymmetries by common interests identically experienced. Only in a more moderate system could such hopes begin to be vindicated. At that point arms control agreements could be policed by international forces. The arms control agreements and discussions of recent years reflect, to be sure, both the existence of moderating factors within the present international system and the need, felt by the super powers, to curb the "mad momentum" of the strategic arms race which has ceased to have any direct relation to political use and achievements. But this is only a beginning—and a slow one at best.

Secondly, the main powers in a moderate system tend to be more able and willing to act together in order to prevent smaller states from upsetting the status quo: the hierarchy becomes again more important than the bloc alliances. Given such a big power consensus, the capacity of the smaller states to resist the pressure from above would decrease, and prospective upstarts would have an advantage in promoting their interests through cunning rather than force. An international military force could be the secular arm of the international legitimacy the big powers would want to enforce.

(2) However, such hopes are not only what the Germans call *Zukunftsmusik;* they must also be tempered by the following considerations. First, there seems to be an inverse ratio between the existence of "permanent" (or let us say lasting) alliances and that of important international forces. A permanent force capable of playing the role theorists of collective security had earmarked for it presupposes an end of alliances that may well be incompatible with a system of separate states. It is easier to imagine a permanent force of interposition.

Secondly, it is just as easy to imagine that contests about its mission will arise in each concrete case, and that the political authority which will supervise its operations will be a major stake in the international competition. For a joint desire to limit the mischief that lesser states can produce, or even a joint desire by the majority of the big powers to prevent a misguided member of the elite from reaping excessive gains through unilateral action,[21] has rarely gone without a private ambition on the part of each of the "responsible" major powers to win special advantages within the concert of the great. Arms control or disarmament measures may not alter this situation, for although the major states will have even more of a joint interest in preserving a hierarchy that the mere superiority of their arsenals may not ensure anymore, the fear of cheating or rearmament by one of them and the desire to escape or to reduce those controls that might hamper one's own freedom of action would also have increased. If the West European community may be cited as a precedent or a model for a more moderate world system, one can envisage a general delegation of authority from the major states (and the others) to the common executive, full exercise of this authority by the executive in instances of low political explosiveness, and a battle for control whenever the political implications of action are high.

Thirdly, the world force's efficiency would remain as dependent as ever on the success of efforts at solving the substantive issues that would have made its intervention necessary. A system in which these substantive issues persisted indefinitely and whose statesmen would dispose of awesome international bayonets to sit on would be just as uncomfortable—and self-defeating—as previous examples. The less adequate the procedures for the settlement of disputes, the less satisfying to the parties the results achieved through such techniques, then the more resort to international force will be required—but the more unstabilizing its long-run effect will be. In a revolutionary system sitting on powder kegs may be defended as a precaution; in a moderate one it is at best a temporary expedient.

[21]This traditional mechanism of imbalance against a stray great power could not function again if that power were in possession of means of mass destruction. A multipolar world in which all the major states would be full-fledged nuclear powers (i.e., had effective invulnerable deterrents capable of inflicting unacceptable damage on any enemy) would not be a moderate one—to say the least (Aron, *Peace and War,* New York: Doubleday, 1966, doubts that such a system could function or that today's super powers would tolerate its emergence). Thus the hypothesis discussed in the text presupposes some degree of arms control. I agree with the champions of arms control when they point out that without such measures moderation will be impossible to achieve; I do not believe, however, that those measures are likely to be explicitly defined and applied so long as the basic conditions of a return to moderation, described in the text as an end of the Cold War, have not been met. Thus we agree about the need, but differ about timing and prerequisites.

Thomas C. Schelling

STRATEGY: A WORLD FORCE IN OPERATION

The relation of an international military authority to the industrial (once nuclear) powers in a disarmed world is an intriguing one. We should not expect much success in finding an ideal strategy for it. It is hard enough to find one for the United States, Britain, or the Soviet Union in the familiar world of competitive military force.

And unless we expect a nationally disarmed world to be a stagnant one—hardly likely in the first few decades, if only because of the novelty of the environment—it might not be wise even to look for an enduring strategy for the international force. If national disarmanent and an internationalization of military force are ever accomplished, it will probably not be as a revealed religion but as a political-military experiment. We had better not burden the organization with the need to know in advance the solution to all its strategic problems, or even what all those problems will be.

The "strategy" of an international armed agency is not just its military techniques. It is also its "foreign policy." The problem is not only one of equipping and training an efficient force that can conquer a country or halt some hastily mobilized army. It includes whom to invade, when, on what provocation, with what "war aim," or whom to defend against what. It involves who the "enemy" would be in a world in which it may be politically awkward to talk about enemies and in which "enemies" may not always be nations but governments or civil-war factions within nations, or movements not identified with territories and nations. The distinction between civil war and international war, not too clear at present, may become less clear. Those who argue today whether it is better to be red or dead may have to decide whether disarmament is worth a war in arriving at a policy for the international force.

If we think of an international authority as a "police force"—to use a term that is often applied—the correct analogy is not overtime parking and burglary, but school integration, general strikes, looting in the wake of a disaster, election frauds, labor racketeering, collusive price fixing, and the problems of jury rigging, police kickbacks, and the third degree. The "policing" function is not just a matter of blue-suited men on motorcycles, but the entire issue of law and order and individual rights. For our international military authority, we do not even know yet what "laws" it will be asked to enforce. And in making its plans to restrain an aggressor or to dampen hostility the internatioanl authority may not be allowed the conceptual advantage of a clearly identified "criminal."

We have at least three areas to explore. One is the *organization* of the force—how it is staffed and financed, where it is housed, where it buys its supplies, and what "security" functions it performs other than tactical military functions. The second is its *foreign policy*—what it is supposed to deter, to compel, or to obstruct, and what its military relations are to be with nations and with other international agencies. Third are the *techniques* by which the threat or application of military (or non-military) violence is to be used to support that policy.

"Strategy" may suggest that we should confine ourselves to the third area. And so we should, if we could, leaving organization and foreign policy to other studies. But the strategy of our international authority, like that of a nation, is constrained by its economic base and internal organization. The strategy of an island nation differs from that of a continental power; the strategy of a rich nation differs from that of a poor one; and the strategy of a unified nation differs from that of one plagued by civil war or dissidents. A nation's strategy depends on whether it can keep secrets, whether its enemies can, and whether it can bluff its enemies, surprise them, keep them guessing, or promote discord among them. The strategy of a nation depends on its vulnerability to sabotage, to paralysis of decision, to inter-service rivalry, and to the desertion or revolt of its troops. The same applies to an international force. We do not know whether an international military organization would have independent financial means of support, secure access to supplies, and its own intelligence service. We do not know because it has not been decided. And some of these decisions should depend on their implications for the organization's strategy.[1]

---

[1]Something else not decided—and the language of this chapter must, for that reason too, be ambiguous—is how the international armed forces will fit into some larger organization. There will be some parliamentary or formalized diplomatic body at the top, and there has to be some executive authority, military or civilian, over the armed forces or over each separate service or command. Whether there will be some executive-administrative body above the armed forces (as with the

(Continued on page 114)

THE ORGANIZATION OF THE FORCE

A good place to begin is with money. We need some idea of how much money the force would require. This depends on which "force" we are talking about—a single international force, a strategic force separate from a tactical or limited-war force, a deterrent force separate from intervention force, or a force that can confront major powers as distinct from the force used to monitor small countries. If it is to be a force that can deter, repel, or conquer one major power or all of them at the same time, it is likely to be expensive enough to dominate the budget.

It will presumably need an "invulnerable nuclear deterrent," probably a more flexible and diversified deterrent than the major powers require now, with some redundancy as a safeguard against defection and sabotage. It will need good armed reconnaissance and worldwide surveillance and some military capability in space. It may also have to consider more selective, discriminating action than national forces have considered necessary. If it is to have a capacity to invade and conquer large and small countries without (or with little) use of nuclear weapons, it will need well trained, well equipped airborne and amphibious troops. And it would probably have to maintain standards of quality and comfort that would meet the highest existing national standards. Such a force would probably cost something closer to $25 billion than to $10 billion (nearer one third the American than twice the British present defense budget).

During the first decade or so of the arrangement there will be a number of countries that can mobilize more than a million men under 35 who have had military training. Some countries, like the United States, China, Britain, or Japan, would require amphibious invasion (unless Canada or Russia accorded unmolested access) or airborne attack. If prolonged war with selective strategic bombing is not to be inevitable, if victim countries are not to be invaded by their main rivals as allies or recruits of the international force, if the force is not to be exhausted in its first campaign and lose control, and if it is to deter adventurism or panic rearmament in other countries while attending to its victim, the force will have to have sizable, professional, peacetime ground-air-naval capability. (In fact, a military organization that can *really* threaten to keep the peace and to prevent rearmament may look so large and so expensive that it is politically unacceptable.)

United Nations Secretariat) or parallel to them (or even subordinate to them for purposes of procurement, research, etc.), whether the international armed forces will be purely military or jointly military and civilian, how much autonomy they will have—even whether, like the Roman senate during Hannibal's invasion, a distrustful political authority will appoint a partnership of generals who rule on alternate days—must go unstipulated.

This cost—$10 to $25 billion—is not just financially significant. It is strategically significant. The money will come mostly from a very few countries—the large industrial countries. In fact, it will come from precisely those countries that are the main potential "enemies" of the strategic force. It will come either through national contributions, through taxes levied by an international agency, or through business enterprises owned by the international agency and operating in those countries. The financial vulnerability of the force to a few major countries is therefore important.

Parliaments have traditionally been reluctant to give military establishments financial autonomy, sometimes on grounds that a self-sufficient military force can be a threat to political institutions while a short financial tether can ensure civilian control. A parliament can starve a military establishment into submission to its wishes (or can provoke, by its attempt, a coup or civil war). So can an international military establishment be starved by a major contributor nation or by several major contributors. It can be starved selectively if some of its contributors can hold up appropriations for particular functions or capabilities.

Not only is this a threat to the military force—a vulnerability to non-violent financial blockade—but it raises questions about the force's authority. Has the military force (or the agency that controls it) the right to collect the taxes to support itself? Can it use military violence to extract the money it needs to maintain itself? Is financial delinquency a *casus belli?* And may the military organization negotiate in the event of a few financial defections, for higher contributions from more willing countries, possibly by the implicit promise of favors to come?

A possibility is to make the armed organization financially independent. It might manage some strategic industries—international airlines and canals, for instance. It might acquire patent rights arising out of its military assets and its research and development, licensing them for commercial use. It might be granted real estate, so that it, too, can become a territorial entity. But it seems unlikely that the armed organization could live off its own assets, though a good many commercial benefits may come out of the multiple technical activities and properties that accrue to the force. But if it depends in part on its own earnings, may it use violence to protect its properties located within nations and to assure their profitable operation? Like the salt tax of earlier times, a few critical monopolies, perhaps especially related to foreign trade, might give a good deal of non-violent leverage to the force. Whether it would want to use it, of course, is another matter.

Next consider how the military authority will spend its money. Most powerful nations have possessed within their territories the industrial base of their war potential. Even countries as dependent on foreign trade as Britain and Japan manufacture most of their own weapons. Control of the industrial base and critical supplies is strategically important to a military force. Without its own industrial base, an international force designed to cope mainly with the big industrial powers would be dependent on its likely enemies not only for money but also for war materials and for research and development of new military capabilities.

Embargo is thus a weapon that can be used against the international force—not just deliberate hostile embargo, but malingering slow-downs and induced difficulties of delivery. Subtle sabotage could be a problem. In a crisis, if a strike occurs at a German or American plant producing re-entry vehicles for the international Polaris force, or if a high incidence of defectives shows up in the delivery of some critical weapons, the organization may have a sticky problem on its hands. And if there is a straightforward denial of access, the international force (or its controlling authority) has to decide not only whether a *casus belli* exists but how long it can afford to negotiate before it feels the pinch of supplies.

Some deliberate dispersal and redundancy of supply would look attractive to the force. It may want to be dependent on no single country for any important military item. It may want to be assured of excess capacity around the world so that, in a crisis, it can forego the output of particular countries. But this raises two problems. One is the high cost of duplicate facilities for complicated items. The second is that a latent "Nth country problem" would be aggravated.

Much that has been said about production and procurement applies to research and development, for which the force would also be dependent on its most likely enemies. If it is to finance all its own research and development outside the major industrial countries, this will probably be at a high cost both in outlay and in reliability. Probably the best that can be hoped for is that some kind of "oligopolistic competition" among three to six major industrial powers would keep the force from being too dependent on any single country or alliance.

In any case, the international force would have to think about the reliability and security of alternative contractors. The letting of a long-term weapon contract will almost surely lead to conjecture as to the political and security motives for choosing one country rather than another. (A country that is interested in the weakening or discrediting of the international force may be tempted to consider bad technological advice to achieve its purpose.) This consideration in turn raises the question whether the force will contract through governments or with private firms, and since the force may want some immunity from strikes and other disruptions in the privately organized economies, the answer is likely to be that it contracts through governments unless it invests in its own "internationalized" arsenals and laboratories on neutral soil.

The loss of industrial secrecy under a worldwide disarmament arrangement might substantially spread military technology around the world. This spread would be relevant to a possible resumption of the arms race as well as to violation of the rules of disarmament. To pose the question in extreme form: how many countries have the right to share in providing nuclear weapons to the international force? Do the present nuclear powers retain, under the heading of "industrial security," the nuclear secrets they possess? Must they share them with each other? Is the technology to be disseminated throughout an "open world" that at some stage, by breakdown or re-negotiation, may begin to rearm itself?

We should keep in mind that it is difficult in any country to divorce military considerations from domestic economics. Any organization that has ten or twenty billion dollars of procurement to undertake will be obliged to think about depressed areas, balance of payments problems, equity in the distribution of contracts, and the industrial growth of more than a hundred countries. What we now call "lobbies" and "military-industrial complexes" may not be purified out of existence by the internationalization of military procurement. And if the United States and the Soviet Union are still in the race to see who will be first on Mars, it is unlikely that an international military procurement organization could stay aloof, and be universally considered aloof, from the impact of its procurement on the relative space technologies of the two countries.

In addition to financial, logistical, and industrial questions, there are some questions of political and administrative organization that would affect the strategy of the force. One is whether it should have its own military intelligence service or should rely on some open "inspection" system to which all nations have equal access. Can it have "spies," and not just "inspectors"?

A second is whether it can keep its military plans and deployments secret from the countries that it works for. Political as well as military secrecy and surprise are involved, because the countries that might be the subjects of military action by the international force would also be represented in the organization. If they know exactly what kind of attack to expect and when, which actions will trigger a response and which will be allowed, or when a military deployment is a bluff and when it means business, the international force will be unlike a national force in its relation to the enemy.

Particularly if the force engages in any kind of "bargaining"—in deterrent threats or ultimatums—it might be embarrassed to have its internal decisions and plans known to its adversary. And if, say, it were about to launch a preemptive invasion intended to be as efficient and bloodless as possible, surprise might be crucial.

Within nations, military organizations usually have secrets that are not available to the voters, political representatives, nor even the entire cabinet. Presumably the chief executive of a country has the right to any information he wants, but he may not know what he wants or whether it exists. The occurrence of military coups and revolts demonstrates that secrets can be held within a military organization. And there can be a legitimate recognition, particularly in times of crisis or war, that since any sharing of secret information with civilian authorities may compromise security, those who have a right to know certain things may prefer not to exercise it.

So we can properly imagine the military organization's having its own intelligence system separate from the intelligence arrangements of the "political authority," or the "inspection force," or whatever else there is. We may also suppose that it can have the legal right to make secret war plans. Whether it could keep secrets in fact, given its non-national personnel system and its political relations with other international agencies, is not easy to say. The answer probably depends on how far one is willing to compromise certain political principles in the interest of military effectiveness. If the organization is confined to a very few nationalities in its top ranks—the nationalities that reflect the former nuclear powers—it may be possible to keep information from the representatives of a hundred other countries. But there is still a problem in keeping secrets from potential adversaries among the major powers.

As Germany, Russia, or the United States becomes a possible target for military action, its representatives may have to be eased out of positions of confidence, their "security clearance" withdrawn, perhaps in a way that did not tip them off to what was happening. This would be difficult, even if one relied on very specially indoctrinated senior personnel who were allowed a good deal of autonomy. If their plans were reviewed by higher civilian authority, the same problem would arise there.

The nature of the problem is suggested by our own government: only the Congress can declare war. If the international force is to be responsive to some representative arrangement, the countries that are most likely to be enemies of the force are precisely the ones most likely to be strongly represented in the legislative branch. The problem is a little like that of a Congressional declaration of civil war against, say, New England. Bargaining between the federal government and a secessionist bloc of states under the threat of war, the development of operational military plans, and particularly any action based on surprise, would be affected by the presence in the Congress of legislators from New England who could not be constitutionally excluded from debate.

While the most tangible problems here may be those of operational secrecy, the more important ones relate to bargaining. Imagine that during the Cuban crisis the Russians by right had had a man sitting beside the President in the White House who not only knew what information was available to the President but also could overhear all the policy discussions. Just what risks to take, how far to let things go, with what limited objectives to take action if action were taken, what minimum Soviet responses would meet our demands, and all that—these are things that one usually wants to keep the potential enemy from knowing.

Of course, it can sometimes help to let the enemy know certain things. If in the Cuban crisis the Russians really miscalculated, and if it was in both our interests that they not miscalculate, it might have been better if they had had better knowledge of how the United States was going to react. When one is not bluffing, it helps if the adversary can authentically learn the fact. (But unless it had secret intelligence in addition, it could not be sure it wasn't being left out of something.)

At some stage, some formality like "declaration of adversary relation" might be required in order to put a country on notice and to exclude it from the inner councils of the organization. The question arises whether at that point the country could cancel its obligations to put up money, sell goods, permit access, provide information, and participate in political-military planning. This not only has to be considered a procedural question, but also as a factor inhibiting the determination of an adversary relationship. How does a legislature deal with illegal secession or civil war by some of those represented in it? (The filibuster comes to mind.)

These questions of security, surprise, and command are affected by another organizational question: whether there is to be a single international military force or several for different purposes. If the latter, what are to be the control and coordination arrangements between the several military organizations?

American forces are now represented in NATO, but there are United States commands, including the Strategic Air Command, to which the North Atlantic Treaty Organization (NATO) countries have had no access by virtue of the NATO treaty. Similarly, an international "strategic force" that is mainly oriented toward deterring the major industrial nations might be quite separate from other international forces whose functions are lower in the scale of violence, oriented toward different areas of trouble, and possibly less concentrated among a few main governments.

From the point of view of military organization, one would probably set up a strategic command separate from the force that is to cope with smaller-scale violence, denying the latter force access to the former. But such a separation of functions does not solve the political problem of who controls the strategic force: whether it tends to be considered the agent of, or the enemy of, the major industrial nations that formerly were (and potentially are) major nuclear powers. If, for the reasons of finance, technology, industrial power, security, and military experience already mentioned, the strategic command is the captive of the United States and the Soviet Union, it may be regarded as a monopoly of force by the great powers. But if control over the strategic command is widely spread, "democratically" or "popularly" diffused among many lesser countries, it may become essentially a device by which a few big nations are policed militarily for the benefit of the small ones. Control over the strategic command will be determined by the arrangements made for its financing, staffing, procurement, and so forth.

THE FOREIGN POLICY OF THE FORCE

These considerations bring into focus the novel position of the force in a disarmed world. We usually think of the Western alliance and the Soviet bloc, or the United States and the Soviet Union, as the principal potential enemies that may need to be deterred, detained, or kept disengaged *from each other* by an international force. But in a disarmed world the United States and the Soviet Union are likely to have a common interest in maintaining their superior mobilization base for the event of war or rearmament. Whether or not they collaborate, they may be of a mind on a number of issues in opposition to lesser countries (including their former allies). Certain preparatory actions that might be considered grounds for military threat and intervention might be available only to the major nations, perhaps the largest two. Threats of intervention might be directed not at one of these countries at the urging of the other, but at both of them at the urging of many other countries, or at the autonomous discretion of an international authority itself. Their maintenance of a technical mobilization base for rearmament, either deliberately or as a natural consequence of industrial and scientific activity, might be an example of such an issue.

Whether the force will be primarily the agent of great or small nations will affect its military strategy, because a main ingredient of that strategy will be threats of intervention. Beliefs about which threats are real and which bluffs, what kind of violence is threatened, and what the likelihood is that the violence will be contained or will get out of hand—these will depend on who controls it. War with a major country or bloc will always be dangerous business no matter what uniform the attackers wear.

An example of such a crisis of credibility is NATO at the present time. There has been much discussion of which deterrent threat will be more credible to the Russians—a United States deterrent "umbrella," independent national deterrents, or a fifteen-nation NATO deterrent. There are also disagreements over the nature of the Soviet threat to be deterred—a large-scale Soviet attack, small Soviet mischief, or Soviet response to an unpremeditated outbreak of violence (like Hungary)—for which appropriate NATO deterrents can be designed. Strategy depends not only on what is credible, but also on what contingencies and actions it is politically possible to contemplate and to plan.[2] And these in turn depend on where political control over strategy lies. Deterrence strategy is at least as much political as military, at least as much concerned with command structure as with the destructive potential of a military force.

There is another important question about the separation of commands. It seems unlikely that an international strategic force would intervene often against major powers. It would be too serious an event. A force may frequently intervene in smaller-scale affairs, of which the Congo, Laos, the Arab-Israeli dispute, Goa, or a Castro revolution might be examples. If there is a single force, its experience is likely to be dominated by small wars, brush fire engagements, police actions, and so forth. Its budgetary orientation may reflect the crises that it is called on to manage during its first several years, unless a "strategic" force is separately emphasized.

At the same time, if we reflect on how an international force might deal with, say, Vietnam, we do not know whether the job would fall under the strategic command or the limited-war or counter-insurgency command. An international force might be no more willing, perhaps less willing, than the United States to support a local force against externally supplied and externally indoctrinated insurgents. An international force might identify the target as Hanoi, Peiping, or Moscow, not the Laotian-Vietnamese border. And if it wanted credibly to threaten that it would not forever tolerate an externally supported revolt but would sooner or later use its military coercive power on North Vietnam or China, it would surely have to coordinate its local actions with its strategic plans. In other words, if most local problems are part of a strategic contest between East and West (or some such blocs) and if a significant element in local wars is some elusive participation of major powers, the relation between local and strategic responsibilities becomes an

---

[2]NATO is seriously precluded from acknowledging certain contingencies and making plans for them by the political sensitivity of the issues. Similarly it is often reported that the Russian and Chinese communists feel constrained—or used to feel constrained—to argue by "proxy," using Yugoslavia or Albania as euphemistic code words for Russia and China.

important matter of policy. It is not a foregone conclusion that in the interest of peace and quiescence the international force should pretend that local violence is a local problem when it is not.

THE TECHNIQUES OF THE FORCE

The techniques by which violence or the threat of violence would be used by the international strategic command should depend on the policy it is supposed to carry out. Even with a fairly explicit idea of what the force is supposed to do, such questions as whether continued disarmament will be worth a war cannot be answered in advance.

The least ambitious purpose that might be served by an international strategic command would be ceremonial. The major nuclear powers might like to support a facade, a pretense that an international force is aimed at them as well as at smaller countries. They might commit themselves to the notion of an international force capable of policing the entire world against everything, adhere nominally to their verbal commitments, and be quite slow about setting up any actual capability. (Some proposals for NATO nuclear forces may serve as illustrations of such an "international" force.) A force might, for example, consist of "national contributions" and solemn declarations by all parties that the progressive integration of the world would bring the force closer and closer to true unification and some eventual autonomy.

At the other extreme the most ambitious goal is probably a force whose primary function is to maintain its military supremacy against all possible adversaries. The critical thing here is the irreversibility of the arrangement. The armed authority would be charged with the mission of making sure that only by sufferance could any nation withdraw from the arrangement and rearm itself. The primary objective of such an organization would not be the deterrence or prevention of war among "disarmed" nations, but the deterrence or prevention of rearmament. As long as significant rearmament was forestalled, the international force would still be in business. It might not win all its wars; it might not prevent wars; but at least it would have the ultimate capability to do so. And as a last resort it could launch preventive war and military occupation against its potential enemies.

A less ambitious objective is to police disarmed nations against the temptations toward violence and aggression, protecting disarmed nations either by active defense or deterrence of attack. This is an easier role to fill because it implies weaponry and tactics effective against disarmed nations and applied in support of an international status quo. The difference between deterring war and deterring rearmament might be compared with the difference between deterring Soviet attack on Europe and deterring Soviet resistance to an armed "rollback" of the Iron Curtain. One is external and passive; the other is internal and active. Rearmament for major industrial countries would be largely an "internal" affair. Except for countries quite vulnerable to blockade, rearmament could be stopped only by force or coercion inside a country, not by containment at its borders.

An important role to consider for an international strategic command is that of a *buffer force.* Instead of being responsible for preventive war against a country that inititated rearmament, it might maintain a protective deterrent shelter within which other countries could catch up. Such a buffer force might not even be obliged to enter an arms race if it could exercise a sufficient deterrent influence—hold a "balance of power" and keep the situation stabilized until the rearmament of other countries had superseded their dependence on the force. Part of its purpose would be to induce or to permit countries to rearm with a view to stabilized deterrence and self-defense rather than with a view to preemptive action. The role of such a buffer force in the event of war itself might not be to win against all countries or against those that start it, but just to make winning a war costly and uncertain for the side that starts it. The international authority might, in other words, pursue a "minimum deterrence" strategy against war itself while providing shelter in the early stages of a rearmament race.

Its role might then be comparable to that of the American armed forces since the end of World War II. The United States has tried to deter, to contain, to guarantee, and otherwise to preserve peace and the status quo. It did not undertake and apparently did not seriously consider preventive war against a nuclear-arming Soviet force. An international force might be equally reluctant or unable to consider preventive war in the face of a large nation's persistent armament program.

If the military organization is intended to guarantee its own supremacy and the irreversibility of the disarmament arrangement by deterring rearmament if it can, and forcibly stopping it if deterrence fails, we get a very different strategy. We get a strategic force absolutely committed to preventive war in the interest of peace and disarmament. (It is even committed to it in the interest of the subjects of the country that it might preventively attack.) And it would confront a dilemma.

The dilemma is that war is war; and to act prematurely, impatiently, and without negotiating not only might create needless violence and damage but also would be a major political act. If instead the force procrastinates, negotiates, provides "one more chance," and waits for internal political decisions or a change of government, it may be confronted with an increasingly difficult military situation. As it waits it will be confronted with an enemy of increasing strength and an increasingly unattractive war, while its threat to initiate a forestalling war becomes less persuasive, and other countries become anxious and hedge against rearmament themselves.

The three main kinds of military action that the force could take against a united country would be pain, conquest, and obstruction. By "pain" I mean sheer coercive damage. Nuclear or other weapons might be used to inflict civil damage at a rate sufficient to induce the government to change its mind and bend to the will of the international authority. By "conquest" I mean invasion or occupation sufficient to put the international authority into the role of occupying power. By "obstruction" I mean military action designed to retard a country's rearmament, to make it more costly than the country could manage, to spoil it altogether or to impede it sufficiently to prevent a major threat to the security of other countries. This might be done either by selective bombing or by selective invasion and occupation of key facilities.

Activities aimed at causing confusion, revolt of the population, civil war, or *coup d'état* could come under any of these three headings but would, of course, involve different tactics.

It is not obvious that we should want a force, even were it charged with the most ambitious responsibilities, to have excellent capabilities to carry out those missions. We might prefer the international force itself (or the nations controlling the decisions) to be deterred by at least some prospect of difficulty or even failure. We might, in other words, want the force itself to be under strong incentive to consider military intervention only as a last resort.

Militarily we can distinguish at least three different kinds of deployment for the international strategic force. In one, strategic weapons and personnel would be kept in neutral territories—on the high seas, in special areas reserved to the international force (perhaps island bases), or perhaps distributed in enclaves in some politically acceptable proportions. Except for contingents that happen to be within the victim country, the international armed force would then be in the same position that national armed forces usually are with respect to war: to conquer they have to penetrate enemy territory.

In a second mode of deployment, forces could be kept deliberately within the countries that are most likely to be "enemies." This would mean keeping strategic forces within the larger industrial countries. It might include the option of moving more forces into a country toward which threats were being made or with which war was imminent. Moving extra forces into the United States or the Soviet Union would of course be a major political move and might be subject to restriction of access. The purpose of being within the country, other than ceremonial, would be to minimize the cost and delay of invasion, occupation, or selective destruction—i.e., of war. Particularly for non-nuclear invasion—a quick capture of strategic points in the country—mobile forces already within the country, properly distributed, might enhance the likelihood of quick success. The force could occupy Moscow more reliably with ground forces located thirty miles away than by relying on airborne troops in bad weather. An amphibious landing on the coast of Japan, France, or the United States would be harder than just moving troops already located within these countries.

The third mode of deployment—and it might look a little unmilitary —would be to put critically vulnerable parts of a country's economy and essential services directly into the hands of an international force. If the force can control the supply of water, electricity, fuel, transport, and communication to American, German, or Soviet cities, it might minimize strategic bombings, selective occupation, and other violence. To coerce a country, like the landlord who shuts off the utilities when a tenant refuses to move, the force could put on the squeeze by shutting down services. Rather than bomb electric power installations the force might press a key that sets off a charge of dynamite already installed.

If one really believed in the reliability and permanence of an international arrangement, such schemes for providing the authority with "hostages" might be more efficient, even more humane, than providing it with bombers and shock troops. One could even go further and let the force have a monopoly of critical medicines to use for bacterial warfare on a transgressor country. As soon as it starts an epidemic, it sends its medical units to make sure that no one suffers who cooperates. Those who oppose it—military forces, government leaders, or anyone else—are without essential vaccines and must decide for themselves whether to stay at large and suffer or to surrender to be cured.

These gimmicks undoubtedly suffer from novelty, even from meanness, and would not be acceptable. They probably also go too far in assuming that the scheme is really for keeps. They give the international force too great an assurance of easy victory. The cards should be stacked in favor of the international force, but not with complete reliability. The decision to intervene by force in a sovereign country should always be a hard one. Furthermore it is worth some extra cost to keep the forces of organized violence out of sight, in reserve, and confined by tradition. No matter how strongly the entire arrangement is opposed to military traditions, uniformed troops are likely to seem more civilized than schemes patterned on the "protection" rackets or a paternalistic big brother.

Nevertheless there may be something in the notion of "prior occupation," i.e., of having strategic forces already located where they can accomplish "strategic" missions by simple tactical means—throwing switches and using only the conventional weapons of armored infantry.

The "enemy" of the force may also look for unconventional techniques of deterrence. One, which works especially well in a totalitarian country, would be a government's using its own population as hostages. If a Chinese government could threaten to hold out in such a way that an international force would have to kill large numbers of Chinese, either directly or in the economic consequences of strategic bombing, the force and its political leadership might be substantially deterred.

A threat of this sort might be implicit in any country's determination to rearm unless stopped by military action. Such a determination presents the international authority with the dilemma mentioned earlier. Shall it inflict war damage on a violator, or should it abandon the disarmament agreement in the interest of peace? It hardly seems possible to answer these questions in advance. The United States government did use Union forces to prevent secession by the Southern states from an agreement they had entered voluntarily, but the basic arrangement had been in effect for over four score years and was a good deal more than a disarmament agreement.

If the victim has nuclear weapons or can acquire them, it can threaten reprisal of its own. Against whom? If the international force has no homeland—no women, children, or industrial assets toward which it feels a strong attachment—there may be no way to hurt it except to engage it militarily. But the force will be acting at least with the acquiescence, and almost surely at the urging, of other major powers. If the victim has nuclear weapons that it can deliver on countries, it need not threaten to seek out the Quonset huts of an international island-based force; it can threaten to detonate weapons in Russia, China, Britain, Ghana, America, or wherever the military move against it originates politically.

Where might the United States, Japan, or the Soviet Union acquire nuclear weapons for reprisal? One possibility is that it retained them, contrary to agreement, in secret and secure locations. If other countries are believed to have hedged in this way, even the "honorable" countries may feel obliged to do likewise. (It is not out of the question that an agreement would even provide for some "minimum deterrent" buffer stock of weaponry, at least in the early stages.)

But if we assume—unreasonable though it may be to assume—that no country has its own nuclear weapons, there are still ways to get them. *Somebody* has them and knows how to use them. If they cannot be stolen from the force by burglary, they may be stolen or access provided by an insider. In a crisis nuclear weapons belonging to the international agency but located within particular countries might be captured or production and assembly facilities taken. Finally, for the most honorable of reasons, part or all of the international strategic nuclear force might secede in favor of the intended victim.

There are those who believe that military officers could be recruited and indoctrinated with exclusive loyalty to the international authority and that their reliability would be unquestioned. It is worthwhile to question whether this is desirable; even so, one must wonder whether it could be accomplished, particularly within the first few decades of the arrangement. Flag officers of the organization are likely to have been loyal and outstanding military officers who had served national governments. It would take the organization some twenty or thirty years to recruit youngsters under twenty, put them through the equivalent of Annapolis, and raise them in an international military tradition to flag rank.

Furthermore, it should not be a foregone conclusion that this kind of abstract loyalty can be bred into military officers, especially if they are born and raised in important countries that command their affection as well as their early allegiance. And even if it can, it remains to be proved that the best personnel of an international force are men who, after reaching maturity, can turn their backs on their homelands and "emigrate" into a government that has no population, no territory, no cultural tradition, and no family ties. The capacity to incur allegiance to an abstract organization, or even to "mankind" generally, may not be a capacity highly correlated with the other qualities we want in our senior military officers or even our junior ones.

But supposing that this abstract loyalty is desirable and that the international authority should appear to have promoted it successfully, we still could not be sure of it. It will be hard to cultivate officers finer than Robert E. Lee, whose devotion to his country has, to my knowledge, not really been questioned. He confronted a dilemma at the peak of his career—one that he could surely never have anticipated by a prior decision—and had to decide where his highest allegiance lay.

We still refer today to the Civil War as a conflict between North and South, rather than between America and the South; a military showdown between an international force and a major country may not appear as a showdown between the United States and mankind, or Russia and mankind, or a United Western Europe and mankind. It may appear as an East-West conflict or a European-Asian conflict, with an international force controlled by one bloc against another.

Similarly, military coups and civil wars throughout history—even in some of the most civilized and idealistic nations—have often found national military establishments not unified on one side or the other. One has to consider therefore the possibility that, in a major showdown between an international force and an important country or a bloc of countries, some of the international military forces or personnel would side with the victim country. They might refuse to take military action against it; they might split off and join it; or they might attempt to take over the international organization itself. So there *are* ways that countries in defiance of the international force could acquire weapons, including some of the best.

If we assume, then, that major countries may get nuclear weapons, "counter-deterrence" against the international authority or its supporters through threat of nuclear reprisal is meaningful. Furthermore, the delivery of these weapons might not be difficult if the nations are themselves substantially disarmed.

It is not likely that the international force would provide every country with an air defense or ballistic missile defense network against the possibility of nuclear attack. (Besides adding tens of billions to the possible cost, an effective system of active defense would look so militarized that countries might prefer to maintain small, national, nuclear deterrent offensive forces instead.) Thus a Soviet Union that got control of some nuclear-missile submarines or bomber aircraft with nuclear weapons and wanted to threaten western Europe or the North American hemisphere might pose a threat against which the international force could provide no direct shelter. The force might hope to *deter* such an attack; but if the result is just mutual deterrence, it has failed in the mission of capturing or disarming the delinquent country.

For a major industrial country a technique of defense against the international force might be sabotage. For two reasons the force might be susceptible. The first, already adverted to, is its likely inability to maintain tight internal security of the kind that national military forces hope to maintain. The problems of security clearance and personnel selection, together with the multi-national political access to information, would pose acute problems. And in an acute crisis of national loyalties the same possibilities of military defection mentioned earlier might provide opportunities for sabotage. In fact "honorable" sabotage of strategic forces might be easier, safer, and more conservative than revolt or defection by military forces.

A second vulnerability to sabotage is in the production process. A military force that buys complex equipment in the major industrial countries might risk certain vulnerabilities that had been embedded in the equipment it purchased. One may suppose that acceptance of complex equipment would be conditional on inspection by officers of a nationality other than the producers'. Nevertheless an "encrypted" vulnerability might be built into certain equipment—that is, secret vulnerabilities that did not affect the reliability of the equipment but could be triggered by those who knew about them. (This might be more likely in unique pieces of equipment—the central command-control headquarters of the international authority or the electronics of a missile force.)

Except for retaliation and sabotage, disarmed countries should be vulnerable to attack by a professional, well equipped, international force. In fact, preventive conquest might be militarily simpler for the force than defense of one country against another. If large numbers of ill-equipped American reservists invade Canada, the force can probably stop them most effectively by occupying critical parts of the United States, taking over or immobilizing government facilities, communications, and other essential services.

Non-violent resistance may be a problem for the force. What can be accomplished by non-violent resistance to the force depends on what the international force is after. That in turn raises the question of the "war aim" of the force when it does take action against a major adversary.

If the most feasible and most humane military action available to the force is pure conquest (military occupation of a country's government) the force will be good at achieving total victory—unconditional surrender—but not lesser objectives. Is the country then to be occupied indefinitely? Is a regime put in that is favorable to the nations that backed the international force? Or are the illegal facilities dismantled, the miscreants punished, and the country turned loose again? The extent of popular resistance may depend on what is expected to happen after the country has suffered a humane blitzkrieg.

It is worth noting that the temptation for the force to launch preventive occupation may be as strongly motivated, perhaps more strongly motivated, when two competing power blocs are both violating the agreement. In fact a force that can painlessly convert a bipolar cold war into victory for one side by invading and conquering either power bloc may ignite the same apprehensions that the possibility of pre-emptive attack does now. If somebody is eventually going to be conquered by the international force, pre-emptive control of that force by one side or the other may begin to appear imperative.

CONCLUSION

To speak of these contingencies may seem contrary to the spirit of a disarmament agreement and a peace-keeping world military organization. The whole arrangement only makes sense if there are decent prospects for the cooperation of the major powers. To suppose that something like the present East-West struggle continues, or that other competing power blocs emerge to continue a cold war, and that some major country or bloc provokes the international force into action, may seem like imagining the worst. In fact, not just imagining the worst but contradicting the premise on which it is all established.

But we are discussing the "strategic problems" of the force. One may hope that the eventual actions of any such military force are purely ceremonial, that its strategic problems never become real. But to the extent that it is meant to be a real force, capable of handling actual problems, we have to ask what those problems might be.

Two tentative conclusions can be put forward. First, it is unlikely that an international strategic command would have a completely reliable, credible capability to intervene and to stop any rearmament of a major industrial power. Its "deterrent" against rearmament will certainly be subject to some doubt. It will suffer from some of the same disabilities as a national deterrence force. As a coercive military organization it will be quite imperfect.

Second, it would probably be unwise and unsafe to have it any less imperfect. The international force can itself be a threat to peace, even to disarmament, and surely to the freedom and independence of nations. The more nearly omnipotent it is, the less reassurance it would provide. The greater its military superiority over individual nations, the more it can be viewed as a potential "enemy" by the nations that it is set up to guard. The more decisive its potential role, the more crucial becomes the capture of its political control or its disablement by those who cannot hope to control it.

If we are to have someday an international military force, we probably want one that is itself deterred. To create an instrument of painless world conquest, one that can overcome both passive and active resistance of national governments and national populations, might be to create extraordinary political instability. Indivisible, centralized, coherent power may be a good deal less conducive to peace and reassurance than a more diffuse, less decisive, less tempting instrument of control.

A world disarmament arrangement is unlikely to be viable if it requires a "perfect" strategic military force to deter violation and secession. Unless a quite imperfect deterrent can be believed adequate to forestall competitive violation, the arrangement should be abandoned or postponed.

Suppose an international strategic force were as likely to split apart as to stay together under crisis. Suppose it were believed appreciably vulnerable to various forms of sabotage. Suppose that individual nations could get hold of nuclear weapons and a capacity to deliver them on population centers. Suppose there were doubts whether the political arrangements were conducive to the force's timely action in a crisis—at least as many doubts as have ever been raised about American intervention on behalf of Europe. What is the consequence?

The consequence may be a significant deterrent, a deterrent based not on the certainty of decisive intervention but on a likelihood of intervention too great to ignore. A deterrent force does not have to *guarantee* that it can win the engagement.

This brings us back to the concept of "buffer." Instead of threatening to intervene against the rearming nation the force might be charged only with maintaining enough deterrence against war itself to permit other nations to take steps for their own protection. In the event of a rearmament race the international buffer force would try to ensure that no nation or group of nations could get a decisive headstart over its rivals.

Particularly since deterrence may depend on the absolute reprisal damage with which a nation can threaten an aggressor, not on just relative strengths, an international buffer might deter a rearming country's aggression long enough to permit other countries to develop at least "minimum deterrent forces" by themselves.

Under this concept the international force might even be authorized to assist in the laggards' rearmament. By simply threatening to facilitate the defensive, deterrent rearmament of the laggards (turning over its own production facilities to them, providing technical assistance, or giving some of its own weapons to them) the force might reduce the attractiveness to any nation of rushing back into an arms race. If this were the expected outcome of a rearmament race, there might appear little advantage in initiating such a race and no desperate haste to join a race that may or may not have begun.

How definitely and exactly can we hope to specify what the force is supposed to do? Can we rule out certain functions, such as its assisting laggards in their own rearmament? Can we make sure in advance that it will intervene (or that it will not intervene) in certain kinds of rearmament? Can we decide that it should engage in nuclear reprisal against a country that starts war, but not against a country that starts rearmament; or, choosing the opposite, can we guarantee that it will use nuclear weapons to deter or obstruct rearmament but not against a country that initiates conventional war?

I suspect we cannot. We can talk about the alternatives and can perhaps arrange weaponry, deployment, doctrine, political controls, and national military capabilities in a way that enhances the likelihood of certain decisions and reduces the likelihood of others. But no one can say in advance whether those who enjoy political control of the force will have the resolve, temerity, prudence, audacity, restraint, brutality, responsibility, or whatever else it takes, to launch war when they ought to, to threaten it credibly, to limit war properly if it occurs, or to abstain in the face of temptation. It is unlikely that we can deny the nations that politically control the force any ability to disband it, to redistribute its assets, or to charge it with grand new responsibilities that were never dreamed of before.

What could be decided in advance, and ought to be decided, is whether the force is to be viewed as an experiment in power politics or as a religious institution. If every war is a holy war, if the force cannot admit compromise or even occasional defeat, if every flaw in its strategy is to be construed as a doctrinal contradiction, if its leadership is to be considered the embodiment of disinterestedness and saintliness, and if any affront to the force is to be considered heresy, the demands on strategy will be exorbitant. The one thing we cannot do is to design a military force and strategy to support a doctrine of absolute self-righteousness.

Henry V. Dicks

NATIONAL LOYALTY, IDENTITY, AND THE INTERNATIONAL SOLDIER

I. INTRODUCTION

This essay attempts to envisage potential conflicts of loyalty in the minds of soldiers of a future international peace force and to review some of the means and steps by which such conflicts might be eased or prevented. For it is a fundamental of collective action that for any group to be effective in pursuing its object its members must be reasonably free from crises of loyalty.

Man has long known that any armed forces in action is only as strong as its group cohesion—its morale. As Napoleon put it: *"A la guerre les trois quarts sont des affaires morales. La balance des forces reelles n'est que pour un quart."* But it was not until World War II that military thinkers, aided by the developing psychological sciences, began to spell out some of the conditions and factors governing military morale and formulated something like this list:

(1) Belief or faith in the cause for which the troops are asked to fight and die.
(2) Conviction of personal and group worth, as shown in the esteem accorded to their forces by the backing population and by the high command.
(3) Confidence in the leadership, especially at the face-to-face level.
(4) Good selection—i.e., the fitting of personal aptitudes to the technical tasks and demands required by the unit's role in battle. This can be held to include a conviction of one's skill and mastery in the role.
(5) Confidence in the superiority and plentiful supply of technical equipment (arms, vehicles, etc.).

(6) Good personal logistic support—food, billets, welfare, medicine, fuel, home links, comforts.

Items 5 and 6 may be interpreted as derivatives of 2 and 3. Any authority or "backer" of troops who esteemed them well and any good commander would see to it that the supplies were the best possible in all respects. One need not waste time considering what would be the morale of a starving, ill-equipped UN detachment used on doubtful legal grounds against a well-fed, better equipped national army full of self-righteousness! Most of this essay, therefore, will be taken up in considering how items 1 to 4 could be applied to a UN force from the experience of analogous provisions in other forces.

When the conditions of good morale are stated in this way, it becomes easy to see how bound up with our theme are "belief in the cause" and a "conviction of personal and group worth." The "good cause" of recent wars for which "national" armies have loyally fought has been the defense or the greater glory of the nation-state. National loyalty and belief in the cause were then almost identical. And what, in psychological terms, is "identity" but the sense of finding oneself and one's role affirmed as "good" or "worthwhile" by one's government and people in answer to the subjective question "What am I like?" The sense of identity requires a congruity of a person's values with his actions and their acceptance by society.

It appears, then, that the UN "cause"—the peace of the world—must become a powerful motivating sentiment analogous to patriotism; and it follows that the crucial task in the welding of supranational or international armed forces is the grafting of new, international loyalties onto national loyalties.

At this point it becomes pertinent to distinguish between national loyalty and nationalism. The distinction will be of some importance in a potential or hypothetical international force. Whereas national loyalty and pride are, in the writer's view, entirely compatible in an individual or group with a wider identification, militant nationalism is not. The former could be illustrated by a young man who has already "found himself," has established his identity by his secure belonging to a reference group, for example his own family, and who can thus meet the wider world with self-confidence; the latter by an insecure young man, ambivalent about his reference group and unsure of his identity, full of mingled feelings of secret inferiority and compensatory, narcissistic self-assertion, with a "chip on his shoulder." The two young men present different risks as recruits for an international force. Aggressive nationalism in the individual would be among the most troublesome difficulties in the creation and effective operation of international projects, especially any such project as a UN armed force acting as the guardian of international law and order vis-à-vis a nation guilty of aggression under the banner of righteous nationalistic aims.

The question is how we might overcome such loyalty troubles in a UN force. But we ought first to examine the pessimistic assumption that national allegiance must constitute a serious weakness in a supranational armed force. Is it possible that we have looked at the motivations of soldiers only in the light of recent wars, when the professional military were greatly outnumbered and all but submerged by the vast armies of non-professional soldiers whose military attitudes and incentives were chiefly those of aroused national loyalty and national identification? We might get a different picture if we consider the problem in the light of "peacetime" forces, dominated of course by professional career soldiers,[1] who would constitute the bulk of any UN force whether temporary or permanent.

II. THE PROFESSIONAL SOLDIER'S ATTITUDES

Military history suggests that the profession of arms has been exercised with valor and proficiency in causes which bear little relation to the national loyalties of the warriors involved. Generals and soldiers have fought and died for empires, religions, and ideologies which were not part of their native background. The motley armies of Tilly and Wallenstein in the Thirty Years' War contained professional mercenaries, little touched by the ideological struggle, who fought and died for loyalty to their generals.

The former British Indian Army, which (like France's former colonial contingents) was recruited from a number of peoples, provides a recent example of the capacity of professional soldiers, even though precluded from the pinnacles of the profession, to identify with and render splendid service for the cause of a remote ruler under competent yet alien leadership. We also recall the "mercenaries" of heroic stature: the O'Higginses and Cochranes, the Barclay de Tollys and MacMahons—foreign professionals who commanded alien national or revolutionary armies or navies with at best only the mild approval of their motherland. Scrutiny of their stories might well reveal conflicts of early loyalties or doubts about identity, some perhaps not laudable. The Foreign Legion illustrates what mixed motives may converge to assemble and to weld diverse deviants into a dedicated force.

It appears that professional soldiers constitute a transnational

---

[1]To save tedium, all groups of fighting men will be called "soldiers," whether naval, marine, air force, or ground force.

professional group in the sense that artists or engineers or doctors do. As the latter have disciplined their talents, so the career soldiers have accepted discipline of their combative tendencies. Moreover, from the study of several groups of professional soldiers certain features of the motivations, personality dynamics, and self-perception of military men emerge which make up a "military profile" which has surprising constancy over wide cultural and national differences. It makes professional soldiers of different national and ethnic origins more akin to each other than many of them would be to some sub-groups of their own people.

It is the writer's opinion that professional soldiers—especially enlisted men—do not choose their roles primarily out of national loyalty. They choose their job because it offers satisfaction for their personal needs. They are no more and no less loyal or nationalistic than their civilian fellow-citizens. It is the political currents of our present phase of history which by and large encourage some nationalistic, authoritarian men to choose the role of brave defender of the nation as a suitable outlet for their super-patriotism or ethnocentricity. Soldiers are, in fact, often more objective and less bigoted about their enemies and can identify with them more readily than the nationally conscious civilian.

The Identity of the Soldier

Morris Janowitz a decade ago described the typical attitudes and motivations of professional officers especially in the highest ranks at the Pentagon in the United States.[2] Even in this relatively "new" corps, formed moreover in a revolutionary setting, Janowitz finds the typical military ethos of Europe well ingrained. The virtues of chivalry and gentlemanly conduct, of personal loyalty to the commander-in-chief, and the acceptance of the brotherhood of disciplined men are characteristic. To this I would add the strong bonds, more typical of enlisted men, within the particular unit (a ship's company, a tank regiment, an air squadron) that identifies the members. In some of the older European as well as Asian armed forces with long traditions of allegiance to a king or feudal overlord these characteristics stand out even more clearly than in the United States. The identity or self-image which is shared by and links the military professions everywhere is among the oldest distinctive life styles in the world. It was described in the tenets of the *Kshattriya* (warrior) caste of ancient India, and in the chivalry which enabled a Crusader baron to establish a sense of gentlemanly understanding with his Saracen opponent.

[2]Morris Janowitz, *The Professional Soldier* (New York: Free Press of Glencoe, 1960), see especially Chapter 2.

Military professionalism embodies a congruence of the social role with personal needs for a manly life of sport and risk, and for being perceived as a standard-bearer of certain virtues. These virtues include both command and loyal obedience, orderliness, and the spurning of materialist or corrupt self-interest. These often—but not always—go with non-political conservatism and a high degree of simple religious faith. We have lately seen radical military fraternities in some new countries take over control as "saviors" of their people from what they conceived to be corrupt and ineffective politicians.

In World War II the operation of the military code of behavior was seen at its best in the small face-to-face combat teams: the bomber crew, the tank crew, the infantry squad manning a pill-box or forward position; the company of a motor torpedo boat or a submarine. Here "the cause" or the political issues were only marginally in mind. It was the loyalty to the leader and to the comrades, the trained mastery of fear, the intense experience of brotherhood and mutual commitment which made what the Germans called *das fronterlebnis* a life-long memory of a man's "finest hours." Military forces everywhere, despite the introduction of machine technology which approximates the skills of a large proportion of soldiers to those of their civilian counterparts, have preserved this central core of their professional ethos by the unifying marks of the military specialist—the smart drill and uniforms, saluting, and so on—which are the symbol of special brotherhood.

III. THE SOCIAL INTEGRATION OF A MILITARY FORCE

If there is truth in our assertion that the professional soldier has certain nearly universal attitudes toward his role and certain personal values around which his identity and self-image are built, then the task of creating an international military constabulary or peace force becomes at the human level that of enlisting and conserving the loyalties of a sufficient number of such soldiers. How this might be done will be discussed under four headings: 1) the creation of a high command and general staff; 2) recruitment and personnel policy for a permanent force, with some references also to short-term task groups; 3) conflicts of national or ideological loyalties within both of these; and 4) the problem of deracination.

1. *Creation of a High Command*

The creation of a world military constabulary dedicated to world peace has been a dream of internationalists since the days of the League of Nations. Since that time we have had experience with loaned detachments of national forces pooled to serve the UN in this way, the most significant being the Korean operation, in which the command structure seems to have functioned effectively. With political progress, a permanent military staff advising and planning for the UN may supersede the improvised forces whose staff officers and units could be recalled at the whim of their governments.

Assuming that political and legal sanction for creating a permanent force under the orders of UN executive organs has been worked out and agreed, the selection and briefing of a high command and general staff will be the key problem. If this body is well formed, it will itself create a force suitable for its mission within the limits of civilian and budgetary control. Ultimately the authority of the UN will come to depend on the loyalty and dedication of this elite body; and its power will be the greater the more the UN replaces sovereign states as the holders of military means of coercion. Checks against abuse of this power, however, need to be worked into its structure.

Where shall we look for people who are sufficiently senior to form first a planning staff and next a field force, and who possess in highest degree the virtues of professional officers? How can this be done without arousing suspicions among the presumably still extant differing ideological camps which might have agreed, grudgingly and on logic rather than from burning idealism, to such a force? There has been wisdom in nominating commanders for *ad hoc* UN troops from among small or uncommitted countries even when their operational experience or skill had not been proved. Can we conceive of a stage of political objectivity or mature rationality when the UN would agree to delegate to an expert body of behavioral scientists the preparation of a "job analysis" and personality criteria for such selection, and then to invite them to cooperate in choosing this all-important staff perhaps from a list of willing "possibles" nominated by member nations? The methods exist and are now in use in the sphere of industrial and military personnel selection. Their use for our purpose would seem essential.

In the light of what was said earlier about the nature of the military code, we need not anticipate severe conflicts of loyalty or difficulties of adaptation in such chosen volunteers to the new commander-in-chief, i.e., the symbolic or real head of the UN. This, one ventures to think, might even be easier with military personalities than with civilians at corresponding levels.

To what image of a universal "good cause" shall we ask our hypothetical guardians of the peace to devote their faith? We can perhaps define their role as that of maintaining, as a last resort when other means have failed, standards of civilized political behavior to be defined in UN statutes. On this "good cause" we may hope for agreement from all ideological and national camps. We may liken this aim of an international staff to that of the uniformed constabulary or police of most countries, who watch for and have authority to prevent breaches of the peace irrespective of the importance or motives of the people committing the acts.

It is the civil power which gives the authority and subsequently adjudicates. As Janowitz[3] argues in the case of the United States officer corps of the future, such a constabulary role is the only possible one to assign to an international force. It alone gives its military elite the sense of guardianship of law and order "on behalf of all the peoples," irrespective of which nationality or territory is involved in breaches, as well as the "built-in" loyalty to civil powers and legal process. Its pride would be in the successful and humane elimination of political and military delinquency against the world order. There could be no old-time "glory" to boast over.

The assimilation of these essentially protective, "parental" values—so well displayed, for example, by many a middle-aged, tolerant London policeman—will be the essential learning process for the international high command. It is in this spirit that they should proceed to build the forces for which their civilian masters will grant them money and sanction.

Given the assurance of the other factors we enumerated as necessary for high morale, namely a relation of mutual trust and esteem with the civilian heads of the UN, a secure and dignified level of remuneration, pension provisions, and not too much interference or cheese-paring at the budgetary or technical autonomy level, one can be optimistic about the prospect of attracting military personalities of high caliber to a task which they might well judge to be more interesting and challenging for the essential qualities of the dedicated disciplined professional soldier than a time-serving job at home.

2. *The Creation of a Permanent International Force*

The formation and nourishing of a permanent force of highly trained, mobile soldiers may be more difficult than recruiting generals and staff officers. One factor favoring recruitment might be the reduction in the level of national forces in countries which accept disarmament, hence making available large numbers of trained officers and enlisted men from such countries for the original force. On the score of role perception and honorable identification with it, it is desirable that, at least to begin with, the top jobs should be filled by able soldiers of smaller

[3]*Ibid.,* Chapter 20.

nations—e.g., the Swedes, the Thais, the Mexicans—whose parent country will be universally accepted as not aspiring to world domination, and whose soldiers have for a long time accepted the role of guardians rather than prestige-creators. It would seem essential too that at the stage when a permanent international high command is allowed to exist by the concert of nations, its personnel should be commited to the UN by the terms of employment and not merely loaned by national forces for a brief period. If the demobilized men were enrolled as "foundation members" with the consent and blessing of their own governments, the primary conflict of loyalty would be minimized. Many good soldiers tend to take the line of least resistance, which is to continue in a congenial role promising some extra rewards. There was no difficulty in Britain in manning various post-World War I control and plebiscite forces on a semi-international level. Let us admit that a considerable number of such men will be time-serving mercenaries, the kind who form the core of most regular armed forces. If the top policy control is safe, we can accept them.

The major problem is how to maintain their cohesion by identifying them with a cause not so easily accepted by such men as the simple one of national power. Let us examine this question under the heads of the major factors listed earlier as contributing to high morale. In addition, we should consider the advantages and disadvantages to morale of units composed on an ethnic basis as against those made up of soldiers recruited at random from anywhere.

a) *"The good cause."* What matters is that in any recruiting campaign as well as throughout training the utmost care should be taken to remind all ranks of their high mission and role. "Where there is no vision, the people perish." In a world in which, so we hope, the military virtues derived from another age will be less and less esteemed, it will be a difficult task to foster the conviction in such a force that it is respected rather than regarded as an archaic minority. In democratic settings especially, soldiers are apt to be personally somewhat on the defensive, hence tending to counter-contempt of democratic values. The soldierly personality is one in which subordination and domination are polarized. It will require the use of much psychosocial skill to reconcile the integration of members of the force and their role values with the pacific surrounding population. The good cause has to be shared by both, but chiefly by the military as its human symbol. We shall recur to this theme later. Here we only stress the crucial importance to morale of the image or sense of identity which such soldiers will feel themselves to embody in the popular mind.

There is an inner conflict of identity common among soldiers (and policemen) especially in peacetime. It is compounded of certain dimly perceived insights of the average man's hate of authority figures, and of their own identification with, or submission to, the paternal super-ego. There results some guilt feeling at being on the side of the boss. Many an intelligent officer will disarmingly say to academic or professional people: "I am only a plain, bluff soldier," implying an apology for having chosen a low-ranking and despised tough occupation, with an underlying note of defiance and pride. He feels his dedication to valor, extraversion, and life on limited pay should mark him as a leader, but that others will not grant this.

b) *Need for sense of worth.* The foregoing remarks bring us to the second important factor in maintaining morale in a regular standing armed force in a civilian world—especially in peacetime. From the point of view of military cohesion all armed and police forces need a sense of forming a special *corps d'élite*. The semi-segregation of the military community is a necessary part of this if the boundaries of their inner group *mores* and loyalties are not to dissolve. And so even national armed forces are, in the main, a community apart. They and their families live in barracks, cantonments, or camps and have a largely self-contained social life, a condition which gives rise to conflicting feelings on the part of the civilian community. The civilian, when he is permitted to visit military installations or when soldiers parade on national holidays, has a sense of national pride in the armed forces. But at other times he commonly looks on the military as living in comparative idleness, with every convenience provided for it at the taxpayer's expense; and he resents its necessary presence.

Ambivalent feelings toward an international force will be much more marked. Contingents of such a UN force will have to be stationed at strategic points in various parts of the globe where they will be in a sense an alien body in the midst of the population; and special efforts at good public relations will be necessary to overcome the mutual sense of strangeness and even of "occupation." The image required for good relationships of this future world constabulary with the host population will be one of self-containment, but a friendly, calculatedly fraternal one.

There are several measures which the force could take to reduce ambivalence and make itself respected and even welcomed by the people among whom it is placed:

i) The force should possess good liaison officers, including experts in the cultural patterns of the area.

ii) The force should be an economic advantage to the area in which it is located. It ought to purchase supplies when possible locally, including leisure facilities.

iii) The manpower and technical resources of the force should be made available for the benefit of the area. Emergencies such as natural catastrophes or epidemics are only the most obvious examples. The force's engineers could also be employed for constructing drainage, bridges, and roads, while its medical and educational staffs would be available to treat, train, and educate underdeveloped populations and upgrade their local services.

Thus the force should be perceived not only as a guardian of peace and a symbol of benevolent authority but also in some sense as UN technical aid, as a sort of resourceful Peace Corps. This kind of relationship, if cultivated with full regard for the self-respect of both parties, will be a help in building the right image of their role both in the soldiers and in the surrounding population.

We must expect a degree of strain in the soldiers even when these good conditions are realized. Few ordinary people can tolerate long spells of expatriation even in married quarters. Two and a half years without change has been considered the maximum in static units a long way from home. And few populations will take readily to having outside groups quartered in their midst, especially if these have higher living standards than themselves, until they understand and share the purposes of the strangers—which will take time.

c) *Face-to-face leadership.* It is not only under combat conditions that face-to-face leadership assumes supreme importance in a soldier's life. We have always known, and now have the evidence from studies of group relations, that the dynamic which binds groups is not chiefly the common task but the shared, family-like loyalty to the leader, which also cements the bonds between the "brothers" in affection and rivalry with one another. This shared identification is seen most clearly in the military group, where it points up the need for careful selection of the junior officers who will mature into captains. It is at platoon and company level that it is essential to create an image of the trusted unit leader role, and this image should be consistently used for recruitment appeals in all countries from which it is decided to seek volunteers. The "profile" of the required qualities must be rigorously applied in choosing candidates. The appeal of the role is likely to be considerable to the kind of young man who might previously have volunteered for his nation's overseas service as an administrator, soldier, or educator. Additional figures who can decisively influence the morale of men are the unit medical officer and the senior non-commissioned officers, who must be carefully selected at first entry and on promotion.

In this connection both politico-social education in the values which the force exists to defend and uphold and the inculcation of the correct attitudes toward the civilian population, whether friendly or the people of a country against whom action is contemplated or going on, are important. Moreover, they must come from the men's own officers. The so-called "education" officer "from above" who goes from group to group is only grudgingly accepted by most soldiers, and his words are discounted as coming from an outsider.

At staff and high echelon levels provision should be made for a guidance or educational directorate with responsibility for morale and human relations which would hold seminars for suitable junior officers. The courses should have the same degree of priority and prestige as technical training and other graduate study. At this level there is ample scope for participation of civilian political and social science experts.

d) *Technical skill and superiority.* These are mentioned again to emphasize the values which soldiers attach to the quality and quantity of their equipment and supply. One need only recall the *élan* of the "invincible" Nazi *Luftwaffe* until it met the British Spitfires, whose pilots in their turn felt tremendous uplift of fighting spirit when they knew that they could outgun and outmaneuver the Germans. In the same way, though soldiers complain of incessant training in arms and tactics, this high pitch of skill also gives them a good feeling of being "a crack team," especially if backed by adequate aptitude selection which has a role to play here as at command levels.

e) *Welfare.* This aspect of morale building includes food, housing, mails, and medical services as well as constructive leisure. The latter comprises further education for its own sake and for helping men on leaving the services to obtain skilled employment in civilian life; it must comprise arrangements, including financial aid, for the soldier's re-integration with his own people on completion of contract. These things, which ought to be in the program of any civilized military force, should be made explicit in the contracts of service in an international force. They could be the responsibility of UN force liaison offices in all parts of the world, who would integrate their social follow-up services with similar services at the national level.

f) *Symbolism and ceremony.* The value of non-rational elements in creating a self-image of worth and group allegiance should not be over-looked. Such elements include the design of special flags, badges, and uniforms and ceremonies ranging from solemn induction to public appearances on parade on suitable occasions—e.g., UN Day and other anniversaries connected with the growth of the world community.

Doubtless some system of awards for good service, bravery, or other distinction would be instituted. The bestowals should optimally be made by representatives of the civil power, who should also show other signs of live concern for and pride in their armed force.

The foregoing are some of the ways in which soldiers serving any given force can be helped to build and maintain a good image of themselves and to feel pride in the unit to which they belong. These methods create conditions which favor good morale and group cohesion in military forces anywhere. Their observance in a new international force *sui generis* is doubly necessary.

We must now attempt a more difficult feat of imaginative prediction and try to weigh the advantages of random individual recruitment on the Foreign Legion model as against those of embodiment by ethnic units—the Gurkha model.

3. Blended or Pure?

From the point of view of morale our concern is with the basic unit of affiliation, the unit with which a man can easily identify at a face-to-face level—let us say the company (200) of land troops, the air squadron, or the crew of a small warship. For operational purposes land units may need to be up to battalion (800) strength. Higher formations in a hypothetical regular UN force will necessarily consist of units internationally composed. In any such force a linguistic and communications problem will exist at all levels, not to mention the problems caused by differing ethnic culture patterns reflected in dietary and religious customs, in attitudes to other people and to authority, and so on. Technological change, secularization, and convergence of patterns of urban life are softening some of these differences, but it would be a mistake to underrate them. Attempting to alleviate them, however, by too narrow selection in hopes of avoiding trouble with communications or "culture clash" might well result in the image of the force as a "Western," or a "white" or an "Asian" enclave and thus in the sacrifice of universal acceptance.

It could be argued that in advanced countries with many avenues of skilled work and upward mobility open to its universally literate populations the armed forces in peacetime have been regarded as "backward" institutions. They have often attracted to their ranks the less resourceful and independent personalities save in times of major unemployment. Yet the military life was often a school where self-respect, discipline, and technical skills were learned. The service was also the mother symbol and nurturant home for many orphans and products of broken families or adolescent revolt. In less developed countries the armed forces, on the contrary, are often the best school that enterprising and independent youth can find. To them military service is an opportunity for modernizing—of learning the three R's, acquiring technological knowledge, having a higher standard of living than at home in the mud village. Nurtured in the universally diffused traditions of military honor and efficiency, the armed forces of such countries often truly represent the most "civilised" and modern-thinking elite group. By the same token, UN soldiers from such countries could become agents of social change and modern ideas for their homeland.

A valuable function of the UN force would be that of a school for men from diverse climes and races brought together and held by a common task-commitment and shared identifications, learning to be "modern men" and rubbing a lot of prejudices and archaisms off each other. They will start with certain similarities—the wish to be soldiers because this answers a personality need. The question is one of how to cushion the culture clash, how to encourage this new image without causing confusion and maladaption leading to loss of identity in many simple men.

a) *Units are homogeneous (the Gurkha model).* The advantage of embodiment in ethnic units is that men with strong elemental national identifications or culture peculiarities can join a unit which is not frighteningly new or strange. They will be with their own kind, have their own sort of food, welfare, and patterns of authority. Recruitment of such units for a UN force might be facilitated by the attraction of friends from the same region. The logistic problem would be simplified if a station-quartermaster knew he had to procure typical diets for a unit of Hindus or for a unit of Nigerians. Although presumably for its commands and communications the force would have one or two compulsory languages mastered by officers, senior non-commissioned officers, and signalers, the life and discipline in the face-to-face units could be conducted in the vernacular. Religious observances and familiar customs could be kept up.

National identity problems might be lessened. The universal "good cause" and high mission of the whole force could still be inculcated by the educational influence of belonging to it, as stressed by the general regime and symbolism already discussed. National loyalties could be turned to good account in healthy inter-unit rivalries and competition for smartness and efficiency and in sports. A given unit could be withdrawn from any military action against its own nationals with its threat of crises in loyalty.

The disadvantages of ethnic units might be a lessened over-all identification with the force, a greater ethnocentric resistance to "modernizing" and becoming a true international soldier. Mass disaffection or rioting might be more likely and more difficult to control. Whereas in a Foreign Legion type of unit such clashes might be confined to a few hotheads, in the ethnic type two companies—say of Danes and Indonesians—might become a real problem if inter-unit hostility broke out. We recall the recent trouble in the "homogeneous" British Army of the Rhine between a unit of Scots and of Lancashire men!

At a higher level, if we suppose that the rival ideologies at present dividing humanity were still active, albeit covered over to the extent of permitting service of the respective nationals in a UN force, ethnic units might bring with them solid political attitudes, prestige claims, and intolerance which might seriously conflict with the objective and non-partisan role of the force. This is another aspect of the dilemma discussed earlier. How does one incorporate into the force men with life-long exposure to totalitarian indoctrination, especially if their rulers see to it that only "the right ones" are permitted to "volunteer"?

b) *Units are of individuals (the Foreign Legion model).* It was stated earlier that the release of many soldiers, both officers and enlisted men, from national forces might offer a ready nucleus of a field force. Such men would volunteer individually and from personal motives ranging from international idealism to mental laziness, the attraction of good pay, and the prospects of adventure. To select and enroll them into units culturally compatible and not too heterogeneous would require language training and a regime—the creation of a climate of tradition—so broad and characterless as to make identifications rather problematic. The Foreign Legion had a clear image to model itself on and give loyalty to—namely the French officers and the President of France. In an international force only exceptional characters somewhat polyglot, rootless, or dedicated are likely to benefit by finding a new identity in a UN force.

We cannot risk the force's becoming a refuge for psychopaths. If, however, it was found that there were enough tough and yet stable military types, such recruits might become the most mobile and dedicated elite group of the force. They would not be bothered by national affiliations or customs since they would be seeking a worthwhile new identity. It is likely that many of them would be deviants, including various political defectors or expatriates whose personalities would create disciplinary difficulties when their high expectations were thwarted; but others would be types who would in any case become soldiers, seamen, or adventure seekers.

On balance it would seem sensible to expect the main structure of the force we envisage to be on a Gurkha model but there should be some experimental units on the Foreign Legion model. In these latter we may have one of the necessary alembics to produce the man of the future, whose home is the world, and who is capable of modifying parochial stereotypes and archaisms on his return to his native land.

4. Conflicts of Ideologies and Identity

We must now turn to what is perhaps the thorniest problem in trying to blend a motley crowd of men reared in widely differing societies and ideologies into a cohesive, disciplined military force. This may take place in the fairly near future, while the world is still profoundly divided as to values, political goals, and in the consequential molding of children to assimilate them.

We said that we could make the ethos of the force non-political, technical, and professional, hoping to gain the allegiance of all to the primary task of enforcing law and order as an instrument in the hands of the civilian executive organs of the UN. We postulated that these organs would act impartially under law and demonstrate the justice and legality of the cause. One can further assume that common training and unit life would foster solidarity and some lasting identifications overriding the more parochial ones. But these parochial loyalties—nationalist and ideological—will be deeper. Even among genuine volunteers, who might come forward precisely because of their revolt against some aspect of their national politics or way of life, the clash with others who might denigrate their country could mobilize unsuspected depths of national feeling. This is most likely to happen in Foreign Legion mixed units— between soldiers originating in different great power countries or between one of them and "unaligned" nationals who detest their pretensions and envy them their national background and power.

Within limits of good fellowship and deeper ties, such barrack room arguments and fights have educational value; and it might be possible to structure such conflicts in debates as part of morale building and training in world citizenship under good leadership. Nonetheless, as long as great power alignments and rivalries exist, a force at UN disposal cannot be permitted to be but another reflection of them. Therefore the wiser plan is initially to confine recruitment not only of staff but also of officers and enlisted men to smaller, non-competing countries as was done in the case of the *ad hoc* task forces at Gaza or in the Congo. It would be easier and even prestigious for nationals of small countries to identify with the new world constabulary concept. Only in the improbable or at least presently unforeseeable event of power politics having manifestly been abandoned in favor of social engineering everywhere could this ordinance be cautiously modified in favor of some experimental toleration of "mixed" units and "great power" ethnic units. The results on the members' identity and morale problems should be carefully assessed as a piece of social research. This caution is preferable to the likely alternative of the staff having to discharge unassimilable men or to disband whole units on grounds of national or political fanaticism, actions which would lead to very awkward and unfortunate charges of partiality in the councils of the UN by offended national delegates.

While any organization must reserve the right to terminate the services of misfits, a UN force should take great care to draft its regulations in terms which will minimize this risk. The desirable goal is a morale structure which includes and respects conflict and tries to deal with it by assimilation. Discharge should be on behavior, not on views. The unit climate should be able to tolerate a few fanatics and agitators.

5. *The Problem of Deracination*

Some social thinkers have been exercised by demoralization resulting from individuals being uprooted from their accustomed milieus and transplanted into strange social and geographical surroundings. Such demoralization, with loss of sense of identity and personal worth, which is called "deracination," is well known to occur not only in forcibly displaced persons. It happens also in volunteers—for example lonely students from remote or underdeveloped countries overwhelmed by the impact of a great Western city, or disenchanted emigrants who have left their native country with a vision of some promised better life. It happens even in UN personnel and especially their families, who can suffer from considerable loss of stable "belongingness" and from homesickness after a long spell of expatriation in what have been called the "international ghettoes" of Geneva or New York.

To what extent is deracination a danger to the potential armed forces we are considering? It would be foolish to underrate the severe personal maladaptations—depression, loss of initiative, resentment, and so forth—which may eventually break to the surface in some people under conditions of expatriation and which lead to disaffection, irrational griping, and desertion. In the introductory section we alluded to two models of behavior, using the paradigm of a secure young man with a good home background incorporated in his personality in contrast to an insecure young man from a problem family who on the surface might seem tougher, more ready to abandon his roots and assert his independence. We know with certainty which of these two is likely to be the better risk as a soldier—the one with sound roots. Hence my stress on good selection and on the need for ethnically homogeneous basic units for our force. The potential sufferer from deracination symptoms is one who unconsciously seeks in each new situation "a better father and mother" and—of course—becomes repeatedly disenchanted because his quest was a projection to the outer environment of an essentially inner, psychic malaise. He began without safe roots; the move to another milieu, intended as a cure by him, emphasized the trouble.

The problem might be most acute for those potential recruits to the UN force whom we described as already somewhat rootless, polyglot characters, who are sometimes the products of forced population movement (such as the sons of anticommunist, east European refugees). It is for the avoidance of such dangers on a large scale that we have tried to build into the envisaged group structure some safeguards against the sense of rootlessness. In contrast to the civilian groups mentioned above, our force was imagined as consciously providing a "parental" function by its personnel policy and by advocating a mainly ethnic pattern for its basic units. It is not proposed that the United Nations should subvert men from their motherlands or drive out their good feelings of national pride and identity, although we hope that they will become good UN men. We have attempted to incorporate into our planned service life respect for the customs and folkways of our soldiers (i.e., their national identity). They would be surrounded by their compatriots, and in static conditions by their families living in suitable cantonments. The contract of service would be for a limited period, during which home furlough and facilities for easy communication with home would be provided. At the end of his period of service a soldier would normally expect to be repatriated with his dependents (if any) and given help to establish himself in his native land as a more educated, modern person with new skills.

It might happen that some such men will have become strangers and feel deracinated only on returning to a home which they had outgrown. The same danger arises in national armed forces, in civilian pioneering projects—in fact, anywhere where people are exposed to new experiences and horizons. We should therefore be prepared to meet the problem but not inflate it. If we can create a focus of international loyalties in men also securely rooted in their own backgrounds, a brotherhood of men-at-arms dedicated to making a safer world, we should not be deterred by the moderate risk involved. The anxieties we feel may well be akin to those aroused in us by the kindred idea of "surrender of national sovereignty"—abolishing "safe" boundaries and so imperiling our sacred national identities—those perilous archaisms of the pre-nuclear age.

IV. CONCLUSION

It remains to sum up what is necessarily a tentative essay in applying the lessons learned from morale problems of national armed forces to a hypothetical international constabulary.

We have proposed that national identity and loyalty do not of themselves constitute a powerful obstacle to securing the services of professional soldiers. Such soldiers' personality structure could be shown to rest on the individual's image of a good self, his identity, and his sense of worth—not so much on primarily national allegiance (with which in recent history it has become confused) as on an almost universal code of professional conduct and honor. We have also attempted to relate the maintenance of this good image to the acknowledged conditions favoring high morale in any military force—the cement without which such a structure does not long survive as an effective instrument.

We have suggested that, in order to lessen conflict between national and international loyalties in future UN soldiers, they should be drawn from countries not in the great-power struggle, whether national or ideological; that they should be given a simple nonpolitical task as the cause with which to identify; and that they should be offered such conditions and publicly perceived status as would assimilate them to a well esteemed constabulary rather than to any army of the old sort. They should be trained to be bringers of peace, order, and modernization to the regions in which they may be stationed, somewhat recalling the great civilizing impact which came as the still visible by-product of Rome's legions upon the barbarians.

In order to reduce conflicts of identity in individual soldiers we have proposed that the initial basis for forming the face-to-face units should be an ethnic one. This would provide a halfway house between international loyalty and continued awareness of belonging to the national or ethnic reference group. With these and general welfare measures it could be anticipated that a regular international force, unified around good leadership and well designed educational and symbolic functions, could be made viable. The problem of penetration of the force by solid, national, ideological groups may perhaps be avoided by reliance on a simple agreed statute of impartial aims and temporary exclusion of soldiers from the camps of great powers who are likely to be the chief carriers of the ideologies and pretensions conflicting with the international order.

Deracination was seen as a danger chiefly if the force recruited, without careful selection, men already somewhat footloose who were seeking escape from inner insecurity and were prone to disaffection. The service could be constructed to deal fairly satisfactorily with the problem of deracination, which was perhaps raised partly because of the opposite fear of loss of national sovereignty if we permitted the international force to become a reality. If the force came into being it could, in competent hands, be made into a workshop for creating a truly modern, international man who would never be the same again after experiencing its fellowship.

In conclusion, it needs to be stressed that a future UN military peace keeping force will only exist so long as the great powers tolerate it. This writer, at least, cannot visualize an international force powerful enough to coerce the nuclear super-powers—nor any advantages for the human race. UN nuclear missiles are no more acceptable. In the last analysis, we can survive only if wisdom and humanity continue to prevail in the counsels of the mighty.

APPENDIXES

1. **Controlling Conflicts in the 1970's,** Report of a National Policy Panel Established by the United Nations Association of the United States of America

2. **Report of the President's Commission for the Observance of the 25th Anniversary of the United Nations: Recommendations**

3. **United Nations Emergency Force** by Dag Hammarskjöld, October 9, 1958

4. **United Nations Peace Force** by U Thant, June 13, 1963

5. **Comprehensive Review of the Whole Question of Peace-Keeping Operations in All Their Aspects,** Report of the Special (United Nations) Committee on Peace-keeping Operations, November 3, 1969

6. **United Nations Charter Articles Related to Peacekeeping**

7. **Consent, Good Offices and the Future of Peacekeeping,** International Peace Academy Committee, February 1971

8. **Peacekeeping:** A Survey and an Evaluation prepared for Friends Peace Committee (Quakers) by Charles C. Walker

APPENDIX 1

Controlling Conflicts in the 1970's, Report of a National Panel established by the United Nations Association of the U.S.A.*

How Strengthen United Nations and Regional Peacekeeping Capabilities?

Regional and even world peace may depend on using a multilateral option in order to insulate or de-escalate a dangerous situation. But multilateral peacekeeping machinery today is weak. Can it be strengthened? If so, how?

Enlarging United Nations Peacekeeping Capabilities

Efforts over the past three years to move United Nations peacekeeping into more dependable patterns have made little progress.

Ten UN member countries have earmarked approximately 11,000 men for United Nations service—a small portion of which are available on a standby basis. These military units are available to the United Nations for a very limited period, some for as little as six months. A UN force composed of such units can be stationed on the territory of a member country for as long as the host government will permit, which in effect gives the latter a veto over the composition of the force as well. In many cases the countries providing units have reserved the right to withdraw those units at any time should circumstances change.

The future of UN peacekeeping is presently being considered in a thirty-three member United Nations committee, established by the General Assembly. Thus far, it has reached no basic agreement on arrangements for future composition of forces, on guidelines for their use, or on arrangements for more secure financing. The furthest it has gone is the modest step of authorizing a Secretariat study of past UN experience with peace observation.

---

*Pp. 38-51 of the report are reprinted here. The complete report can be obtained from the U.N.A. of the U.S.A., 345 East 46th Street, New York, N.Y. 10017 for $1.00.

If the revived interest in multilateral peacekeeping is to be translated into effective United Nations capabilities, prompt and major moves will need to be made to develop United States proposals, to discuss these with the Soviet Union and other principal powers, and to determine the forum in which they should be formally considered.

There is one development in the important relationship between the two superpowers which may point the way to a new opening in the peacekeeping deadlock. This is through Article 43* of the UN Charter under which member states, particularly the "Big Five," originally were to make available armed forces for Security Council collective action.

The failure of the Security Council to develop such forces, to oppose aggression and to keep the peace, was a casualty of the Cold War.

More recently both the Soviet Union and the United States have indicated a willingness to reopen negotiations under Article 43, to see if it would be possible to work out arrangements for more effective United Nations collective peacekeeping action. In July 1964 the Soviet Union suggested that such UN forces be composed of units *not* from the Permanent Members of the Security Council but rather from the middle and smaller powers. More recently Moscow has suggested that the UN Military Staff Committee, which was created for the purpose of advising the Security Council with regard to the force arrangements, should be enlarged to include not just Permanent Members of the Council but non-Permanent Members as well.

The Panel believes that these are potentially promising lines for serious exploration.

Successful UN peacekeeping depends to a substantial degree on super-power cooperation. It is increasingly unrealistic to think in terms of any major UN operation which either superpower strongly disfavors. Moreover, even if the general emphasis in the future continues to be on peacekeeping with the consent of the parties, rather than the less realistic enforcement action, the U.S., Soviets and British have agreed to a

---

*Article 43 of the United Nations Charter provides:

"1. All Members of the United Nations, in order to contribute to the maintenance of international peace and security, undertake to make available to the Security Council, on its call and in accordance with a special agreement or agreements, armed forces, assistance, and facilities, including rights of passage, necessary for the purpose of maintaining international peace and security.

2. Such agreement or agreements shall govern the numbers and types of forces, their degree of readiness and general location, and the nature of the facilities and assistance to be provided.

3. The agreement or agreements shall be negotiated as soon as possible on the initiative of the Security Council. They shall be concluded between the Security Council and Members or between the Security Council and groups of Members and shall be subject to ratification by the signatory states in accordance with their respective constitutional processes."

new form of security assurance through the Security Council for Members that are threatened with nuclear attack after signing the Non-Proliferation Treaty. This agreement on the part of three Permanent Members of the Security Council could in itself open the way to a new set of international security considerations involving UN deterrent capabilities.

The Panel believes the time has come for a major initiative by the United States to strengthen the peacekeeping and crisis management capabilities of the United Nations.

The objective should be the conclusion of arrangements between the Security Council and member states under which these states make forces available to the UN on a more reliable basis and for a wider range of peacekeeping activities than is feasible under the present pattern.

The initial effort should be to reach an understanding with the Soviet Union and other key members of the Security Council on the principles that would underlie the development and use of greatly strengthened United Nations forces. This might be done within the general framework of Article 43.

One central principle, that makes such forces usable in the present international peacekeeping context, is the suggestion that the military units should come from *non-great power* countries. We interpret the Soviet proposal to this effect as a signal that they too may be willing to consider more effective UN peacekeeping capabilities.

A second principle is that the primary role of the Security Council should be emphasized. We believe the United States can accept this further emphasis on the Security Council's primary role in peacekeeping, since it reflects the reality of great power influence. Moreover, the U.S. itself could be faced in the future with a situation in which the majority of UN Members desired a peacekeeping operation which the United States strongly opposed.

A further governing principle, however, should be the retention of the present right in any international emergency to turn to the General Assembly if action in the Council is blocked. Keeping this option open is of general importance, but it could be of particular importance if Peking ever takes China's seat in the Security Council. Under these circumstances, it might be in the interest of both the United States and the Soviet Union, as well as other UN Members, to make frequent use of the General Assembly.

If the preliminary talks we suggest prove fruitful, then we recommend more general negotiations within the framework of Article 43 with all interested UN Members.

While it would be desirable if all national units could be made available to the Council under a standard Article 43 agreement, it is unlikely that this would prove possible, or indeed that all national units would have capabilities for the variety of assignments to which the Council would, at one time or another, be directing its efforts. Some national units would be suitable only for limited observation or police-type action; others could be available for more general types of UN deployment.

A More Capable United Nations Standby Force

The Panel suggests that the new UN negotiations be directed to the following principal objectives:

(1) The establishment of a standby United Nations peacekeeping force of 20,000 to 25,000 men, composed of land, sea and air units from non-Permanent Members—the standby units to be supported by adequate earmarked reserves with both specially trained for UN service.* The standby units would represent four or five regiment/brigade task groups of approximately 5,000 men each—3,000 active ground forces with 2,000 men in air, naval, logistic and staff support.

These standby units, which would approximate in size the UN force assembled in the Congo, should be available promptly on the UN's call and would enable the United Nations to cope with most of the crisis-type situations for which UN peacekeeping action, in the foreseeable future, is likely to be effective. The force would represent a doubling of the presently available units and would, the Panel believes, represent an appropriate and manageable next step in the development of the UN's capabilities.

In the UN operation in the Congo, one of the major problems was the unavailability of adequate earmarked reserves and replacements. If arrangements can be made for the national contingents to be available for longer than six months, which is the period of availability of most of the present national units, a 100 per cent reserve would not be necessary. In that case a 75 per cent reserve of earmarked units might prove adequate.

We have suggested that not all standby or earmarked units would be suitable or available for all types of situations with which the Council would be faced. However, with 20,000 to 25,000 men on standby, and an earmarked reserve of at least 15,000 men, an overall UN capability of a trained force of 35,000 to 40,000 men would be a reasonable initial objective.

---

*We distinguish between *standby* units from UN member governments, i.e., units such as the one infantry battalion presently maintained by Canada and available for UN service on one week's notice, and *earmarked* units which would be available on two to eight weeks notice.

(2) Arrangements between the Security Council and the countries providing the military units under which, whenever possible, the latter would be available to the Security Council for a minimum of one year's service in whatever capacity the Security Council and its executive agent, the Secretary-General, might direct.

(3) UN Members not in a position to provide military units would supply bases and other facilities, including overflight privileges and pre-arranged rights of passage. Member countries having bases not presently used in connection with their national defense requirements could earmark certain of these bases to be made available to the Security Council as staging or storage points for future UN operations.

(4) Certain member states would provide officer personnel on a more individual basis for UN fact finding and observation, and for the nucleus of elite cadres which could be of particular help in situations requiring fast UN reaction. A larger UN force would require a larger number of "support personnel" for staff, communications and security functions. This would make necessary an increase in recruiting and training of civilian personnel—including an increase in size of the UN Field Service.

(5) UN Members having military assistance programs which permit assistance to countries participating in international peacekeeping under the United Nations should conclude with interested countries arrangements for the training and equipping of forces to be available to the Security Council. This might best be done on the recommendation of some appropriate UN body, or through third parties where UN peacekeeping training programs already exist. Under such arrangements it might also be possible to underwrite the training of individually recruited volunteers for UN service.

Middle powers with peacekeeping experience would be asked to give special technical training in language, civic action, communications, logistics and other peacekeeping arts, to officers and non-commissioned personnel from other countries. Training programs for middle-level officers and for civilian personnel might well be established by the United Nations.

(6) The Permanent Members of the Security Council would undertake to maintain in a state of readiness and to provide logistic support for specified types of situations. One way would be to designate a specified number of types of aircraft, ships, etc. to be available on short notice if required—but not permanently tying up specific items of equipment.

The Management and Control of UN Forces

The Secretary-General has thus far served as executive agent in the management of UN peacekeeping operations.

He derives his general responsibility from the Charter which charges him with being the "chief administrative officer of the Organization" (Article 97). But in peacekeeping operations he derives his special authority from the authorizing resolutions of the Security Council or the General Assembly.

In order to implement these resolutions charging the Secretary-General with responsibility for organizing and managing such forces, a general management system has been developed within the UN Secretariat. Under this system, first Dag Hammarskjöld and subsequently U Thant have delegated much of the principal operational responsibility to one of the Under-Secretaries for Special Political Affairs. The military commander in the field reports to the Secretary-General through the Under-Secretary, who in his work has had the counsel of the Secretary-General's Military Advisor and his staff.

The UN Charter, under Article 47, provides for the establishment of a Military Staff Committee "to advise and assist the Security Council on all questions relating to the Security Council's military requirements for the maintenance of international peace and security, the employment and command of forces placed at its disposal, the regulation of armaments, and possible disarmament."

The Panel believes there can be an enhanced role for the Military Staff Committee to advise the Security Council in peacekeeping operations. However, Article 47 is ambiguous as to the role of the Military Staff Committee in the management of United Nations forces once they have been activated under the Council's authority.

Sub-paragraph 3 of the Article suggests that the MSC shall be responsible "under the Security Council for the strategic direction of any armed forces placed at the disposal of the Security Council." It then goes on, however, to say that "questions relating to the command of such forces shall be worked out subsequently."

It is obvious that no Committee composed of the Chiefs of Staff of the five Permanent Members of the Security Council (or a larger group if the recent Soviet suggestion for enlarging the Committee were to be accepted) could effectively "command" UN military forces. "Strategic direction" would be workable only in the sense of the wartime combined Chiefs of Staff, or the former NATO Standing Group. **We believe it important to emphasize that the Military Staff Committee's function must be purely as an advisory body to the Security Council.**

The Panel believes it is crucial that a clear chain of command be retained by the United Nations in its peacekeeping operations. The Secretary-General's role as executive agent for all UN field operations must be maintained.

To reinforce the administration of peacekeeping forces, the Panel believes a **Special Peacekeeping Section** should be established within the **UN Secretariat** to **assist** the **Secretary-General.** It should be headed by an Under Secretary-General for Special Political Affairs. The Section would be composed of personnel seconded from the UN departments with specialized experience and with functions directly related to the field operation.

The tasks of the Special Peacekeeping Section would include:

(a) The administration, under the Secretary-General of field peace-keeping operations;

(b) Assistance to Member States which are providing standby or ear-marked contingents;

(c) Initiation of an in-service training program;

(d) Establishment of appropriate liaison arrangements with regional organizations.

The Secretary-General and the Under Secretary-General in charge of the Special Peacekeeping Section should be aided by an Advisory Board chaired by the Secretary-General and composed of the senior Under Secretaries—General and Assistant Secretaries-General whose departments are most directly concerned with peacekeeping operations. The Military Advisor to the Secretary-General should be an ex officio member.

Effective United Nations Communications Facilities

The United Nations at the present time has a short-wave communications network with which it keeps in touch with its peacekeeping and peace observation activities. There is little comparison between this limited but still effective system and the advanced communication networks now employed by the great powers for keeping in touch with their own defense installations in various parts of the world.

Recent UN requests for funds to improve the efficiency and capability of the UN system have been refused on budgetary grounds.

There is no reason why the United Nations should be handicapped in any way by a lack of resources in this essential field. Indeed, if additional countries are to make national units available to the United Nations on a standby basis, and if proper arrangements are to be made for the use of bases, staging areas and overflights, a more capable network should have a higher priority.

The Panel believes that the member governments should make available to the United Nations the financial resources to support more effective peacekeeping communication facilities and equipment.

The Panel recommends that a United Nations Committee on Communications be established promptly to make recommendations as to the type of additional facilities required and to prepare estimates of their cost.

Peacekeeping, Peaceful Settlement and Peaceful Change

The United Nations is often brought into a dispute only after fighting has broken out. In these situations it is natural that the focus of attention should initially be on a cease-fire. The UN's record in this respect is good—witness its effective work in Indonesia, in Kashmir, and twice in the Middle East in bringing general hostilities to a close.

There is a growing conviction within the international community that UN peacekeeping efforts in any particular situation must be linked more directly with efforts at peaceful settlement of the issues underlying the dispute. Unless this is done the peacekeeping operation may cause both the UN and the parties in conflict to relax their efforts to resolve the dispute. Indeed, the incentives to settle such conflicts may be greater when fighting is still in process.

Related to the settlement of disputes is the issue of peaceful change.

Peacekeeping must not be a reason for failing to settle a dispute. Nor should it be a device for suppressing legitimate i.e. popular pressures for social, economic or political change. The West has been acutely suspicious that the Communist nations cause much of the contemporary violence. On the other hand, left-of-center criticism suspects UN peacekeeping of being a cover for "capitalist anti-revolutionary activities."

The purpose of UN peacekeeping is not to impose—or oppose—any ideological system. It should be to insulate the processes of internal politics from outside interference which may threaten international peace and security. In no event should it be used to freeze a situation in such a way that social and political change cannot take place. The concept of peaceful change signifies the hope that the needed economic and social changes can be brought about without violence.

The problem for the instrumentalities of international peacekeeping is to permit the necessary change, while at the same time limiting international disorder and reducing violence.

The Panel therefore recommends that:

(1) UN peacekeeping activities be linked more immediately and directly with vigorous efforts to resolve the basic issues that gave rise to the conflict;

(2) UN's peaceful settlement capabilities be strengthened by additional advance identification of individuals of exceptional talent and experience to assist the UN in its conciliation and mediation work. The UN's conflict control work has been enhanced by many men with extensive diplomatic experience. The Panel believes, however, the Organization should proceed, in advance of future crises, with the identification of additional talent and ensure that more such individuals gain experience in the work of the Organization;

(3) Such individuals, having been identified, should be brought together in occasional informal conferences with persons who have had successful UN negotiating experience, so that they may become more familiar with UN procedures and practices, and with the resources upon which they would need to draw should they at some point be asked to take on special assignments for the Secretary-General, or for one of the UN political organs;

(4) A greater effort be made to identify "justiciable" issues even in political quarrels and to encourage their adjudication by the International Court of Justice, by special chambers of the ICJ (as permitted by the Court's Statute) or by impartial arbitration.

The Financing of UN Peacekeeping

The legacy of debt left over from the United Nations Congo operation, exacerbated by the constitutional crisis over Article 19, has made the general question of financing UN peacekeeping a major issue clouding all discussions of strengthening the UN's general capabilities. No significant progress can be expected without some mutually satisfactory answer as to how future forces are to be financed and how past debts are to be met.

Three general methods have been used by the United Nations for financing peacekeeping operations:

(1) regular or special assessments; (2) costs divided between the parties to the dispute; and (3) voluntary contributions by governments.

Regular budget assessments are suitable for only the smaller UN operations, such as those on the Kashmir cease-fire line ($1,028,100), and the UN Truce Supervisory Organization in the Middle East ($4.2 million). It was the arrearages under special assessments which precipitated the UN financial crisis of 1965. Payment by the parties to a dispute has proven workable for operations which were limited in size, cost and duration, such as those in West Irian and in Yemen. The Secretary-General's experience with the UN Cyprus Force has highlighted the inadequacies of purely voluntary financing. The Force costs about $11 million a year. The UN Cyprus account is now $14 million in debt.

Of the methods which thus far have been used by the United Nations for financing peacekeeping operations a variation of the voluntary method, apportionment by the General Assembly, is the only one likely to produce anything like the funds needed for the larger UN operations. It combines the basic principle of voluntarism with some guidelines on fair sharing, based upon ability to pay—and presents the package to the Members as a recommendation from the General Assembly. This was the method of financing UNEF in recent years. A substantial UNEF debt suggests, however, that even this method of financing is inadequate.

Each UN peacekeeping operation to date has, the Panel believes, been clearly in the United States interest. In each case, if it had been necessary for the United States to deal with the crisis through unilateral means, the costs would have been far greater.

In order to ease certain of the financial difficulties, under which the UN has labored, the Panel recommends that a United Nations Peace Fund be established primarily with voluntary governmental contributions. Funds would thus be available for the initial financing of a peacekeeping operation and to meet continuing costs. The Fund would be replenished as needed.

The Fund should be established at a level which would provide adequate funding of UN peacekeeping operations in the period between annual General Assemblies. This would suggest an initial Fund goal of $60 million. Past UN peacekeeping operations have been so clearly in the United States interest that the U.S. should be willing to provide 50 per cent of this amount. The ultimate size of the Fund would depend upon future levels of UN operations.

The establishment of the Fund should be accompanied by the setting up of a Special Finance Committee by the General Assembly, under rules permitting the Secretary-General to spend up to $10 million from the Fund for authorized peacekeeping operations but requiring that additional expenditures from the Fund would be made on the recommendation of the Special Finance Committee. The Committee might either have the same membership as the Security Council, or be composed of those countries which are Permanent Members of the Council plus other UN Members selected on the basis of past contributions to peacekeeping.

This would retain the basic Charter responsibility of the Assembly for financial matters, while at the same time making certain that these decisions are effectively shaped by, and properly coordinated with, what is likely to be the larger future role of the Security Council in decisions on the disposition and use of UN peacekeeping forces.

Estimates of the amount required to meet the Organization's peacekeeping debts range from $38 million to $60 million. The UN has received something over $23 million in pledges to a "Rescue Fund." Despite a succession of promises on the part of France and the USSR to make pledges toward this fund after the U.S. gave in on the Article 19 deadlock, neither has done so.

If the United Nations is to make constructive moves toward a safer world through improved peacekeeping—and we strongly urge that it do so—it is essential that France and the Soviet Union do their part in making progress possible, and do so before additional delay further clouds the prospects for international peacekeeping arrangements that will benefit all.

Once this is done, the Panel believes that the United States should contribute not more than one third of the amount needed for a package settlement covering the payment of overdue UN peacekeeping assessments and the liquidation of UN debts—including the bond issue floated as one means of helping finance the Congo operation.

The Future of Regional Peacekeeping

There would appear to be little which the United States can do in the immediate future in moving to strengthen the direct military capability of either the Organization of American States or the Organization of African Unity. This is not to say, however, that at some point in the future, possibilities might not emerge for increasing the military capacities of at least the OAS. The United States should be alert to such possibilities, keeping in mind that the initiative should come from other members of the Organization.

In the meantime, however, the Panel believes it may be possible to enhance the capability of both the OAS and the OAU for the conciliation of difficult and pressing disputes among their Members. This could be done through strengthening the fact-finding, peace observation and communication facilities of the two organizations. In both cases the United States could offer to make communication equipment available which would become a part of their permanent operational equipment.

The OAS could be a genuinely important instrument for crisis management in the Western hemisphere. The Panel believes its principal current need is for renewed assurance that it will have a significant role in future conflict control.

The Panel also believes we are moving into a decade likely to be characterized by a more sophisticated set of relationships than has existed in the past between regional organizations and the United Nations—with closer working relationships between the two sets of institutions.

On several recent occasions representatives of OAU, in one case four foreign ministers, were asked to represent the Organization at meetings of the Security Council when a dispute of special concern to the OAU was before the Council. There is no reason why a similar procedure should not be followed when disputes of special concern to the OAS are before one of the United Nations political bodies. The OAS, the OAU and the Arab League all maintain accredited observers at the United Nations. As we have pointed out earlier in this report, the Dominican

Republic crisis was concurrently before both the Organization of American States and the United Nations, and the UN Secretary-General at the request of the Security Council sent an observer unit which for over two years was stationed in Santo Domingo at the same time that the OAS forces were active on the island.

Chapter VIII of the Charter sets forth general relationships between the UN and regional organizations. Within this Chapter, Article 54 provides that "the Security Council shall at all times be kept fully informed of activities undertaken or in contemplation under regional arrangements or by regional agencies for the maintenance of international peace and security."

While the kind of reporting arrangement envisaged under the Charter has not developed in the manner anticipated, it would seem likely that in the future, dispute settlement in the areas in which regional organizations are concerned is likely to involve a much more differentiated and mutually reinforcing set of relationships between the global organization and the regional ones than was envisioned when the Charter was drafted.

Should a more substantial set of UN peacekeeping arrangements be developed, with a larger number of UN Members designating earmarked forces available for United Nations service, a pattern might ultimately develop in which certain of these forces were also earmarked for service with a regional organization—in case a decision was made that the dispute could better be handled on a regional basis. A reverse arrangement might be equally appropriate. A system of double earmarking has already developed on a limited basis in the European area where Holland has earmarked a force as available either to NATO or the United Nations.

The Panel believes that a system of double earmarking, while it has certain obvious limitations, is nevertheless a pattern which could over time develop to the benefit of both regional organizations and the United Nations.

PANEL MEMBERS

KINGMAN BREWSTER, JR., *Chairman*
President, Yale University

HARDING F. BANCROFT
Executive Vice President
The New York Times

JOSEPH L. BLOCK
Chairman, Executive Committee
Inland Steel Company

ROBERT S. BENJAMIN
Chairman of the Board
United Artists Corporation

LINCOLN P. BLOOMFIELD
Professor of Political Science
Massachusetts Institute of Technology

WILLIAM K. COBLENTZ
Partner
Jacobs, Sills and Coblentz
San Francisco

BISHOP JOHN J. DOUGHERTY
President
Seton Hall University

SHELTON FISHER
President
McGraw-Hill, Inc.

MRS. ALBERT M. GREENFIELD
Philadelphia, Pennsylvania

ERNEST A. GROSS
Partner
Curtis, Mallet-Prevost, Colt & Mosle

NAJEEB E. HALABY
President
Pan American World Airways

PATRICIA ROBERTS HARRIS
Professor of Law
Howard University

JOSEPH E. JOHNSON
President
Carnegie Endowment for
International Peace

ROBERT H. KNIGHT
Partner
Shearman and Sterling

J. IRWIN MILLER
Chairman
Cummins Engine Co.

CHARLES P. NOYES
Formerly, Counselor
United States Mission to the
United Nations

JOHN N. PLANK
Senior Staff
The Brookings Institution

GENERAL MATTHEW B. RIDGWAY
Formerly, Supreme Commander
Allied Powers in Europe, and
Army Chief of Staff

NICHOLAS A. ROBINSON
Student, Columbia University Law
School

ROBERT V. ROOSA
Partner
Brown Brothers Harriman & Co.

KENNETH W. THOMPSON
Social Scientist and Administrator
New York City

HOWARD S. TURNER
President
Turner Construction Co.

CYRUS R. VANCE
Partner
Simpson, Thacher and Bartlett

JEROME B. WIESNER
Provost
Massachusetts Institute of
Technology

JOSEPH C. WILSON
Chairman of the Board
Xerox Corporation

CHARLES W. YOST*
Senior Fellow
Council on Foreign Relations

Affiliation indicated for purpose of identification only.

*Served until assuming office as United States Permanent Representative to the United Nations. Did not participate in the drafting of the final report.

APPENDIX 2

Report of the President's Commission for the Observance of the Twenty-Fifth Anniversary of the United Nations, Henry Cabot Lodge, Chairman

*Peace, Security, and Strengthening International Law**

The UN's Peacekeeping Capabilities

Drastic steps by the world community, especially by the great powers, will be required to establish the vitality of the United Nations to maintain international peace and security. As the American people become increasingly uneasy about any direct U.S. involvement in overseas conflicts, multilateral substitutes to defuse dangerous situations and keep local conflicts from escalating to wider war become an urgent necessity rather than a luxury.

THE COMMISSION RECOMMENDS that the United States undertake bold new initiatives to revitalize the peacekeeping and peacemaking capabilities of the UN.

Most important in reversing the present unproductive trends in UN peacekeeping is a new *attitude* among the great powers, including the United States, that should be based on the following elements:

—acceptance at all levels of decision-making of the importance of *multilateral* substitutes for unilateral involvement in local conflicts;

—acceptance of the principle that UN peacekeeping operations should be considered as a means for defusing and insulating a conflict area so that procedures of pacific settlement can take place without outside interference; and

—greater emphasis on conflict prevention, through early warning

*pp. 4-12 of the report are reprinted here. The complete report can be obtained from the Government Printing Office, Washington, D.C., 20402—Price 60 cents, Stock Number 4000-0261.

techniques, improved observation and reporting capabilities, and above all a willingness to involve the UN in actions to keep the peace early rather than dangerously late.

For UN peacekeeping to have any chance of success will require cooperation between the United States and the Soviet Union.* The two superpowers should exercise restraint and not encourage, interfere, or participate in local conflicts but rather work to the greatest extent possible through the UN system to control conflicts and promote peaceful change.

The obstacles to great-power agreement on revitalizing the UN's peacekeeping capabilities are well illustrated by the long drawn out negotiations at the UN on guidelines for future peacekeeping operations. There has been painfully slow—almost imperceptible—progress in these negotiations.

THE COMMISSION RECOMMENDS that in order to make a fresh start toward reviving the UN's capability for peacekeeping the United States announce specific steps it is willing to take or support in order to overcome the crucial weaknesses in the present UN system. These should include:

—the establishment of a UN Peace Reserve;

—the development, through a training program of a permanent UN corps of military observers; and

—the creation of a UN Peace Fund.

Some states already maintain contingents in their armed forces earmarked for service in UN peacekeeping operations. Additional measures should be taken by the UN and by members to insure that an adequate number of trained contingents are available to carry out future peacekeeping operations. States should be asked to inform the Secretary-General of (*a*) the size, character and degree of readiness of organized contingents they are prepared to make available to the Security Council for peacekeeping operations, and (*b*) the facilities, logistic support, and other services they are willing to provide. The aim should be a Peace Reserve of 25,000 trained troops, earmarked in battalion strength by countries in various parts of the world, plus a cadre of highly trained staff officers and specialized units for signals, transport, medical, and civil police duties.

THE COMMISSION RECOMMENDS that the United States:

---

*"Peacekeeping" in this context does not encompass collective measures to repel acts of aggression.

—indicate its readiness to cooperate fully with the UN and other countries in developing contingents and specialized units for a UN Peace Reserve;

—pledge air/sealift facilities for immediate transport of UN peace troops;

—earmark within the U.S. defense forces specialized units in signals, transport, and logistics for backstopping UN peacekeeping operations and for possible participation in such operations;

—insure through existing and/or new legislation that the U.S. is fully prepared to support UN peacekeeping operations, including assistance in training and equipping contingents for UN service through use of existing (but unused) provisions of the Foreign Assistance Act; and

—assist the UN in taking full advantage of developments in science and technology that might improve its peacekeeping capabilities, including new techniques in aerial surveillance and improvements in the UN's communication system through priority access to communication and observation satellite systems.

Thirty-six members of the UN have made military observers available for service with various UN missions. This aspect of the Organization's activities would be greatly strengthened by the development of a corps of a few hundred military officers, fully trained and readily available, for dispatch to troubled areas to observe and report to the UN and carry out such other functions as may be assigned to them.

THE COMMISSION RECOMMENDS that the United States offer to work with the UN and other countries in a collaborative effort to plan, train, and equip a corps of UN military observers.

Equitable and reliable financial arrangements for future peacekeeping operations are needed now. Repetition of the serious financial problems the UN has experienced in the past must be avoided. While UN missions utilizing a limited number of military observers should be financed out of the UN's regular budget, special methods of financing have to be developed for large-scale operations involving contingents of troops.

THE COMMISSION RECOMMENDS that the United States:

—propose the creation of a special fund to meet the costs of initiating large-scale peacekeeping operations;

—announce its readiness to contribute its fair share to such a fund, provided the other major powers do likewise, and also indicate its willingness, under the same condition, to accept a special scale of assessments for peacekeeping operations; and

—support the establishment of a Special Finance Committee in the UN in which the larger contributors to peacekeeping operations would have a voice commensurate with their contributions.

Prospects for effective UN peacekeeping in any particular crisis would be greatly improved if the flow of arms into areas of conflict or potential conflict were severely restricted. The UN could monitor arrangements to this effect and give maximum publicity to the dangers of arms races. There is an urgent need for reliable agreements to limit and reduce both conventional and nuclear armaments. The Commission wishes to draw attention to the useful role the UN has played in connection with such arms control agreements as the nonproliferation treaty, the treaty banning nuclear weapons in outer space, and the recently concluded treaty prohibiting the emplacement of nuclear weapons on the seabed beyond national jurisdiction. The United States should continue to utilize all appropriate forums for seeking to curtail the dangerous and costly buildup of armaments. In this process, the unique capacity of the UN to focus world attention upon particular problems and the importance of its contribution in affecting broad acceptance of arms control agreements should not be overlooked.

Procedures of Pacific Settlement

In emphasizing the need to strengthen the UN's peacekeeping capabilities, the Commission is fully aware that this is but one aspect of the larger problem of the more effective discharge by the Security Council of its primary responsibility for maintaining international peace and security. Peacekeeping must be accompanied by continuing efforts by the United Nations and the parties themselves to resolve the underlying causes of conflict. Prompt action must be taken to resolve conflicts *before* they reach the stage of open hostilities.

The disappointing record of the UN in resolving disputes does not stem from lack of machinery but from the unwillingness of states to submit to the judgment of the UN and the inability of a fragmented Security Council to put pressure on them to do so.

THE COMMISSION RECOMMENDS that the United States urge the Security Council to undertake a comprehensive reexamination of its practices with respect to the peaceful settlement of disputes with emphasis upon the need for

—speedy and thorough investigation of the facts by impartial agents;

—improved procedures of good offices and mediation; and

—bolder use of the Council's power to recommend terms of settlement.

The Council should not act upon the substance of a dispute unless it has before it a thorough report on the facts based upon impartial investigation by its own representatives, those of the Secretary-General, or another UN agency on the spot. The Secretary-General should be encouraged to use his good offices for resolving disputes and assisting parties in implementing agreements they may reach.

THE COMMISSION RECOMMENDS that the United States reiterate its position that measures directed toward supplying the Security Council with the facts of a situation should not be subject to a veto by one of the permanent members and that all states are under a positive obligation to cooperate fully with UN factfinding bodies.

THE COMMISSION FURTHER RECOMMENDS that the United States continue to support the Secretary-General's efforts to assist parties in resolving their disputes and encourage the development of a stronger research and advisory staff within the Secretariat for these purposes.

As a general practice the Security Council should, upon the submission of a complaint, immediately designate one of its members, or an *ad hoc* committee of members, to meet with the parties directly involved with a view to exploring procedures and, if possible, terms for bringing about a settlement of the controversy. For the Council to take bolder and more forceful action in recommending terms of settlement requires that the legitimate interests of *all* parties be adequately considered. The Council is prevented from adopting "balanced" recommendations when it is clear that a permanent member will veto any resolution not completely acceptable to one side in a dispute.

THE COMMISSION RECOMMENDS that the United States repeat its offer to forego the use of the veto on recommendations for procedures and terms of peaceful settlement, provided the other permanent members do the same. In the absence of such an agreement, the United States should make clear that it is prepared to use its veto to block recommendations that are patently one-sided.

While assigning primary responsibility for maintaining peace to the Security Council, the Charter recognizes the important role regional organizations should play within the UN system. It is highly desirable that relationships between the UN and regional organizations, such as the Organization of American States and the Organization of African Unity, be placed on a truly cooperative basis.

THE COMMISSION RECOMMENDS that the United States:

—support arrangements that will encourage systematic peacekeeping and peacemaking by regional organizations as agents of the world community with their actions closely coordinated with the UN; and

—provide advice and assistance to regional organizations, where appropriate, to strengthen their capabilities for carrying out such functions within the framework of the UN.

Finally, the Commission welcomes the recent decision of the Security Council to hold the high-level "periodic meetings" called for in the Charter. The unique character of these meetings should be emphasized. Their usefulness would be maximized if a small informal committee of members that can make a particularly significant contribution to the Council's work were to meet throughout the year to consider developments on the international scene and make suggestions as to the topics that might be most fruitfully considered at the periodic meetings.

THE COMMISSION RECOMMENDS that the United States:

—urge that the "periodic meetings" of the Security Council be utilized to examine incipient conflict situations, new approaches to old problems, and innovations in the Council's practices;

—propose the establishment of an executive committee, composed of the United States, the Soviet Union, and three or four other members, to follow world developments and report thereon to the periodic meetings; and

—suggest that at least some of these periodic meetings be held outside the UN headquarters and that members invite the Council to hold such meetings in their countries, preferably at sites away from major population centers.

The holding of periodic meetings of the Council at the foreign minister level is a promising new development that needs to be fully explored. In appropriate circumstances and with adequate preparation, this instrumentality might be utilized for meetings of heads of state.

The International Court of Justice

Except for a request by the Security Council for an advisory opinion on Namibia, the docket of the International Court of Justice, the principal judicial organ of the United Nations, is empty. The failure of UN members, all of whom are parties to the Court's Statute, to resort to the Court despite the multitude of problems that could be settled by litigation hardly helps the cause of international peace. In a world gravely in need of international law and legal procedures as substitutes for the use or threat of force in the settlement of international disputes, the Court must be invigorated.

Faults have been attributed to the organization, structure, and procedures of the Court. But every organizational remedy plainly requires greater confidence by states in judicial procedures to settle matters that are subject to international law.

THE COMMISSION RECOMMENDS that, as first steps in revitalizing the International Court of Justice, the United States support measures to make the Court more accessible and more responsive to the needs of states, especially the developing states. The Court should be willing to:

—meet away from The Hague at places more convenient to non-European parties to the Statute;

—set up regional chambers, or chambers to deal with specific disputes at the request of the parties with judges selected by agreement of the parties to sit at any location convenient to them; and

—adopt procedures which will reduce the costs of litigation.

Litigation before the Court has been tedious and inordinately drawn out because of archaic procedural rules and the practices and attitudes of the Court. A thorough revision of the Court's rules is long overdue. They must be adapted to the needs of today. Both the length and costs of litigation must be cut.

Costs could be reduced through the use of special chambers, through briefer proceedings, and through the reduction of printed documents. The Court's excessive generosity in extending time limits for its proceedings has been widely criticized. Reasonable and close time limits must be set and adhered to.

THE COMMISSION RECOMMENDS that the United States and the UN impress on the Court the need not merely for extensive reform of its procedures, but for a fresh look at the responsibilities and opportunities of the Court as the principal judicial organ of the UN.

Under the present practice, states are not permitted to approach the Court for *advice* on legal problems in a dispute; they can seek only a final and irrevocable *decision.* While the Court is not expressly authorized to give advice to states, it is not forbidden to do so. The Court has on occasion, at the request of states, performed functions neither authorized nor prohibited by the Statute.

THE COMMISSION RECOMMENDS that the United States urge the

Court to make known its willingness to give advice on legal problems to states that are parties to a dispute.

The Statute stipulates that only states may be parties to cases before the Court, although various organs of the UN and the specialized agencies are authorized to request advisory opinions. Recognition that international organizations are legal personalities has been an important development in world order.

THE COMMISSION RECOMMENDS that the United States support amendment of the Court's Statute to permit the UN, regional, and other specially authorized international agencies to appear as parties to a case before the Court.

THE COMMISSION FURTHER RECOMMENDS that the United States encourage the establishment of regional international courts which could serve as courts of original jurisdiction while allowing appeals to the International Court of Justice.

No state can be brought before the International Court of Justice without the consent of that state. Consent may be given specifically for an individual case, or in advance by a clause in a treaty or through adherence to the so-called "optional clause" of the Statute. Under this clause, states declare "that they recognize as compulsory *ipso facto* and without special agreement, in relation to any other state accepting the same obligation," the jurisdiction of the Court in all legal disputes, such as the interpretation of a treaty or a question of international law.

Forty-eight states have, under the "optional clause," accepted the Court's compulsory jurisdiction in legal disputes, but various reservations severely limit the effectiveness of many acceptances. The United States virtually nullified its acceptance of the Court's compulsory jurisdiction by its reservation (Connally) stating that the United States itself would determine whether any complaint against it was a matter of domestic jurisdiction and thus beyond the jurisdiction of the Court.

Since 1946 the United States has committed itself, without reservation, to the jurisdiction of the Court in over 20 multilateral treaties and 20 bilateral agreements with respect to disputes arising from those agreements. This is a commendable way for widening the Court's jurisdiction, but these agreements are only a small portion of the more than 200 bilateral and multilateral treaties subscribed to by the United States since 1946. The United States should lead the way in encouraging all states to recognize the jurisdiction of the Court as compulsory, without special agreement, for legal issues.

THE COMMISSION RECOMMENDS that the United States continue

its policy of seeking to incorporate in treaties, where appropriate, provisions accepting the jurisdiction of the Court in disputes arising under those treaties.

THE COMMISSION FURTHER RECOMMENDS that the United States withdraw its reservation (Connally) to the compulsory jurisdiction of the Court in disputes concerning the interpretation of a treaty or a question of international law.

Commission Members

AMBASSADOR HENRY CABOT LODGE, *Chairman*
FREDERICK L. EHRMAN, *Vice-Chairman*
FRANCIS O. WILCOX, *Chairman of the Working Group*

SENATOR GEORGE D. AIKEN
DR. RUTH E. BACON
GEORGE F. BAKER, JR.
MRS. BERNICE W. BEHRENS
JOSEPH L. BLOCK
DR. LINCOLN P. BLOOMFIELD
DR. LANDRUM R. BOLLING
ERWIN D. CANHAM
MISS SUSIE A. CHAN
RICHARD TALBOT CLARK
HIS EMINENCE TERENCE
   CARDINAL COOKE
SENATOR JOHN SHERMAN COOPER
AMERICO V. CORTESE
DR. LEE A. DUBRIDGE
JUSTICE ROBERT M. DUNCAN
JOHN CLIFFORD FOLGER
SENATOR J. WILLIAM FULBRIGHT
CONGRESSMAN CORNELIUS E.
   GALLAGHER
JAMES C. HAGERTY
MISS MARIE-LOUISE HANDAL
HON. BOURKE B. HICKENLOOPER
DR. JOHN R. HOWARD
JOHN T. ISAACSON

WILLIAM D. JACKSON
JOHN H. JOHNSON
DR. ROBERT B. KAMM
RABBI BERTRAM W. KORN
ANDRE LE TENDRE
ARTHUR G. LINKLETTER
CONGRESSMAN SHERMAN P. LLOYD
MRS. MARY P. LORD
BENJAMIN M. McKELWAY
PAUL MILLER
CONGRESSMAN THOMAS E. MORGAN
EUGENE ORMANDY
THOMAS A. PAPPAS
DR. NORMAN VINCENT PEALE
MRS. MILDRED EMORY PERSINGER
CHARLES S. RHYNE
DR. WALTER ORR ROBERTS
MRS. MARY LOUISE SMITH
SENATOR JOHN J. SPARKMAN
VERNON STOUFFER
RONALD F. STOWE
SENATOR ROBERT TAFT, JR.
THOMAS VAIL
ANDREW N. WYETH

APPENDIX 3

United Nations Emergency Force by Dag Hammarskjöld,

*Summary study of the experience derived from
the establishment and operation of the force.
"Concluding Observations and Principles"
from the Report of the Secretary-General**

A. OBSERVATIONS

148. In the preceding pages of this report a summary has been given of the experience of the United Nations derived from the establishment and operation of the United Nations Emergency Force. In advance of the conclusions, certain observations are called for regarding the specific circumstances in which the experience with UNEF has been gained, since those circumstances definitely limit any detailed application of that experience to the general problem of United Nations operations of this character. It is useful, in this context, also to note and compare the subsequent experience with United Nations operations in relation to Lebanon and Jordan.

149. UNEF was brought into being to meet a particular situation in which a United Nations force could be interposed between regular, national military forces which were subject to a cease-fire agreed to by the opposing parties. UNEF has continued to function along the "dividing line" between the national forces. It follows that in UNEF there has never been any need for rights and responsibilities other than those necessary for such an interposed force under cease-fire conditions. The Force was not used in any way to enforce withdrawals but, in the successive stages of the withdrawals, followed the withdrawing troops to the "dividing line" of each stage. It is also to be noted that the Force has functioned under a clear-cut mandate which has entirely detached it from involvement in any internal or local problems, and also has enabled it to maintain its neutrality in relation to international political issues.

*UN Document A/3943, October 9, 1958.

The fact that UNEF was designed to meet the needs of this specific situation largely determined its military components, geographical composition, deployment and status, and also its effectiveness.

150. A further factor of significance in the evaluation of the UNEF experience is that in Gaza the Force is in an area having special status under the Armistice Agreement. In Gaza and elsewhere in its area of operations, UNEF has been able to function without any question arising of its presence infringing upon sovereign rights, on the basis that, at the invitation of the Egyptian Government and in accordance with the decision of the General Assembly, the United Nations assists in maintaining quiet on the Armistice Demarcation Line around the Gaza Strip and along the international line to the south. The Government of Egypt has co-operated by taking necessary steps to facilitate the functioning of UNEF in the Gaza area. The same is true of the position of the Egyptian Government in keeping its limited military units in the Sinai Peninsula away from the area in which the UNEF chiefly functions.

151. Obviously, some of the above-mentioned circumstances are of such a nature that it could not reasonably be expected that they would often be duplicated elsewhere. Nor can it be assumed that they provide a sufficient basis to warrant indiscriminate projection of the UNEF experience in planning for future United Nations operations of this kind. Indeed, the more recent experiences in Lebanon and Jordan serve only to emphasize the uniqueness of the UNEF setting, which, in part at least, explains the success of this pioneer venture. Neither in Lebanon nor in Jordan would it have been possible to interpose a United Nations force between conflicting parties. Nor would it have been possible in either of those situations to preserve a natural distinction between the presence and functions in various areas of any United Nations force and the presence and functions of government troops. In Lebanon, it is unlikely that a United Nations force could have operated without soon becoming a party to the internal conflicts among nationals of the country. In Jordan, the presence of a United Nations force has been regarded by the Government as difficult to reconcile with its own exercise of full sovereignty over the people and territory of the country. United Nations experience with these three Middle East operations justifies the assumption that, in each new conflict situation in which the United Nations might be called upon to intervene with military personnel, the nature of the actual organization required and its paramilitary aspects would be determined by the particular needs of the situation and could not, therefore, be anticipated in advance. Thus, for example, stand-by arrangements for a force designed for a UNEF-type operation would not have been of practical value in either of the situations in

Lebanon or Jordan, where conditions required an approach in all relevant aspects quite different from that employed in UNEF.

152. The foregoing leads to the obvious conclusion that, in considering general stand-by arrangements for United Nations operations of the kind envisaged in this report, a course should be followed which would afford a considerable degree of flexibility in approaching the varying needs that may arise. This could be achieved if stand-by arrangements were to consist of an approval of those general conclusions regarding principles which can be reached in the light of the UNEF experience, and which would provide a setting within which, with the necessary variations of approach, personnel in units or otherwise could be recruited and an operation organized without delay and with full adjustment to the specific situation requiring the action.

153. Further support for the position here taken is found in that the type and rank of military personnel required, the need for specialists and for supporting units, as well as the vehicle and equipment demands, as experience has shown, also vary so much from case to case that more far-reaching and firm arrangements—as, for example, the maintenance of a nucleus United Nations force of the type generally envisaged—would be without great practical value and certainly would not warrant the substantial sacrifices involved. By way of illustration of this point UNEF has been able to use enlisted men with short military experience under the command of experienced officers; the recruitment of personnel for the United Nations Observation Group in Lebanon has been limited largely to officers, who, however, with few exceptions, did not have to be rigorously screened for the mission; while the arrangements in relation to Jordan may involve, if any, only a very limited number of military personnel, all of officer rank but individually and carefully chosen for the purpose. Similar differences are apparent as regards the need for matériel with UNEF being adequately served by, in military calculations, a quite modest number of aircraft and vehicles, while UNOGIL has had to operate with a considerably higher ratio of planes and vehicles to the men involved, because of the specific tasks with which it has been entrusted.

B. BASIC PRINCIPLES

154. In view of the impossibility of determining beforehand the specific form of a United Nations presence of the type considered in this report, which would be necessary to meet adequately the requirements of a given situation, a broad decision by the General Assembly should attempt to do no more than endorse certain basic principles and rules which would provide an adaptable framework for later operations that

might be found necessary. In a practical sense, it is not feasible in advance of a known situation to do more than to provide for some helpful stand-by arrangements for a force or similar forms of a United Nations presence. In the following paragraphs, certain principles and rules are laid down in the light of the experience gathered in the past years, which, if they were to meet with the approval of the General Assembly, would provide a continuing basis on which useful contacts in a stand-by context might be established with interested Governments, with the aim of being prepared for any requests which might arise from future decisions by the Assembly on a force or similar arrangements to deal with a specific case.

155. As the arrangements discussed in this report do not cover the type of force envisaged under Chapter VII of the Charter, it follows from international law and the Charter that the United Nations cannot undertake to implement them by stationing units on the territory of a Member State without the consent of the Government concerned. It similarly follows from the Charter that the consent of a Member nation is necessary for the United Nations to use its military personnel or matériel. These basic rules have been observed in the recent United Nations operations in the Middle East. They naturally hold valid for all similar operations in the future.

156. The fact that a United Nations operation of the type envisaged requires the consent of the Government on whose territory it takes place creates a problem, as it is normally difficult for the United Nations to engage in such an operation without guarantees against unilateral actions by the host Government which might put the United Nations in a questionable position, either administratively or in relation to contributing Governments.

157. The formula employed in relation to the Government of Egypt for UNEF seems, in the light of experience, to provide an adequate solution to this problem. The Government of Egypt declared that, when exercising its sovereign right with regard to the presence of the Force, it would be guided by good faith in the interpretation of the purposes of the Force. This declaration was balanced by a declaration by the United Nations to the effect that the maintenance of the Force by the United Nations would be determined by similar good faith in the interpretation of the purposes.

158. The consequence of such a bilateral declaration is that, were either side to act unilaterally in refusing continued presence or deciding on withdrawal, and were the other side to find that such action was contrary to a good faith interpretation of the purposes of the operation, an exchange of views would be called for towards harmonizing the positions. This does not imply any infringement on the sovereign right of

the host Government, nor any restriction of the right of the United Nations to decide on termination of its own operation whenever it might see fit to do so. But it does mean a mutual recognition of the fact that the operation, being based on collaboration between the host Government and the United Nations, should be carried on in forms natural to such collaboration, and especially so with regard to the questions of presence and maintenance.

159. It is unlikely that any Government in the future would be willing to go beyond the declaration of the Government of Egypt with regard to UNEF. Nor, in my view, should the United Nations commit itself beyond the point established for UNEF in relation to the Government of Egypt. In these circumstances, I consider it reasonable to regard the formula mentioned in paragraph 158 above as a valid basis for future arrangements of a similar kind.

160. Another point of principle which arises in relation to the question of consent refers to the composition of United Nations military elements stationed on the territory of a Member country. While the United Nations must reserve for itself the authority to decide on the composition of such elements, it is obvious that the host country, in giving its consent, cannot be indifferent to the composition of those elements. In order to limit the scope of possible difference of opinion, the United Nations in recent operations has followed two principles: not to include units from any of the permanent members of the Security Council; and not to include units from any country which, because of its geographical position or for other reasons, might be considered as possibly having a special interest in the situation which has called for the operation. I believe that these two principles also should be considered as essential to any stand-by arrangements.

161. Given the two principles mentioned in paragraph 160, in actual practice the area within which conflicting views may be expressed will in all probability be so reduced normally as to facilitate the harmonizing of the rights of the United Nations with the interests of the host country. It would seem desirable to accept the formula applied in the case of UNEF, which is to the effect that, while it is for the United Nations alone to decide on the composition of military elements sent to a country, the United Nations should, in deciding on composition, take fully into account the viewpoint of the host Government as one of the most serious factors which should guide the recruitment of the personnel. Usually, this is likely to mean that serious objections by the host country against participation by a specific contributing country in the United Nations operation will determine the action of the Organization. However, were the United Nations for good reasons to find that course inadvisable, it would remain free to pursue its own line, and any result-

ing conflict would have to be resolved on a political rather than on a legal basis. I would recommend that the basis thus laid in the case of UNEF be considered as the formula on composition applicable to similar operations in the future.

162. The principles indicated in the four points discussed above (paragraphs 155-161 inclusive) were either established by the General Assembly itself, elaborated in practice or in negotiations with the Government of Egypt. They have served as the basis for a status Agreement which applies to the United Nations personnel in the Force in Egypt. In its entirety, this status Agreement has stood up well to the test of experience. Its basic principles should be embodied in similar agreements in the future, and their recognition, therefore, would seem necessarily to form part of any stand-by arrangements for a force. The Agreement regarding the presence of UNOGIL in Lebanon, although much less elaborate because of the modest size of the operation and the fact that normal immunity rules could be applied to the bulk of the personnel, also reflects the basic principles I have in mind.

163. The most important principle in the status Agreement ensures that UNEF personnel, when involved in criminal actions, come under the jurisdiction of the criminal courts of their home countries. The establishment of this principle for UNEF, in relation to Egypt, has set a most valuable precedent. Experience shows that this principle is essential to the successful recruitment by the United Nations of military personnel not otherwise under immunity rules, from its Member countries. The position established for UNEF should be maintained in future arrangements.

164. Another principle involved in the UNEF status Agreement, and which should be retained, is that the United Nations activity should have freedom of movement within its area of operations and all such facilities regarding access to that area and communications as are necessary for successful completion of the task. This also obviously involves certain rights of over-flight over the territory of the host country. These principles have been maintained in the case of UNOGIL. Their application requires an agreement on what is to be considered as the area of operations and as to what facilities of access and communications are to be considered necessary. On the assumption that, like UNEF, any similar United Nations operation in the future would be of assistance to the nation on whose territory it is stationed, it is not to be expected that the necessary process of agreement will give rise to any serious complications in the interpretation of the principle.

165. Apart from the principles thus established in negotiated agreements or formal decisions, a series of basic rules has been developed in practice. Some of these rules would appear to merit general application. This

is true especially of the precept that authority granted to the United Nations group cannot be exercised within a given territory either in competition with representatives of the host Government or in co-operation with them on the basis of any joint operation. Thus, a United Nations operation must be separate and distinct from activities by national authorities. UNEF experience indicates how this rule may apply in practice. A right of detention which normally would be exercised only by local authorities is extended to UNEF units. However, this is so only within a limited area where the local authorities voluntarily abstain from exercising similar rights, whether alone or in collaboration with the United Nations. Were the underlying principle of this example not to be applied, United Nations units might run the risk of getting involved in differences with the local authorities or public or in internal conflicts which would be highly detrimental to the effectiveness of the operation and to the relations between the United Nations and the host Government.

166. A rule closely related to the one last-mentioned, and reflecting a basic Charter principle, precludes the employment of United Nations elements in situations of an essentially internal nature. As a matter of course, the United Nations personnel cannot be permitted in any sense to be a party to internal conflicts. Their role must be limited to external aspects of the political situation as, for example, infiltration or other activities affecting international boundaries.

167. Even in the case of UNEF, where the United Nations itself had taken a stand on decisive elements in the situation which gave rise to the creation of the Force, it was explicitly stated that the Force should not be used to enforce any specific political solution of pending problems or to influence the political balance decisive to such a solution. This precept clearly imposes a serious limitation on the possible use of United Nations elements, were it to be given general application to them whenever they are not created under Chapter VII of the Charter. However, I believe its acceptance to be necessary, if the United Nations is to be in a position to draw on Member countries for contributions in men and matériel to United Nations operations of this kind.

168. Military personnel employed by the United Nations in paramilitary operations are, of course, not under the same formal obligations in relation to the Organization as staff members of the Secretariat. However, the position must be maintained that the basic rules of the United Nations for international service are applicable also to such personnel, particularly as regards full loyalty to the aims of the Organization and to abstention from acts in relation to their country of origin or to other countries which might deprive the operation of its international character and create a situation of dual loyalty. The observance of this rule is

not only vital for good relations with the host country, it is also to the benefit of the contributing countries concerned, as any other attitude might involve them in responsibilities which would be undesirable in the light of the national policies pursued.

169. In setting up UNEF, the General Assembly appointed a Commander of the Force with the position of an international civil servant responsible for discharge of his task to the Assembly, but administratively integrated with the United Nations organization, and under instructions from the Secretary-General on the basis of the executive authority for the operation vested in him by the Assembly.

170. A somewhat different procedure was followed in the case of UNOGIL, where the Security Council delegated to the Secretary-General the responsibility for constituting the Observation Group. However, basically the same principle employed in UNEF is applied to UNOGIL, for the Group is responsible for the conduct of its business to the Security Council, while administratively it is under the Secretary-General, who is charged with its organization. A basically similar pattern finds reflection also in the arrangements being made by the United Nations in relation to Jordan.

171. The innovation represented by the constitutional pattern thus followed in recent United Nations field operations has, in experience, proved to be highly practical and, especially, politically of decisive importance, as it has provided for an integration giving the operation all the advantages of administrative co-ordination with the Secretariat and of the fully internationalized status of the Secretariat. As pointed out in my "Second and final report on the Emergency Force," on which the General Assembly based its decision to organize the Force, the appointment by the General Assembly of a Commander determined the legal status of the Force. The other arrangements, mentioned above, reflect the same basic concept.

172. In full recognition of the wide variety of forms which decisions on a United Nations operation may take in seeking to fit differing situations calling for such an operation, the underlying rule concerning command and authority which has been consistently applied in recent years, as set out above, should, in my view, be maintained for the future. Thus, a United Nations operation should always be under a leadership established by the General Assembly or the Security Council, or on the basis of delegated authority by the Secretary-General, so as to make it directly responsible to one of the main organs of the United Nations, while integrated with the Secretariat in an appropriate form.

173. Were soundings with Member Governments, based on the aforementioned legal and political principles and rules and on the regulations regarding financial responsibilities set out below, to show that a number

of Governments in their planning would be willing to take into account the possibility of having to provide promptly—on an emergency basis, on specific appeal from the United Nations—men and matériel to a United Nations operation of the kind envisaged in this report, a question arises regarding the conditions under which such a desirable stand-by arrangement could be utilized.

174. Under the Charter, and under the "Uniting for Peace" resolution, a formal decision on a United Nations operation must be taken by the General Assembly or by the Security Council. It must be regarded as excluded that the right to take such a decision, in any general terms, could properly be considered as delegated to the Secretary-General. Short of an explicit decision by the General Assembly or the Security Council with a specific authorization, the Secretary-General, thus, cannot be considered as entitled to appeal to a Member nation for military personnel to be dispatched to another Member country in a United Nations operation.

175. The terms of the delegation in each operation thus far have set the limit of the Secretary-General's authority. Thus, for example, as apparent from the description of the new body, the decision relating to UNEF, which was to be implemented by the Secretary-General, qualified the operation as being one of a paramilitary nature, while the absence of an explicit authorization for the Force to take offensive action excluded the organization by the Secretary-General of units for such action, and consequently, the units generally were equipped only with weapons necessary for self-defence. Had there been any remaining doubts in this respect, the legal basis on which the General Assembly took its decision would have made this limitation clear.

176. Similarly, the Security Council decision on the United Nations Observation Group in Lebanon qualified the kind of operation that the Secretary-General was authorized to organize by the very name given to the unit to be established. That name excluded the creation of a paramilitary force and imposed, in fact, such limitations on the operation as to call for great restraint regarding the arming of the unit and its right of self-defence.

177. The General Assembly decision concerning the arrangements in relation to Jordan was in such broad terms as to provide possibilities for the organization of any kind of operation, short of one possible only under Chapter VII. In this case, however, as in the case of UNEF, a certain incompleteness in the terminology of the decision was covered by the conclusions following from the legal basis on which the decision was taken.

178. Confirmation by the Assembly of the interpretation of the question of authority given above would be useful. This interpretation would

signify that a Member country, in deciding upon a contribution of men or matériel to a United Nations operation on the basis of such stand-by understandings as may have been reached, could rely upon the explicit terms of the executive authority delegated to the Secretary-General in determining the use which could be made of the units provided; it being understood, naturally, that in the types of operation with which this report is concerned this could never include combat activity. There will always remain, of course, a certain margin of freedom for judgement, as, for example, on the extent and nature of the arming of the units and of their right to self-defence. In the case of UNEF, such questions of interpretation have been solved in consultation with the contributing Governments and with the host Government. The Advisory Committee on UNEF set up by the General Assembly has in this context proved to be of especially great assistance.

179. In the preceding paragraph I have touched upon the extent to which a right of self-defence may be exercised by United Nations units of the type envisaged. It should be generally recognized that such a right exists. However, in certain cases this right should be exercised only under strictly defined conditions. A problem arises in this context because of the fact that a wide interpretation of the right of self-defence might well blur the distinction between operations of the character discussed in this report and combat operations, which would require a decision under Chapter VII of the Charter and an explicit, more far-reaching delegation of authority to the Secretary-General than would be required for any of the operations discussed here. A reasonable definition seems to have been established in the case of UNEF, where the rule is applied that men engaged in the operation may never take the initiative in the use of armed force, but are entitled to respond with force to an attack with arms, including attempts to use force to make them withdraw from positions which they occupy under orders from the Commander, acting under the authority of the Assembly and within the scope of its resolutions. The basic element involved is clearly the prohibition against any initiative in the use of armed force. This definition of the limit between self-defence, as permissible for United Nations elements of the kind discussed, and offensive action, which is beyond the competence of such elements, should be approved for future guidance.

180. The clear delimitation of the right to use force which has been set out above as a basic rule for the type of operations discussed in this report should dissipate any objections against the suggested stand-by arrangements which would be based on the view that they go beyond the measures which the Charter permits the General Assembly to take and infringe upon prerogatives of the Security Council. The principles

outlined above put UNEF at the same level, constitutionally, as UNOGIL, for example, qualifying it so as to make it an instrument of efforts at mediation and conciliation. It may be noted in this context that UNOGIL has not given rise to any constitutional objections; the fact that the Group was created by the Security Council is in this case irrelevant, as the Council acted entirely within the limits of Chapter VI of the Charter, and as a similar action obviously could have been taken by the General Assembly under Article 22.

181. In the case of UNEF, the General Assembly decided to organize an Advisory Committee under the chairmanship of the Secretary-General, to assist the operation. In practice, this arrangement has proved highly useful. In principle, it should be accepted as a precedent for the future. Extensive operations with serious political implications, regarding which, for practical reasons, executive authority would need to be delegated to the Secretary-General, require close collaboration with authorized representatives of the General Assembly. However, it would be undesirable for this collaboration to be given such a form as to lead to divided responsibilities or to diminished efficiency in the operation. The method chosen by the General Assembly in the case of UNEF seems the most appropriate one if such risks are to be avoided. The Committee is fully informed by the Secretary-General and his associates. There is a free exchange of views in closed meetings where advice can be sought and given. But ultimate decisions rest with the Secretary-General, as the executive in charge of carrying out the operation. Dissenting views are not registered by vote, but are put on record in the proceedings of the Committee. It is useful for contributing countries to be represented on such an advisory committee, but if the contributing States are numerous the size of the committe might become so large as to make it ineffective. On the other hand, it is obviously excluded that any party to the conflict should be a member. Normally, I believe that the same basic rule regarding permanent members of the Security Council which has been applied to units and men in the recent operations should be applied also in the selection of members for a relevant advisory committee.

182. In the administration of UNEF at Headquarters, certain special arrangements were made on an ad hoc basis to provide expert military guidance. Thus, a senior Military Adviser and three officer assistants were attached to the Executive Office as consultants. The Military Adviser, and the Under-Secretary representing the Secretary-General on current matters relating to the Force, were assisted by a group of military representatives from the countries providing contingents, sitting as an informal military advisory committee. Once the operation was firmly established, these arrangements could be and were reduced and simpli-

fied, but in the initial stage they proved to be of great value organizationally and also as an added means of maintaining close contacts with contributing Governments.

183. A parallel arrangement was that by which, for a period, a personal representative of the Secretary-General was stationed in the capital of the host country as a liaison officer directly in contact with the Government.

184. In view of the very great diversity likely to characterize the experience in practice of using United Nations units within the scope of this report, it is impossible to enunciate any principles for organizational arrangements at Headquarters or in the host country that should be made in anticipation of each case. There will always be developed, as a matter of course, the forms of liaison for which there will be a clear need.

185. The question, however, is of interest in this context, as it has a bearing on the problem whether or not such stand-by arrangements as those for which the principles and rules set out here would provide, would call for any kind of nucleus of military experts at United Nations Headquarters. At some stage, a standing group of a few military experts might be useful in order to keep under review such arrangements as may be made by Member Governments in preparation for meeting possible appeals for an operation. I would consider it premature, however, to take any decision of this kind at the present time, since the foreseeable tasks that might evolve for the Secretariat do not go beyond what it is now able to cope with unassisted by such special measures. Were a more far-reaching understanding than I have indicated to prove possible, the matter obviously would have to be reconsidered and submitted again in appropriate form to the General Assembly, which then might consider the organizational problem. Pending such a development later, the present working rule, in my view, should be that the Secretariat, while undertaking the soundings mentioned above and the necessary continuing contacts with the Governments, should not take any measures beyond keeping the situation under constant review, so as to be able to act expeditiously, if a decision by the General Assembly or the Security Council should call for prompt action.

186. It may be reiterated in passing that the United Nations Secretariat has by now had extensive experience in establishing and maintaining United Nations operations involving military personnel and, without improvising or augmenting unduly, can quickly provide any operation of that nature with efficient communications service in the field and with Headquarters, with transportation and vehicles for local transport, with well-tested administrative and accounting systems and expert personnel to man them, and with effective procurement and security arrangements.

187. The financial obligations of Member countries to the United Nations are of two kinds. On the one hand, there are such obligations as are covered by the scale of contributions established by the General Assembly; on the other, there are certain voluntary commitments outside that scale, such as United Nations technical assistance or the United Nations Children's Fund. While, of course, contributions from individual Member nations to United Nations units for field operations may always be made on a voluntary basis, thus being lifted outside the scale of contributions, the principle must be that, as flowing from decisions of one of the main organs of the United Nations, such contributions should be subordinated to the normal financial rules. Any other principle would seriously limit the possibility of recruiting the necessary personnel from the most appropriate countries and achieving the best geographical distribution, since most countries are not likely to be in a position to assume the additional financial burdens involved and since, unless otherwise agreed, all contributing countries should be treated on the same basis.

188. In the initial stages of UNEF, Member nations assumed certain additional burdens beyond those which would follow from the application of normal rules governing contributions to the United Nations. Later, financial relations were adjusted so as to be based on full compensation for extra and extraordinary costs, financed under the normal scale of contributions. The underlying rule is that a contributing country, by such action, should not be subjected to financial sacrifices beyond those obligations which would be incurred if it were not contributing directly to the operation. On the other hand, naturally, contributing countries should not shift to the United Nations any costs which, in any case they would have had to meet under their normal domestic policy.

189. I believe that, as part of the stand-by arrangements, it should be established that the costs for United Nations operations of the type in question, based on decisions of the General Assembly or the Security Council, should be allocated in accordance with the normal scale of contributions. The United Nations in this way should assume responsibility for all additional costs incurred by a contributing country because of its participation in the operation, on the basis of a cost assessment which, on the other hand, would not transfer to the United Nations any costs which would otherwise have been incurred by a contributing Government under its regular national policy.

190. With relation to the men engaged in one of its operations, the United Nations should naturally assume all responsibilities necessary to safeguard the normal interest of those so employed. Thus, they should be fully compensated by the United Nations for any losses of earning

power or social benefits which may be suffered because of their service with the United Nations. In view of the great variety of regulations applied by various countries, it is impossible to go beyond this general statement of principle; the details would have to be worked out with each contributing Government, as appropriate.

191. With relation to a host Government, it should be the rule that as the United Nations units are dispatched to the country in the interest and with the consent and co-operation of the host Government, that Government should provide all necessary facilities for the operation. This, in principle, should be done without any compensation, in case such facilities are in the possession of the host Government itself. Thus, for example, contributions of government services or government-owned property placed at the disposal of the United Nations for its operation should not be subject to compensation.

192. Concerning the claims of private citizens in the host country, the applicable rule is that the United Nations should pay compensation for the use of their property or services, whenever the host Government would have been obligated to pay for similar services or uses. The question whether the United Nations, in its turn, should be reimbursed by the host Government for such outlays would properly be settled through negotiation, in the light of the circumstances in each separate case.

193. The approach indicated in this chapter suggests a way in which the United Nations, within the limits of the Charter, may seek the most practical method of mustering and using, as necessary, the resources—both of nations and its own—required for operations involving military personnel which may be conceived in response to the needs of specific conflict situations. The national resources likely to be available for such purposes, if our limited experience is a gauge, are no doubt substantial, but they cannot now be calculated or even estimated, and even their availability at any particular time would probably be subject to considerable fluctuation, for political and other reasons. Formalizing the principles and rules outlined above, however, would afford a strengthened basis on which to expedite the mobilization of voluntary aid towards meeting urgent need. Their approval by the Assembly, thus clarifying and regularizing important legal and practical issues, would also ensure a more efficient use of any aid extended to the Organization, were it again to have to appeal to Member nations for such assistance.

APPENDIX 4

United Nations Peace Force by U Thant

The development of an international order, enshrined in an accepted code of world law and guaranteed by an effective world police force, has long been a human aspiration. This dream is based upon the very reasonable idea of projecting the stability and orderliness of a well-governed State onto the relations between nations.

In the history of most nation-States, there came a time when the feuding of a few powerful interests or personages, in disregard of the welfare of the majority, and the ensuing chaos and disaster, became intolerable. From this situation, there was the evolution in due course of a strong central authority, based on popular representation, a sound system of law and a reliable police force. In our world, we reached a similarly intolerable situation many years ago and have twice in this century paid a terrible price for having failed to draw the necessary conclusions.

Most sensible people now agree that some reliable system of ensuring world peace is essential. But, as in most situations involving great and conflicting interests and very large numbers of people, there is all the difference in the world between the need and the practical fulfilment of the need. That fulfilment will be a long and complicated process, requiring a degree of confidence and understanding which we have not yet established in our world.

Few would deny that, if we are to look forward with confidence to the future, we have to take a great step forward in regulating the relations of nations and produce workable institutions for that purpose. One should not, however, underestimate the difficulties of such a step or the inevitable risks which attend it.

Nations and Governments, taking a great step forward, face imponderables and unknown dangers which no research or scientific test can resolve, for these unforeseeable events will be the result of the actions, reactions and interactions of hundreds of millions of human beings, and the human mind and human behaviour are still perhaps the most

An address to the Harvard Alumni Association, delivered June 13, 1963.

mysterious and awe-inspiring force in our world. Statesmen are wise, therefore, to view the future with caution and to examine proposals for fundamental change with more than usual care.

While we are making this step forward towards a new world order, we need guarantees, we need moderating influences and we need some commonly operated and accepted agency to share the risks and make the necessary tests and experiments, and even mistakes. Certainly we need an agency through which the necessary confidence and contact among nations can be built up and maintained. The United Nations is the nearest thing we have to such an agency, and I believe that it is beginning to play an important role of the kind I have just described.

It is no doubt true that there are certain great problems, such as the struggle between the greatest powers and the related problem of disarmament, which may be with us for a long time and which, perhaps, cannot be tackled head-on by the United Nations. We must, of course, do everything that we can to avoid adding fuel to the great power struggle.

There are, however, a large number of important problems and situations which *can* usefully be tackled and, if this is done, the greatest problems themselves can be isolated, if not resolved. We should, in this process, begin to develop the necessary institutions and practices by which, at a later stage, a more stable world order can be ensured.

I am going to talk today about one particular aspect of our problems, namely, peace-keeping and the use of international peace forces by the United Nations. Due partly to the lack of unanimity among the great powers ever since 1946, and partly to the radical change in the nature of war resulting from the development of atomic and hydrogen weapons, there has been a gradual change in thinking on questions of international security in the United Nations.

There has been a tacit transition from the concept of collective security, as set out in Chapter VII of the United Nations Charter, to a more realistic idea of peace-keeping. The idea that conventional military methods—or, to put it bluntly, war—can be used by or on behalf of the United Nations to counter aggression and secure the peace, seems now to be rather impractical.

There also has been a change in emphasis from the use of the military forces of the great powers, as contemplated in the Charter, to the use, in practice, of the military resources of the smaller powers, which has the advantage of not entangling the United Nations actions in the antagonisms of the cold war.

Although there has been one collective action under the aegis of the United Nations—Korea—and although in 1951 the Collective Measures Committee, set up by the General Assembly under the Uniting for Peace resolution, actually published in its report a list of units earmarked by Member States for service with the United Nations in actions to counter aggression, actual developments have in practice been in a rather different direction.

The nature of these developments is sometimes confused, wittingly or unwittingly, by an attempt to relate them to the use of force to counter aggression by the Security Council provided for in Chapter VII of the Charter. In fact, the peace-keeping forces I am about to describe are of a very different kind and have little in common with the forces foreseen in Chapter VII, but their existence is not in conflict with Chapter VII. They are essentially *peace* and not fighting forces and they operate only with the consent of the parties directly concerned.

In this context, it is worth noting that *all* of the permanent members of the Security Council have, at one time or another in the past 15 years, voted in support of the creation of one or other of these forces, and that none of them has in any case gone further than to abstain from voting on them.

Since 1950, the United Nations has been called to deal with a number of critical situations of varying urgency. The most urgent of these have been what are sometimes called "brush-fire wars," meaning, I take it, small conflagrations which, unless controlled, may all too easily ignite very much larger ones.

If we briefly look through the United Nations experience with this kind of operation, we can see that from small and informal beginnings a useful body of precedent and practice has grown up over the years of using military personnel of Member States on peace-keeping operations. In Greece in 1947, the United Nations Special Committee on the Balkans found that professional military officers were invaluable as an observer group in assessing the highly complicated and fluctuating situation. The Security Council itself set up an observer group of military officers in India and Pakistan to watch over the Kashmir question. This observer group, which was set up in 1948, is still operating.

A much larger use of military observers by the United Nations was made when, in July 1948, the first truce agreements in the Palestine war were supervised on the ground by some 700 United Nations military observers working under the United Nations Mediator and the Chief of Staff. This team developed into the United Nations Truce Supervision Organization after the armistice agreements between Israel and her Arab neighbours were concluded in the period from February to July 1949.

This organization of officers from many countries still plays a vital role in keeping the peace in the Middle East and in reporting on and dealing with incidents which, though small in themselves, might all too easily become the cause of far larger disturbances if not dealt with. Its indefatigable members in their white jeeps are now a familiar and welcome part of the Middle Eastern landscape.

A peace-keeping organization of a different nature made its appearance as a result of the Suez crisis of October 1956. Confronted with a situation of the utmost urgency in which two of the permanent members of the Security Council were directly involved, the General Assembly voted for the urgent creation of a United Nations force. This was essentially *not* a force designed actively to fight against aggression.

It went to Egypt with the express consent of the Egyptian Government and after the other parties concerned had agreed to a cease-fire. It was designed not to fight but rather to allow those involved to disengage without further disturbance. It allowed for the peaceful resolution of one of the most dangerous crises which had faced the world since the Second World War. It also, incidentally, allowed for the clearance by the United Nations of the Suez Canal, which had been blocked during the previous military action.

The United Nations Emergency Force in the Middle East has for six years watched over the borders of Israel with the United Arab Republic in the Gaza Strip and through the Sinai Desert. It also watches over the access to the Gulf of Aqaba and to the Israeli port of Elath. What was once a most troubled and terrorized frontier has become peaceful and prosperous on both sides, and the very presence of the United Nations Force is both an insurance against a resumption of trouble and a good excuse not to engage in it. It presents us with one serious problem. To maintain an army of over 5,000 men costs money, but at present the parties concerned have no wish to see it removed.

In 1958 another very tense situation, with quite different origins, occurred in Lebanon. After the success of UNEF, there were suggestions in many quarters that another United Nations force should be collected and dispatched to that country. Here, however, the problem, though aggravated by external factors, was essentially a domestic one.

The Security Council therefore set up a three-man observer group and left the Secretary-General considerable latitude as to the methods to be employed to make this group effective in watching over the possibilities of infiltration from outside. A highly mobile group of 600 officers was quickly organized to keep watch from ground and air, while the crisis itself was resolved by negotiation and discussion. By the end of 1958, it was possible to withdraw the United Nations Observer Group from the Lebanon altogether.

The greatest and most complex challenge to the United Nations in the peacekeeping field arose a few days after the Congo gained its independence from Belgium on 30 June 1960. The general proportions of this problem are sometimes obscured by a wealth of dramatic detail and are worth restating. Harassed by mutiny, lawlessness and the collapse of public order and services from within, and afflicted by foreign military intervention as well as by ominous threats of other forms of interference from without, the new Government of the Congo appealed to the United Nations for help.

The Security Council committed the United Nations to respond to this appeal and thus made the Organization not only the guarantor of law and order and the protector of the Congo against external interference from any source, but also the adviser and helper of a newly independent State which had had virtually no preparation for its independence.

By filling, in the space of a few hours, the very dangerous vacuum which existed in the Congo in July 1960, the urgent danger of a confrontation of the great powers in the heart of Africa was avoided and the territorial integrity of the Congo preserved. The new leaders of the Congo have been given at least a short breathing-spell in which to find their feet. Despite its shortcomings, which must be judged in the light of the fearsome complexity of the problem, the United Nations Operation in the Congo is, in my opinion, a promising and encouraging experiment in international responsibility and action.

The blue helmets of the United Nations Force are known throughout the Congo as the symbol of security. Its soldiers have given protection at one time or another in the last three years to almost every Congolese public figure and almost every group, both African and non-African, when danger and violence threatened them. It is worth noting that, now that the withdrawal of the United Nations Force in the Congo is in sight, the deepest regret, and even alarm, is expressed by the very groups who used to be its most hostile critics and detractors.

In the Force, soldiers from other African countries work side by side in this vast tropical country with those from farther away. Their loyalty to the United Nations, their team spirit and comradeship have been an inspiration to all those who value the peace-keeping role of the United Nations.

I will end my catalogue with two more operations, one of which has already been successfully concluded, and which also involved an unprecedented role for the United Nations. I would like to refer first to the transfer of West Irian from Dutch rule, through a temporary period of United Nations executive authority, backed by a United Nations Security Force, to the administration of Indonesia. This entire operation has taken place with the agreement of the parties concerned, and in consultation with them.

The second is the dispatch to Yemen of an observer team as a basis for the disengagement of the United Arab Republic and Saudi Arabia from the affairs of Yemen. This operation will be paid for by the two parties concerned, and has been undertaken at their request and that of the Government of Yemen.

Although these are peace forces, service in them is hard and can be dangerous. In the Middle East, the United Nations has registered casualties not only from accidents and disease, but from mines. Both there and in West Irian, as also in Yemen, the terrain and the climate are inhospitable. In the Congo, we have had, unfortunately, serious casualties from unwanted fighting as well as from other causes, and I very much hope that we shall have no more.

I have only mentioned here the peace-keeping activities which have involved the use, in one way or another, of military personnel. If I were to mention the many other tense situations in which the United Nations, and my office in particular, have been used as a meeting-ground and as an instrument for mediation and peaceful settlement, the list would be much longer.

To sum up, we have now had experience of three major peace-keeping forces and a variety of military observer and truce supervisory operations. Each of the three forces has been different in composition, nature and task, but they have shared certain common characteristics.

All three were improvised and called into the field at very short notice; all three were severely limited in their right to use force; all three were designed solely for the maintenance of peace and not for fighting in the military sense; all three were recruited from the smaller powers and with special reference to their acceptability in the area in which they were to serve; all three operated with the express consent and co-operation of the States or territories where they were stationed, as well as of any other parties directly concerned in the situation; and all three were under the direction and control of the Secretary-General acting on behalf of the organs of the United Nations.

These facts may now seem commonplace; it is a measure of the progress that has been made that even ten years ago they would have seemed very unusual.

By the standards of an efficient national military establishment, these forces have considerable disadvantages. Obviously, a force put together only after the emergency with which it is to deal is in full swing, will inevitably have some shortcomings. There is difficulty in recruiting at very short notice exactly the right kind of units for the work in hand, and in operating a force whose units and officers meet each other for the first time in the midst of a delicate operation. There are differences not only of language and tradition but of training, equipment and staff procedures. There are differences in pay and emoluments which, if not handled carefully, can cause considerable problems of discipline and morale. Staff-work and command are especially difficult where every decision has important political implications.

Although these contingents from Member States are under the operational control of the United Nations, disciplinary powers are still vested in the national authorities and this could be, although in fact it never has been, the cause of very serious difficulties for the United Nations Force Commander and for the Secretary-General.

The fact that the military establishments of the permanent members of the Security Council cannot be used cuts us off from the most obvious sources of equipment and personnel. The improvised nature of these operations also gives rise to various problems of logistics.

In our experience, these difficulties, which are inherent in the pioneering nature of these operations, have been offset by the enthusiastic co-operation of Member States and by the spirit and comprehension of the officers and men of the contingents which have made up the United Nations forces. It is an encouraging thought that in the military establishments of some 30 or more countries in the world there are now large numbers of officers and men who have served the United Nations with distinction in one or other of these operations and have added thereby a new dimension to their military experience.

The improvised approach also makes it possible on each occasion to make up the United Nations force from the countries which are, politically and in other ways, most suitable for the operation in hand, and at least the United Nations is not afflicted with the age-old problem of having on its hands a standing army with nothing to do.

In my opinion, a permanent United Nations force is not a practical proposition at the present time. I know that many serious people in many countries are enthusiastic about the idea, and I welcome their enthusiasm and the thought they are putting into the evolution of the institution which will eventually and surely emerge. Many difficulties still stand in the way of its evolution.

Personally, I have no doubt that the world should eventually have an international police force which will be accepted as an integral and essential part of life in the same way as national police forces are accepted. Meanwhile, we must be sure that developments are in the right direction and that we can also meet critical situations as and when they occur.

There are a number of reasons why it seems to me that the establishment of a permanent United Nations force would be premature at the present time. I doubt whether many Governments in the world would yet be prepared to accept the political implications of such an institution and, in the light of our current experience with financial problems, I am sure that they would have very serious difficulties in accepting the financial implications.

I believe that we need a number of parallel developments before we can evolve such an institution. We have to go further along the road of codification and acceptance of a workable body of international law. We have to develop a more sophisticated public opinion in the world, which can accept the transition from predominantly national thinking to international thinking.

We shall have to develop a deeper faith in international institutions as such, and a greater confidence in the possibility of a United Nations civil service whose international loyalty and objectivity are generally accepted and above suspicion. We shall have to improve the method of financing international organization. Until these conditions are met, a permanent United Nations force may not be a practical proposition.

But we have already shown that, when the situation demands it, it is possible to use the soldiers of many countries for objectives which are not national ones and that the soldiers respond magnificently to this new challenge. We have also seen that, when the situation is serious enough, Governments are prepared to waive certain of the attributes of national sovereignty in the interest of keeping the peace through the United Nations. We have demonstrated that a loyalty to international service can exist side by side with legitimate national pride.

And, perhaps most important of all, we have shown that there *can* be a practical alternative to the deadly ultimate struggle and that it is an alternative which brings out the good and generous qualities in men rather than their destructive and selfish qualities.

Although it is perhaps too early, for the reasons I have already given, to consider the establishment of a permanent United Nations force, I believe there are a number of measures which could be taken even now to improve on our present capacity for meeting dangerous situations. It would be extremely desirable, for example, if countries would, in their national military planning, make provision for suitable units which could be made available at short notice for United Nations service and thereby decrease the degree of improvisation necessary in an emergency.

I take this opportunity to publicly welcome and express my appreciation for the efforts of the Scandinavian countries in this direction. Denmark, Norway and Sweden have for some time now engaged in joint planning of a stand-by force comprising various essential components to be put at the disposal of the United Nations when necessary. It would be a very welcome development if other countries would consider following the lead of the Scandinavian countries in this matter.

At present, the activities of the United Nations are overshadowed by a very serious financial crisis, a crisis which stems directly from the costs of the special peace-keeping operations in the Middle East and the Congo and from the failure of some Members to pay their assessments for those operations. Although the sums of money involved are small in comparison to the sums spent by many countries on military budgets, they do, nonetheless, present a very serious financial and political challenge to the stability of the United Nations.

The United Nations is the sum of all its Members and, to develop in the right direction, it must maintain this global character. On the other hand, I am convinced that the Organization must maintain and develop its active role in keeping the peace. I therefore view with the gravest concern the prolongation of the financial crisis of the United Nations with its very serious political overtones, and I trust that we may see a solution of the problem before too long.

I am concerned at this financial crisis more particularly because I see, in the long run, no acceptable alternative method of keeping peace in the world to the steady and sound development of the peace-keeping functions of the United Nations. It is no longer possible to think rationally in terms of countering aggression or keeping the peace by the use of the ultimate weapons.

However improvised and fumbling the United Nations approach may be, we have to develop it to deal with the sudden antagonisms and dangers of our world, until we can evolve more permanent institutions. There has been already a great advance in the world towards co-operation, mutual responsibility and common interest. I have described some of the pioneering co-operative efforts made by the United Nations to keep the peace.

I believe that these efforts constitute vital steps towards a more mature, more acceptable, and more balanced world order. We must have the confidence and the means to sustain them and the determination to develop out of them a reliable and workable system for the future.

I am a firm believer in the organic development of institutions. I also firmly believe that, if the United Nations is to justify the hopes of its founders and of the peoples of the world, it must develop into an active and effective agency for peace and international conciliation by responding to the challenges which face it. May we have the courage, the faith, and the wisdom to make it so.

APPENDIX 5

Comprehensive Review of the Whole Question of Peace-Keeping Operations in All Their Aspects

Report of the Special Committee
on Peace-keeping Operations

Rapporteur: Mr. Abel Halim Badawi (United Arab Republic)

1. At its twenty-third session, the General Assembly, following its consideration of the reports of the Special Committee on Peace-keeping Operations,[1] adopted resolution 2451 (XXIII) of 19 December 1968, which read as follows:

> "*The General Assembly,*

> "*Recalling* its resolutions 2006 (XIX) of 18 February 1965, 2053 A (XX) of 15 December 1965, 2249 (S-V) of 23 May 1967 and 2308 (XXII) of 13 December 1967,

> "*Having received and examined* the reports of the Special Committee on Peace-keeping Operations of 2 July 1968 and 12 December 1968,

> "*Mindful* of the importance which Member States attach to the comprehensive review of the whole question of peace-keeping operations in all their aspects,

> "*Noting* that the Special Committee has appointed a working group for the preparation of working papers for the study that the Special Committee was requested to submit to the General Assembly in accordance with paragraphs 3 and 4 of its resolution 2308 (XXII)

> "*Noting* that the *Special Committee has approved, as a first model in the programme of its working group, a study of the United Nations military observers established or authorized by the*

[1] *Official Records of the General Assembly, Twenty-third Session. Annexes,* agenda item 32, documents A/7131 and A/7396.

Security Council for observation purposes pursuant to Council resolutions,

"*Noting further* from the report of the Special Committee of 12 December 1968 that preliminary work has been undertaken in the preparation of the above-mentioned study,

"1. *Requests* the Special Committee on Peace-keeping Operations to continue its work under General Assembly resolution 2308 (XXII), including the provisions of paragraphs 3 and 4 of that resolution;

"2. *Reiterates* its request to the Special Committee on Peace-keeping Operations to keep the General Assembly regularly informed about its progress in the comprehensive review of peace-keeping operations in all their aspects;

"3. *Further requests* the Special Committee on Peace-keeping Operations to submit to the General Assembly as soon as possible, and not later than at its twenty-fourth session, a comprehensive report on the United Nations military observers established or authorized by the Security Council for observation purposes pursuant to Council resolutions, as well as a progress report on such work as the Special Committee may be able to undertake on any other models of peace-keeping operations;

"4. *Transmits* to the Special Committee on Peace-keeping Operations the records of the debates at the present session on the item entitled 'Comprehensive review of the whole question of peace-keeping operations in all their aspects,' with the request that the suggestions and proposals contained therein be taken into account."

2. At its 37th meeting, on 14 February 1969, the Special Committee on Peace-keeping Operations unanimously elected Mr. Yvon Beaulne (Canada) as one of the two Vice-Chairmen of the Special Committee to succeed Mr. George Ignatieff (Canada), and Mr. Abdel Halim Badawi (United Arab Republic) as Rapporteur to succeed Mr. Shaffie Abdel-Hamid (United Arab Republic).

3. At the same meeting, the Chairman drew the attention of the Special Committee to the terms of General Assembly resolution 2451 (XXIII), particularly as it related to the study of military observers authorized or established by the Security Council pursuant to Security Council resolutions. He also informed the Committee that the material prepared by the Secretariat on the United Nations military observers, including the additional information requested of the Secretariat by the

Working Group, would be placed at the disposal of the members of the Committee as soon as possible. The Special Committee then agreed that the Working Group should continue its work and keep the Committee informed of its progress.

4.   At the 38th meeting, on 25 June 1969, the Chairman informed the members of the Special Committee of the progress of the work of the Working Group. He stated that, by a letter dated 23 May 1969, he had informed the members of the Committee that the material on the United Nations military observers established or authorized by the Security Council for observation purposes pursuant to the Security Council's resolutions was available to them. He also stated that the Secretariat had been authorized to make this material available to Members of the United Nations who are not members of the Special Committee, if they so requested.

5.   With regard to the drafting of model I, dealing with military observers established or authorized by the Security Council for observation purposes pursuant to Security Council resolutions, the Chairman stated that the Working Group had begun its work. The Chairman added that the members of the Working Group were conscious of the fact that the Working Group was a subsidiary body of the Special Committee charged with a specific mandate and that it was endeavouring in the best way possible to facilitate the work which was within the purview of the Committee as a whole.

6.   At the 39th meeting of the Special Committee, on 15 September, the Rapporteur submitted the first report of the Working Group (A/AC.121/L.8), which is reproduced as annex I of this report. In introducing the Working Group's report, the Rapporteur stated that it described in general terms the progress achieved thus far. He added that the brevity of the report should not be construed as denoting lack of progress, for the exchanges of views in the Working Group had been very valuable and had dealt with substantive issues.

7.   The Chairman, in commenting on the work done by the Working Group, said that it had hoped to submit to the Special Committee a complete draft of model I, as well as a schema for model II. Unfortunately, that had proved to be impossible. However, in his view, the Working Group had made a certain amount of progress which, although limited, was none the less significant. Speaking of chapter II, dealing with the *Establishment* (formation, strength, composition and command), *direction and control,* chapter III, dealing with *Legal arrangements,* and chapter IV, dealing with *Financial arrangements,* of the schema of model I, the texts of which the Working Group was not able to complete, the Chairman stated that the Working Group had discussed in depth all the questions to be covered in those chapters. In connexion

with model I, the Chairman stressed that it referred exclusively to military observer missions established or authorized by the Security Council and did not constitute a precedent that would affect other types of peace-keeping operations.

8. In the course of the discussion, which took place at the 39th to 42nd meetings, some members of the Special Committee expressed regret that, despite its hard work, the Working Group had been unable to submit to the Committee a complete draft of model I. They noted, however, that the Working Group had to deal with questions of principle which were complex and delicate and in connexion with which serious differences had existed in the past which affected the United Nations fundamentally in its existence. It had been estimated that these problems could not be resolved except through a patient approach and in an atmosphere of mutual understanding and goodwill. They had declared that these conditions appeared to have the best chances of realization within the Working Group. Some members, while noting that progress had been slow, also expressed the view that some real advance had finally been made. They noted in particular that, while not all the problems had been solved, the issues involved had been fully and frankly discussed in the Working Group. They felt that there was more reason now than in the past for believing that the fundamental problems facing the Committee would be solved. Some other members expressed satisfaction at the progress so far made. They felt that the Working Group had no need to apologize for the results achieved. The Working Group had completed five chapters, and on the remaining three it had held intensive negotiations and had reached a substantial measure of agreement. They believed that if the Working Group's mandate was continued, it might be able to solve hard-core problems. References were also made to closer co-operation among all members of the Special Committee. The Chairman recalled that the meetings of the Working Group were open to the members of the Special Committee, who could attend, and he stated that, in order to facilitate this closer co-operation, future meetings of the Working Group would be announced in the *Journal of the United Nations.*

9. Consultations have been under way concerning the possible title and framework of a model II, *which would deal with United Nations peacekeeping operations on a larger scale.* The Committee hopes to be able to begin study of such a model at an early date.

10. The Special Committee on Peace-keeping Operations therefore recommends that the General Assembly authorize it to continue its work in order to present a comprehensive report to the Assembly at its twenty-fifth session.

Annex: First Report of the Working Group

Rapporteur: Mr. Abdel Halim Badawi (United Arab Republic)

1.   The Special Committee on Peace-keeping Operations, in its first report to the General Assembly at its twenty-third session,* dated 2 July 1968, stated that on 8 April 1968 it had established a Working Group composed of the four officers of the Committee (*Mexico*—Chairman; *Canada* and *Czechoslovakia*—Vice-Chairmen; and the *United Arab Republic*—Rapporteur) and four other members, France, the Union of Soviet Socialist Republics, the United Kingdom of Great Britain and Northern Ireland and the United States of America. It also stated that the Working Group had approved "as the first model in its programme of work a study of the United Nations military observers established or authorized by the Security Council for observation purposes pursuant to the Council resolutions." It may be recalled that the Special Committee decided that this would mean studying the following:

(a)   The strength and equipment of the group of observers; their recruitment and organization; facilities and services; financial questions;

(b)   The relationship between observers and the State or States on the territory or territories of which they have to operate;

(c)   The status of observers; privileges and immunities; duration and termination of the mission of observers.

Further, it was stated that the Working Group had requested the Secretariat to provide the following material: first, a compilation of the statements made in the Security Council and in the Special Committee on the military observers established or authorized by the Security Council; and second, a report containing all the documents and materials available in the Secretariat which refer to the military observers established or authorized by the Security Council.

2.   In a second report to the General Assembly at its twenty-third session,* dated 12 December 1968, the Special Committee stated that the material requested by the Working Group had been made available to it by the Secretariat in two volumes in September 1968, and that in the course of a preliminary consideration of that material the Working Group had made observations concerning the material and had requested that the Secretary-General supply additional factual information.

3.   During the discussion of the above-mentioned reports of the Special Committee on Peace-keeping Operations by the Special Political

---

*Official Records of the General Assembly, Twenty-third Session, Annexes, agenda item 32, document A/7131.

*Ibid., document A/7396.

Committee at the twenty-third session and in response to expressions of interest in the material prepared by the Secretariat, the Chairman of the Special Political Committee stated that an understanding had been reached that as soon as the additional factual material was provided by the Secretariat, appropriate steps would be taken by the Special Committee on Peace-keeping Operations to make the material available without delay, for information, to any other interested delegations.

4. The General Assembly in its resolution 2451 (XXIII) of 19 December 1968, requested, *inter alia*, "the Special Committee on Peace-keeping Operations to submit to the General Assembly as soon as possible, and not later than at its twenty-fourth session, a comprehensive report on the United Nations military observers established or authorized by the Security Council for observation purposes pursuant to Council resolutions, as well as a progress report on such work as the Special Committee may be able to undertake on any other models of peace-keeping operations."

5. At its 37th meeting, on 14 February 1969, the Special Committee on Peace-keeping Operations agreed that the Working Group should continue its work and keep the Special Committee informed of its progress.

6. The Working Group resumed its work on 25 March 1969. During the period from 25 March to 11 September 1969, the Working Group held forty-nine meetings. In addition, the members of the Working Group held a number of informal meetings for the purpose of consultation.

7. The additional factual information referred to in paragraph 2 above had been presented to the members of the Working Group by the Secretariat in February 1969. This additional information, together with the original material made available by the Secretariat in September 1968, was considered by the Working Group at its meetings in March and the first half of April. After consideration, the Working Group agreed to request the Secretariat to incorporate the additional information into the original material and also to make certain revisions, including the deletion of some passages. On 15 April 1969, the Working Group further agreed that the revised material should be reproduced. Subsequently, by a letter dated 23 May 1969, the Chairman informed the members of the Special Committee on Peace-keeping Operations that in accordance with the statement made by the Chairman of the Special Political Committee, referred to in paragraph 3 above, and with the approval of the members of the Working Group, the material would be available to the members of the Special Committee. Further, the Working Group authorized the Secretariat to make this material available to Members of the United Nations who are not members of the Special Committee, if they so requested.

8.   In drafting model I (Military observers established or authorized by the Security Council for observation purposes pursuant to Security Council resolutions), the Working Group had before it the following three working papers covering various aspects relating to that model:

(a) Working Paper submitted by Canada on 26 March 1969;

(b) Working Paper submitted by the United States of America on 3 April 1969;

(c) Working Paper submitted jointly by Czechoslovakia and the Union of Soviet Socialist Republics on 23 April 1969.

9.   On the basis of these three working papers, of drafts covering specific questions submitted by its members and of views expressed during the discussion, the Working Group first agreed on a schema of the model containing eight chapters. It then proceeded to elaborate the text of these chapters. In the course of its work, the *Working Group was able to complete the text of five of the eight chapters.* With regard to the three other chapters, namely chapter II, dealing with the Establishment (formation, strength, composition and command), direction and control, chapter III, dealing with Legal arrangements, and chapter IV, dealing with Financial arrangements, the Working Group has not yet been able to work out complete texts. However, the Working Group has had valuable discussions on all elements to be included in these chapters and has indicated the general direction to be followed in completing the work on them. It believes that a continuation of its work along these lines will help promote the completion of model I.

10. In the course of its discussion on chapter III, dealing with Legal arrangements, the Working Group also considered the draft of a standard agreement between the United Nations and the host country on the status of military observer missions.

11. The schema of model I is contained in the appendix to this report.

12. Consultations have been under way concerning the possible title and framework of a model II, which would deal with United Nations peacekeeping operations on a larger scale. The Working Group hopes to be able to begin study of such a model at an early date.

Appendix: Model I

*United Nations military observers established or authorized
by the Security Council for observations purposes pursuant
to Security Council resolutions*

CONTENTS

CHAPTER II   Establishment (formation, strength, composition and command), direction and control

    A. *General considerations*

      1. Promptness of the Security Council's actions

      2. Assistance to the Security Council on military questions

      3. Role of the Secretary-General

    B. *Strength and structure of the Military Observer Mission*

    C. *Composition of the Military Observer Mission*

      1. Earmarked personnel and technical services

      2. Concurrence of host country

      3. Participation of Member States

    D. *Appointment of the chief of the Military Observer Mission and staff officers*

    E. *Direction and control*

CHAPTER III   Legal arrangements

    A. *General principles*

    B. *Agreement on the status of military observer missions between the United Nations and the host country*

    C. *Agreement between the United Nations and States providing personnel, equipment facilities and services*

CHAPTER IV   Financial arrangements

    A. *Responsibility for over-all cost of the Military Observer Mission*

      1. Advance estimate

      2. Method and sources of financing

    B. *Responsibility of costs to participating States over and above the costs of maintaining the same military personnel and equipment in their own countries*

CHAPTER V   Organization, development and functioning of the Military Observer Mission

CHAPTER VI   Operating procedures

CHAPTER VII   Equipment, facilities and services

A. *Equipment*

B. *Facilities and services*

1. Medical services

2. Communications within and outside the Military Observer Mission

3. Buildings and accommodation

4. Supplies

5. Storage facilities

6. Maintenance

CHAPTER VIII   Administrative matters

A. *Conditions of service*

B. *Training*

C. *Accounting procedures, pay and allowances*

D. *Physical fitness*

E. *Postal*

APPENDIX 6

United Nations Charter Articles Related to Peacekeeping

Article 1

The Purposes of the United Nations are:

1. To maintain international peace and security, and to that end: to take effective collective measures for the prevention and removal of threats to the peace, and for the suppression of acts of aggression or other breaches of the peace, and to bring about by peaceful means, and in conformity with the principles of justice and international law, adjustment or settlement of international disputes or situations which might lead to a breach of the peace;

2. To develop friendly relations among nations based on respect for the principle of equal rights and self-determination of peoples, and to take other appropriate measures to strengthen universal peace;

3. To achieve international cooperation in solving international problems of an economic, social, cultural, or humanitarian character, and in promoting and encouraging respect for human rights and for fundamental freedoms for all without distinction as to race, sex, language, or religion; and

4. To be a center for harmonizing the actions of nations in the attainment of these common ends.

Article 11

1. The General Assembly may consider the general principles of cooperation in the maintenance of international peace and security, including the principles governing disarmament and the regulation of armaments, and may make recommendations with regard to such principles to the Members or to the Security Council or to both.

2. The General Assembly may discuss any questions relating to the maintenance of international peace and security brought before it by any Member of the United Nations, or by the Security Council, or by a state which is not a Member of the United Nations in accordance with Article 35, paragraph 2, and, except as provided in Article 12, may make recommendations with regard to any such questions to the state or states concerned or to the Security Council or to both. Any such question on which action is necessary shall be referred to the Security Council by the General Assembly either before or after discussion.

3. The General Assembly may call the attention of the Security Council to situations which are likely to endanger international peace and security.

4. The powers of the General Assembly set forth in this Article shall not limit the general scope of Article 10.

Article 12

1. While the Security Council is exercising in respect of any dispute or situation the functions assigned to it in the present Charter, the General Assembly shall not make any recommendation with regard to that dispute or situation unless the Security Council so requests.

2. The Secretary-General, with the consent of the Security Council, shall notify the General Assembly at each session of any matters relative to the maintenance of international peace and security which are being dealt with by the Security Council and shall similarly notify the General Assembly, or the Members of the United Nations if the General Assembly is not in session, immediately the Security Council ceases to deal with such matters.

Article 14

Subject to the provisions of Article 12, the General Assembly may recommend measures for the peaceful adjustment of any situation, regardless of origin, which it deems likely to impair the general welfare or friendly relations among nations, including situations resulting from a violation of the provisions of the present Charter setting forth the Purposes and Principles of the United Nations.

Pacific Settlement of Disputes

Article 33

1. The parties to any dispute, the continuance of which is likely to endanger the maintenance of international peace and security, shall, first of all, seek a solution by negotiation, enquiry, mediation, conciliation, arbitration, judicial settlement, resort to regional agencies or arrangements, or other peaceful means of their own choice.

2. The Security Council shall, when it deems necessary, call upon the parties to settle their dispute by such means.

Article 34

The Security Council may investigate any dispute, or any situation which might lead to international friction or give rise to a dispute, in order to determine whether the continuance of the dispute or situation is likely to endanger the maintenance of international peace and security.

Article 36

1. The Security Council may, at any stage of a dispute of the nature referred to in Article 33 or of a situation of like nature, recommend appropriate procedures or methods of adjustment.

2. The Security Council should take into consideration any procedures for the settlement of the dispute which have already been adopted by the parties.

3. In making recommendations under this Article the Security Council should also take into consideration that legal disputes should as a general rule be referred by the parties to the International Court of Justice in accordance with the provisions of the Statute of the Court.

Action with Respect to Threats to the Peace, Breaches of the Peace, and Acts of Aggression

Article 39

The Security Council shall determine the existence of any threat to the peace, breach of the peace, or act of aggression and shall make recommendations, or decide what measures shall be taken in accordance with Articles 41 and 42, to maintain or restore international peace and security.

Article 40

In order to prevent an aggravation of the situation, the Security Council may, before making the recommendations or deciding upon the measures provided for in Article 39, call upon the parties concerned to comply with such provisional measures as it deems necessary or desirable. Such provisional measures shall be without prejudice to the rights, claims, or positions of the parties concerned. The Security Council shall duly take account of failure to comply with such provisional measures.

Article 41

The Security Council may decide what measures not involving the use of armed forces are to be employed to give effect to its decisions, and it may call upon the Members of the United Nations to apply such measures. These may include complete or partial interruption of economic relations and of rail, sea, air, postal, telegraphic, radio, and other means of communication, and the severance of diplomatic relations.

Article 42

Should the Security Council consider that measures provided for in Article 41 would be inadequate, it may take such action by air, sea, or land forces as may be necessary to maintain or restore international peace and security. Such action may include demonstrations, blockade, and other operations by air, sea, or land forces of Members of the United Nations.

Article 43

1. All Members of the United Nations, in order to contribute to the maintenance of international peace and security, undertake to make available to the Security Council, on its call and in accordance with a special agreement or agreements, armed forces, assistance and facilities, including rights of passage, necessary for the purpose of maintaining international peace and security.

2. Such agreement or agreements shall govern the numbers and types of

forces, their degree of readiness and general location, and the nature of the facilities and assistance to be provided.

3. The agreement or agreements shall be negotiated as soon as possible on the initiative of the Security Council. They shall be concluded between the Security Council and Members or between the Security Council and groups of Members and shall be subject to ratification by the signatory states in accordance with their respective constitutional processes.

Regional Arrangements

Article 52

1. Nothing in the present Charter precludes the existence of regional arrangements or agencies for dealing with such matters relating to the maintenance of international peace and security as are appropriate for regional action, provided that such arrangements or agencies and their activities are consistent with the Purposes and Principles of the United Nations.

2. The Members of the United Nations entering into such arrangements or constituting such agencies shall make every effort to achieve pacific settlement of local disputes through such regional arrangements or by such regional agencies before referring them to the Security Council.

3. The Security Council shall encourage the development of pacific settlement of local disputes through such regional arrangements or by such regional agencies either on the initiative of the states concerned or by reference from the Security Council.

4. This Article in no way impairs the application of Articles 34 and 35.

Article 53

1. The Security Council shall, where appropriate, utilize such regional arrangements or agencies for enforcement action under its authority. But no enforcement action shall be taken under regional arrangements or by regional agencies without the authorization of the Security Council, with the exception of measures against any enemy state, as defined in paragraph 2 of this Article, provided for pursuant to Article 107 or in regional arrangements directed against renewal of aggressive policy on the part of any such state, until such time as the Organization may, on

request of the Governments concerned, be charged with the responsibility for preventing further aggression by such a state.

2. The term enemy state as used in paragraph 1 of this Article applies to any state which during the Second World War has been an enemy of any signatory of the present Charter.

Article 54

The Security Council shall at all times be kept fully informed of activities undertaken or in contemplation under regional arrangements or by regional agencies for the maintenance of international peace and security.

APPENDIX 7

**Consent, Good Offices and the Future of Peacekeeping,
International Peace Academy Committee**

The Future of Peacekeeping

A unique transnational experiment was undertaken at the Austrian Diplomatic Academy in Vienna during the summer of 1970: a pilot program in education and training for peace-related responsibilities. More than 140 individuals from fifty countries were involved. Thirty governments sponsored participants and observers. A four-week training project for practitioners and scholars with limited experience was followed by a shorter seminar for experienced professionals.

The program stressed three specialized fields: international control of violence ("peacekeeping"), mediation, and peaceful social change. Theories drawn from peace research were brought to bear on these practical concerns. The purpose of the program was to initiate the active development of an International Peace Academy and its training plans.

The following special report focuses on only one aspect of the content—the future of United Nations peacekeeping operations. The full **Report from Vienna** is available from the International Peace Academy Committee.* It reflects the richness of our experience in Vienna, and the long stride that has been taken toward the establishment of the proposed Academy.

> Major-General Indar Jit Rikhye (Ret.)
> Chairman, International Peace
>   Academy Committee
> Former Military Adviser to the
>   Secretary-General of the United Nations

Full text of message is reprinted at the end of this report.
*International Peace Academy Committee
 of the International Research Fund, Inc.
 1865 Broadway
 New York, New York 10023
 U.S.A.

In the personal message that the Secretary-General of the United Nations addressed to the participants attending the International Peace Academy Committee's pilot program in Vienna, he raised a number of issues which were pertinent to the implementation of peace initiatives and actions, and commented on the role that he felt the Secretary-General should play in them. These issues had a distinct relevance to the studies and research with which the Vienna experiment was concerned, and they were debated vigorously in both seminars, as part of a general consideration of the problems and shortcomings of the peacekeeping machinery of the United Nations. It is therefore appropriate and valuable that the views and recommendations put forward should be summarized and published as a special report.

The penultimate paragraph of the Secretary-General's message expressed the hope that the "deliberations will throw light on some of these issues and that they may lead to a better understanding of the various problems involved in the conduct of the United Nations peacekeeping operations." What follows is not intended by the Committee to represent a direct answer to the Secretary-General, nor does it attempt to offer specific solutions to the questions inherent in the issues raised by him. It was not to be expected that solutions would emerge from the deliberations; it was enough that the problems were comprehensively discussed and argued and that the participants, both young and old, went away with a clearer appreciation of what is involved. Certainly many of those who participated returned home with a better balanced judgment as to the value and potential of international control of violence, and of what is required to make the machinery of peacekeeping more efficient and more effective. To this extent the Secretary-General's hopes were fully realized. It can also be claimed that the views and opinions expressed by the participants of the project in regard to the content of the Secretary-General's message, though formulating nothing new, were constructive and helpful and indicated a consensus that advocated a realistic and critical study of the weaknesses, so that peacekeeping operations of the future do not suffer from the continuing mistakes of the past, but are provided with all the means and resources that are necessary to ensure their complete effectiveness. The mood of the participants was more one of seeking improvements and revisions rather than one of doubting the potency and desirability of the United Nations peacekeeping machinery.

The issues raised by the Secretary-General can be summarized as follows:

1. The plain fact that peacekeeping missions often can only be undertaken at the request of or with the consent of governments, and

therefore these governments have the option to request their removal at any time they consider appropriate.

2. The continuing debate over the specific provisions of the Charter under which peacekeeping missions are undertaken.

3. A greater involvement by the Military Staff Committee and other competent United Nations organs, such as the Security Council, in the day to day administration of peacekeeping operations.

4. The practicability of pre-planning for peacekeeping missions, and the extent to which the Military Staff Committee should be responsible.

5. Freedom of action for the Secretary-General to offer his good offices without being dependent on the prior approval of the Security Council, General Assembly or any other competent principal organ.

6. The need for a firmer attitude in regard to financial dues and the requirement that permanent member governments of the Security Council should be expected to make appropriate financial contributions towards the cost of any peacekeeping mission for whose establishment they have voted in the Security Council.

7. The desirability of establishing stand-by United Nations peacekeeping forces.

Taken together they add up to a formidable set of questions which contain the whole essence of the controversy that exists over the use of United Nations peace forces for the settlement or reduction of international conflicts. For the purpose of this commentary, each particular issue will be treated individually under separate headings, with the hope that the end result will be an overview of the peacekeeping machinery as a whole expressed by the participants in Vienna.

The Charter and Peacekeeping Missions Today

The considerations currently affecting the organization of United Nations peacekeeping operations differ in a number of respects from those that were in the minds of the men who drew up the provisions of the Charter twenty-five years ago (other than enforcement measures under Chapter VII to maintain or restore international peace and security). It is not therefore surprising that there are member states who argue that the concept of peaceable intervention, as the present day basis for peacekeeping, is not legally constituted under the provisions of the Charter. They are therefore hesitant in their support of some Security Council resolutions and of any General Assembly resolution establishing peacekeeping missions. Despite the fact that certain types of peacekeeping have acquired a different connotation from the first concept of twenty-five years ago, it is probably expecting too much to believe that agreement could be reached within the United Nations that there should be a revision of those provisions of the Charter to bring them into line with modern requirements. Nevertheless, the need for up-dating the Charter was considered and debated in Vienna.

There was no real division of opinion on whether or not there should be a revision or modification of the Charter to bring it up to date. It would be accurate to state that not one of the participants considered it either advisable or practical to revise the Charter in order to accommodate the principles on which a number of peacekeeping operations have been normally based. There was, however, a major expression of opinion that advocated most strongly that at the Security Council level, where the authority lies for the implementation of peacekeeping measures, more decisiveness was required in the formulation of resolutions authorizing peace operations and more single-minded attention should be given to the provisions of the mandates and directives under which peace forces were required to carry out their responsibilities, to ensure beyond any doubt that the peacekeepers' authority could not be so easily flouted as had been the case so often in the past. Although recognizing the overriding authority of the Charter, some felt that a review of its provisions from time to time could help to remedy the existing anomalies, to the extent of ensuring that the principles under which United Nations' peacekeeping missions were implemented would be constantly in tune with progressive development and change. Whether this might take the form of a set of Standing Procedures for the mounting of peacekeeping operations or whether it would be a statement of guiding principles on which Security Council resolutions and the mandates would be based was not a subject that was discussed. But clearly, any document of such a nature would of necessity have to be recognized as an authoritative instrument set within the framework of the Charter's provisions and accepted as one which the Security Council could legally use as a basis for its actions.

The fundamental point with which most participants agreed was that the form of United Nations peacekeeping which has developed in the past fifteen years should be continued and improved—that of *peaceable, impartial, multilateral* intervention. This conclusion was reached in full recognition of the political and legal arguments against revising the United Nations Charter, the different interpretations placed on Charter provisions by member states, and the fact that the "Committee of 33" has not yet made its recommendations to the General Assembly. It was regarded as imperative that United Nations peace forces be given the kind of mandate and directives sufficient for them to carry out their responsibilities with full effect, not through enforcement action but

through the essential legal rights of investigation, inspection and prevention, accepted and recognized by all nations and states, and respected by
them as being the terms of reference under which peacekeeping forces
will be empowered to operate.

Consent, Status and Withdrawal

It is doubtful whether any peaceable intervention by a United Nations peace force could be achieved without the request or consent of
governments. But obviously such conditions can impose certain limiting
factors on the composition, status, freedom of action and security of
tenure of the force.

When wholly dependent upon their acceptability to the host country,
the provision of contingents can become a major manning problem. The
Congo was cited as a case in point. The size of the force required was
such that a total of thirty-three countries provided contingents to
ONUC. The wide extremes of military experience and training caused
major problems. While recognizing the right of the host country to
approve what countries should or should not be in the force, it was felt
that the arbitrary use of such an option could pose severe limitations on
the quality of the United Nations force provided, in terms of efficiency
and training, and thereby reduce its effectiveness. This point of view was
not expressed exactly in these terms, but it is relevant to the general
opinions voiced during the seminars. It is important that this viewpoint
should not be regarded as an attempt to override the accepted rights of
the host country, nor as an obstacle to the acceptance by the host
country of a peace force within its borders. A certain prerogative should
be open to the United Nations. The world organization should not be
entirely dictated to by the host country, which has presumably either
requested or consented to a peacekeeping force being stationed on its
soil.

The status that the force should enjoy and the freedom of movement
it needs to carry out its responsibilities are normally agreed upon beforehand with the host country, and are the subject of a legal undertaking
between it and the United Nations. Experience has shown that this
special status and the right to freedom of movement are not always
subsequently respected. This drew major criticism from the participants,
who were convinced that these essential requirements of the peacekeeper
must be firmly established from the beginning and under no circumstances be abused or diminished. Numerous references were made to the
difficulties placed in the way of the United Nations Force in Cyprus
(UNFICYP), as well as reference to the many interferences which frus-
trated operations in the Congo. Participants were firmly of the opinion

that the status agreements should be constantly under review so that they could, where necessary, be modified to meet changing circumstances. Where attempts are made to obstruct or interfere with the peacekeeping force's ability to fulfill its tasks, the Security Council and/or the Secretary-General should have the power to intervene and insist that the obstructions be removed and that the interference of whatever kind should cease, whether it comes from individuals, dissident groups inside or outside the country, or external influences from other countries, aligned with one or other of the parties in the dispute.

It was natural that in this context of request and consent the question of the withdrawal of the United Nations Emergency Force from Gaza in 1967 should have been seriously debated—not so much in terms of whether the Egyptian government's request to withdraw should have been honored, but from the angle of what was needed to avoid a similar circumstance arising again in the future. It was agreed that there must be built-in provisions in any Force Agreement to guard against abrupt withdrawal. While recognizing the principle that the host country should have the right to request the withdrawal of a specific country's contingent or of the whole force, a proper and reasonable period of notice was necessary and should be required to be given by the host government before such a withdrawal took effect. This would allow for diplomatic approaches to be made and for negotiations to take place if the Security Council or General Assembly considered that the withdrawal would result in a renewed threat to international peace. It would also allow sufficient time for the withdrawal of the United Nations force to be carried out in an orderly and secure manner. It was a matter of considerable concern that the safeguards hitherto provided for the security of United Nations' soldiers have not always been adequate.

Planning and Preparation for Peacekeeping

Whenever and wherever peacekeeping is discussed, and Vienna was no exception, the present system of raising ad hoc forces at short notice is subjected to highly critical scrutiny. It is an inefficient and uneconomic method, and to say that it inevitably brings in its wake a multitude of operational and administrative difficulties is no misstatement of fact. On the other hand, what is the alternative when the existing political climate is such that any attempt to increase the military influence in the United Nations by bringing in military planners would be strongly contested? This resistance is probably why the Military Staff Committee has always been so inactive and ineffective—an advisory staff in name only. In fairness it must be said that the decision to mount and deploy peacekeeping forces is a political one and the responsibility of a political body—the Security Council. Once the force is established the Secretariat manages its logistic and manning needs. However well intentioned, no central civilian executive, particularly of the size and diversity of the United Nations Secretariat, can be considered to be the ideal machinery for coordinating and administering the requirements of a military force in the field; nor can it be expected to understand completely the special logistic and operational requirements of each force. It is not surprising therefore, that most peacekeeping operations have suffered in their early days from these weaknesses in planning and preparation. The military staffing problem in the Congo, and the confusion when half a dozen battalions of UNEF found themselves in the Gaza desert with food and rations for only ten days and without vehicles, supplies, medical services and staff, are just two examples of the way things can go sadly wrong at the beginning.

In Vienna opinions were divided on whether or not it was politically acceptable to establish a military planning staff at United Nations headquarters, but there was agreement that some kind of planning department was necessary in order that the weaknesses and mistakes of the past could be avoided in the future. It was thought that this might take the form of a department in the Secretariat or of an advisory group responsible to the Security Council. The former would presumably be a fully representative branch working with the Under Secretary General's Department for Special Political Affairs, and would be responsible for studying the implications of possible United Nations peacekeeping operations in conflict or potential conflict areas of the world. It could also act as the coordinating department for the existing peace missions. A Security Council advisory group on the other hand, would act more as 'an early warning system' on potential conflict rather than a pre-planning staff, but in so doing could focus attention on the build-up of tensions so that the Security Council would be better prepared to moderate dangerous tendencies before they went beyond the point of prevention.

Those among the participants who had served in United Nations peacekeeping forces and experienced the disadvantages of ad hoc planning and preparation, were clear in their minds that efficient operations can only come from adequate advance planning. This planning could only be done at United Nations headquarters and should be a joint civilian and military responsibility. It would be of a contingency nature and designed to plan the requirements of a peacekeeping operation in any given situation anywhere in the world. If a United Nations intervention were called for, the plans would be available. The difficulty in naming advisory organs in the Security Council or the Secretariat that could authorize studies was recognized by the participants, as was the necessity to avoid inflaming the political sensitivities of the parties to a dispute.

Others considered it likely that neither idea would be acceptable politically, though an advisory group formed within the Security Council might have the greater appeal of the two. It would therefore be more realistic to consider how the deficiencies in planning could be minimized through training. The training of contingents for peacekeeping tasks was a national affair, but there would be an advantage in combined studies and even exercises with other national armies so that there could be the broadest exchange of experience and technique. Although this kind of multinational training could best be based on a geographical regional grouping, there was no reason why it should not go outside regional boundaries so that the less experienced countries could benefit from the experience of others. Standards of training and efficiency could be greatly improved and a common understanding of the responsibilities and relationships of a multinational peace force built up. For all armies, training for peace would be a comparable objective to training for war.

The training of staff and commanders should be based on an even broader concept, since at this level a requirement exists for training in "jointmanship." This calls for diplomats, civil servants and soldiers in training—the main human ingredients of a peacekeeping force, though other professionals could very easily become involved in time. A transnational training establishment—of which the International Peace Academy is a first example—was considered to be an important requisite to peace training.

In considering the question of a standby force, some doubts were expressed as to the practical benefit this would have. So long as the option of choice rested squarely with the host governments, there would be the likelihood of contributing countries maintaining standby contingents which would never be called upon. Austria is a ready example, for she has kept a United Nations infantry battalion in existence for eleven years and it has never been used. The earmarking of units or sub-units could be a more profitable answer, though this could only apply to national armies of sufficient size to do this. Where earmarking is not possible, then the Scandinavian system of calling up of volunteers as a form of reserve service in specific types of military units which these countries have undertaken to provide, could overcome the problem for the less militarily endowed countries who wish to participate in United Nations peacekeeping. No one was particularly in favor of the formation of a "blue beret" army in the immediate future but agreed that the idea should not be dismissed as a long-term objective. It was thought that it would have all the disadvantages that earmarking would not have and a command structure which could be potential dynamite. There was however a constructive suggestion that a small independent unit might be raised to act as an optimum task force and an advance guard to the arrival of the main peacekeeping force. It would be multinational and might comprise anything from a battalion to a brigade. It is an idea that is worth developing further. At the same time, the possibility of any kind of "UN Corps" becoming a breeding ground for mercenaries should not be overlooked.

Use of the Secretary-General's Good Offices

There was understandable sympathy for the view taken by the Secretary-General that he should be able freely to offer his good offices whenever or wherever they were requested, without necessarily having first to obtain the approval to do so from the Security Council or General Assembly. Most people considered that any efforts that could contribute to the maintenance of peace and to the furtherance of peaceful settlements should be encouraged. Such initiatives at the request of or with the consent of the parties could well achieve quick and advantageous results, while possible delays arising out of a division of opinion among the members of the Council or the Assembly, could have the effect of postponing action until it was too late for the initiative to take place. It goes without saying that as a matter of procedure, both the Council and the Assembly would have to be informed of the Secretary-General's intentions and of the progress subsequently made as a result of such initiatives. Any initiatives of this kind would be expected to fall within the mandate of the Secretary-General, who would act within his terms of reference as provided for in the Charter. Although the Charter does not make specific provision for cooperative action of this kind by the Secretary-General, it comes within the general scope of Article 33 and is, therefore, within the Charter framework. Those member states who have criticized the Secretary-General in the past for what they call 'exceeding his responsibility' do not adequately recognize the unique contribution of the Secretary-General in reducing tensions and providing mediatory initiatives. This role of personal diplomacy is a complementary aspect of the way the establishment and deployment of peacekeeping forces have developed over the past twenty years.

There is a growing tendency for the United Nations to be by-passed in favor of unilateral intervention of the Great Powers. This was considered to be a wholly undesirable development, though it was realized that sometimes it could be the only way to peace. Many would prefer to see these problems handled by an effective United Nations. Unilateral efforts will not add to the United Nations' effectiveness but will detract from it. In making the United Nations more effective, the role of the

Secretary-General in the field of diplomacy and mediation would be given fresh significance. Over the years, the Secretary-General's duties and responsibilities have developed beyond those of a chief administrator. Because of recurring critical situations of worldwide concern, such as the Cuban missile crisis, the participants believed strongly that the Secretary-General should be able to undertake a wider personal diplomacy which was not necessarily subject to the prior approval of the General Assembly or Security Council. Indeed, approval for his assistance in arriving at peaceful settlements is rendered unnecessary by Article 33 of the Charter.

Paying for Peacekeeping

The difficulties experienced in the financing of United Nations peace operations were felt to represent a real danger to the future of international peacekeeping. It was deemed a justifiable criticism that the Security Council should authorize a peacekeeping operation and then expect the Secretary General to find the money for it from voluntary contributions, particularly when some of its members are not listed among the voluntary subscribers. This cannot, by any stretch of the imagination, be regarded as a viable method of doing peacekeeping business. What is more, it cannot be expected that voluntary contributions will always be forthcoming; and those that have been made have never even approximately covered the total financial commitment for any of the peacekeeping operations so far. The record shows that for each of the three major operations, UNEF, ONUC and UNFICYP, only eight member states in each case provided the bulk of the financial support; the United States, the United Kingdom, Canada and Italy being the common denominators, with India, Japan and Sweden contributing to two of the three. It is not to be expected that these countries, or any others which have contributed, will be prepared to continue indefinitely acting as the sole source of funds for peacekeeping operations, which should be the responsibility of all member states.

Realizing that the crux of the problem lay in the fact that the concept of modern peacekeeping was not accepted by a number of member states as being legal within the provisions of the Charter, the participants were dubious of the effect that the positive enforcement of Article 19 might have. Efforts to persuade all member states to meet their financial commitments as required by Article 19 had failed in the past and were likely to continue to be unsuccessful for obvious political reasons. Something in the way of a new payments system was thought to be necessary, and was needed quickly if future peacekeeping operations were to be financially viable. It is to be hoped that the Committee of the

General Assembly entrusted with the responsibility for finding solutions to the constitutional, financial and administrative problems of the United Nations, will provide a workable solution to this critical issue.

*   *   *

This was the view from Vienna that took shape during the discussions and debates on the issues raised in the Secretary-General's message. It was explained at the beginning that no attempt has been made to answer the Secretary-General directly. But because of the importance of the issues he raised, it seems worthwhile to record the opinions and thoughts that were expressed in response to them. The liveliness of debate underlined forcibly the interest and concern with which all of the participants viewed these problems and the need for their solution. No one shut his eyes to the dangers inherent in the present weaknesses in the machinery of peacekeeping, or to the consequences were it not to be strengthened. Nor was the complex political aspect of the problem sidestepped. Everyone recognized the need to overcome or accommodate the political issues which stand in the way of establishing the appropriate authority and procedures for future peacekeeping operations.

If this commentary does nothing else, perhaps it will evoke among those who read it a realization that there is nothing to replace the peacekeeping machinery we have in the United Nations—no international, no transnational substitute. It is essential that this machinery be made as workable as possible. The will of the international community must be aroused on matters of vital future interest to the world— including the role of United Nations peacekeeping in restricting and ending violence, in helping to create the conditions in which change can take place peacefully and just settlements can be reached.

Message from the Secretary-General of the United Nations

(Read by Ambassador V. Winspeare Guicciardi, Director-General of the United Nations, Geneva, at the opening session of the International Peace Academy Committee's 1970 Pilot Projects.)

Vienna, 20 July 1970

I AM GLAD to greet the participants in the seminar and training program organized under the auspices of the INTERNATIONAL PEACE ACADEMY COMMITTEE in Vienna. I regret that I am unable to do so personally, but I am very glad that it has been found possible for Mr. Vittorio Winspeare Guicciardi, Under-Secretary-General and Director-

General of the United Nations Office at Geneva, to represent me on this occasion.

The subject of peacekeeping, which is one of the main themes of your discussion, is one about which there are many misconceptions. It is not often realized that in some cases peacekeeping missions are undertaken at the request of governments or with their consent and therefore these governments have the option, at an appropriate time, of requesting the winding-up of the mission or withdrawal of a peacekeeping force.

There is also considerable debate as to the specific provisions in the United Nations Charter under which these peacekeeping missions are undertaken.

Questions are also raised as to why the Military Staff Committee and competent United Nations organs, such as the Security Council, should not take a more direct interest in the day-to-day administration of such operations. These are important questions and they deserve detailed consideration.

Following the crisis over the interpretation of Article 19 of the Charter in the context of the discussions during the nineteenth session of the General Assembly, these questions have been studied at length for the last five years by a committee of the General Assembly established to consider this question in all its aspects, especially the constitutional, financial, and administrative ones.

So far as the constitutional aspects are concerned, I do not wish to pronounce any particular view except to state my conviction that, when so requested by the parties concerned, the Secretary-General should have the freedom to offer his good offices without any specific prior approval by a competent principal organ, be it the General Assembly or the Security Council. I have pursued this course in the past and intend to do so in the future.

With regard to the financial aspects, one must, of course, await the outcome of the deliberations of the special committee on peacekeeping operations. I would, however, like to share one thought with you. I regard it as entirely unsatisfactory that the Security Council should authorize a peacekeeping operation and then expect the Secretary-General to finance it from voluntary contributions. This reduces the Secretary-General almost to the position of a mendicant seeking alms. In this context, I would like to put forward my view in regard to the special role of the permanent members of the Security Council. I strongly believe that their position involves special responsibilities, especially in regard to the implementation of decisions of the Council. I also believe that when those governments cast an affirmative vote for the establishment of a peacekeeping mission or its continuation they may reasonably be expected to make an appropriate financial contribution to defray its costs.

Concerning the adminstrative aspect, various helpful suggestions have been made in regard to the establishment of a stand-by United Nations peacekeeping force and detailed advance planning of peacekeeping missions. In actual fact, my experience has been that the nature of each crisis is somewhat unique and the peacekeeping mission undertaken in the context of that crisis has to be tailored to fit the needs of that particular situation. I also believe that it is quite proper for the Security Council to give directives from time to time as to the broad policy to be followed by the Secretary-General, but in the light of my experience over the last nine years I feel that the responsibility for the day-to-day administration must still be exercised by one person. In particular, I must confess that I fail to see how, in the prevailing circumstances, the Military Staff Committee could administer a peacekeeping operation.

I hope that your deliberations will throw light on some of these issues and that they may lead to a better understanding of the various problems involved in the conduct of United Nations peacekeeping operations.

I wish you a successful seminar and training program.

U Thant
Secretary General
United Nations

APPENDIX 8

Peacekeeping: A Survey and an Evaluation prepared for Friends Peace Committee (Quakers) by Charles C. Walker*

Foreword

Peacekeeping, as the term is generally used in the United Nations, includes two kinds of operations:
Noncoercive: to mediate, conciliate, observe.
Coercive: to deploy armed forces.
A UN force may be mandated to:
1. Observe, investigate and report: Kashmir, Lebanon, Yemen
2. Aid in mediation: Greece
3. Police a demarcation line: India-Pakistan
4. Patrol a demilitarized zone: Sinai
5. Maintain law and order, and normalize conditions: Cyprus
6. Secure peace and stability in an area: Congo
7. Effect a transfer of authority: West Irian (West New Guinea).

The mandates have varied widely in scope. In West Irian (1962-1963) it was clear and limited, carried out by a Canadian contingent of 5 officers and 8 ground crew with two Otter aircraft. On the other hand, in the Congo (1960-1964) it was broad and ambiguous, enforced by 93,000 military personnel from 35 countries.

The degree of force permitted or used has also varied considerably. The missions have:
1. Worn side-arms only, as in the Middle East, to be used for individual self-defense, with no authority to threaten force to accomplish or frustrate an action.
2. Forcibly disarmed soldiers or irregulars, as in Cyprus, but have kept military actions to very low levels.
3. Engaged in sporadic military operations, as in the Congo, usually in pacification efforts.
4. Carried out full-scale military operations, as in Korea.

*The complete pamphlet, "Peacekeeping 1969" may be obtained for $.30 from the Friends Peace Committee, 1520 Race Street, Philadelphia, Penna. 19102.

The Korea intervention was possible because the Soviet Union had walked out of the Security Council and could not exercise a veto. Secretary-General U Thant, speaking at Harvard University in June 1963, said:

> The idea that conventional military methods—or, to put it bluntly, war—can be used by or on behalf of the United Nations to counter aggression and secure the peace seems now to be rather impractical.

The Congo operation is unlikely to be repeated. A temporary and uncertain mandate was possible, says a leading expert, "because the United States and the Soviet Union for a brief period believed that UN intervention was the least costly way to prevent the other from realizing its objectives in the Congo."[1] Member states held conflicting views about what the mandate directed or implied. The lessons of that venture argue strongly against sending substantial military forces into collapsing or fragmented situations, or without a firm political consensus. . . .

World Peacemakers Association (WPA)

The World Federalists of Canada have proposed an association of nations within the UN to train for and carry out peacekeeping and peacemaking tasks.

The Federalists presented a Brief to Canada's Minister of External Affairs on August 14, 1968, asking the Canadian government to initiate the plan.[2] The key paragraph in the Brief says:

> We propose that Canada should immediately take the initiative in forming within the United Nations a grouping of nations which might be called the World Peacemakers Association (WPA). These nations would pledge their support to UN peacekeeping operations, and train their forces with UN duties in mind. They would also train teams of mediators to help settle particular conflicts. In return, these nations would ask the UN to provide for their security from aggression.

Canada has participated in more UN peacekeeping missions than any other country. This experience has been summarized and analyzed by

---

[1] Ernest W. Lefever, in a conversation with the author.

[2] "Toward an Association of World Peacemaker Nations," with a reply by Hon. Mitchell Sharp, published in the *World Federalist*, Canadian edition, Aug./Sept. 1968, pp. C-2 through C-5.

J. L. Granatstein in the book *Peacekeeping: International Challenge and Canadian Response.*[3]

The Canadian government had sponsored the Ottawa Conference of November 1964, attended by diplomats and military officers from 23 countries. They discussed coordination, training and logistics. One outcome of the conference was U Thant's initiative in the UN to establish the Special Committee on Peacekeeping Operations (Feb. 1965).

The Federalists suggested several nations as initial or early participants along with Canada: Sweden, India, Czechoslovakia, Japan. Since then, they have consulted with some Scandinavian and other countries. A continuing consultative arrangement has been set up, to advance the idea when and where possible, and especially to coordinate their strategy and tactics in the 1969 fall UN meetings.

It is natural for the Canadians to turn to the Scandinavian countries who have also contributed heavily to past missions. Since 1960, Sweden, Norway and Denmark have discussed earmarking special contingents for the UN. In 1963, Finland joined them in planning for a Nordic Standby Force which would provide more than 4500 military personnel.[4] In 1964, the various parliaments provided enabling legislation. Iran has also offered earmarked forces.

The Norwegian Institute of International Affairs sponsored a conference in Oslo in 1964, to evaluate the experience thus far in peacekeeping, and to consider plans for organization and training.[5] Another conference on earmarking was held in Oslo in 1965. Col. Bjørn Egge, of the Norwegian Defense Research Establishment, has been a leading figure in many of these efforts.

The World Peacemakers Association was conceived in a context where the emphasis had been placed on powers other than the Big Five in the Security Council. The new developments in the UN Special Committee suggest that, if the new impasse can be overcome, the US and USSR may assume a major role in the next phase. It remains to be seen how the Canadian-Scandinavian and the Finger-Mendelevich initiatives relate to each other. . . .

Peacekeepers Staff College

Maj. Gen. Frederick S. Carpenter, former commandant of Canada's

---

[3]By Alastair Taylor, David Cox and J. L. Granatstein, published in 1968 by the Canadian Institute of International Affairs.

[4]The Scandinavian Force is described by Per Haekkerup, former Foreign Minister of Denmark, in *Foreign Affairs*, July 1964.

[5]*Peacekeeping: Experience and Evaluation* (The Oslo Papers), edited by Per Frydenberg, includes conference addresses and summarizes discussions. Norwegian Institute of International Affairs, 1964.

National Defense College, proposes that standby and earmarked forces be trained and prepared at a Peacekeepers Staff College operated by any nation(s) willing to do so.

He recommends that some nation initially—it could be Canada—renounce unilateral use of its military forces and turn them over to the UN for exclusively peacekeeping functions. He suggests that this nation "vacate" its seat at the UN to avoid taking sides in disputes where it may serve a peacekeeping role, and to be "truly servants of the UN."

The staff college would initially be outside UN authority. However, it should be developed so that the UN would find it easy to cooperate and to use its services. After the initial step, other nations might join the operation and provide officials for the governing board.

Maj. Gen. Carpenter has been in charge of air transport for several UN peacekeeping operations. Since retirement he has been a faculty member in the Department of Political Studies of Queen's University, Kingston, Ontario.

The college, as he envisages it, would be part civilian, part military. It would develop and teach SOPs (Standard Operating Procedures) in peacekeeping. He does not regard achieving cooperation of military personnel from different countries as a primary problem. The major problem, he claims, is developing a good working relationship among the top military and the top civilian personnel. This relationship could start in the staff college.

He says: "The technical problem is really quite complex, but easy to solve. The political problem is quite simple, but terribly difficult to solve."[6]

One purpose of this proposal is to provide a transitional step between unilateral military action and a system where the UN plays a much more vital role in international conflict. The dynamics of such a transitional period should be thought through carefully. The all-important question is whether this new UN role is indeed in the making. If not, at least in the foreseeable future, then the idea could play into the hands of those who seek new and updated roles for the military at a time when its traditional functions are becoming unacceptable.

The dilemma for such a staff college, and its role, is symbolized in General Carpenter's suggestion that the uniform for field personnel be of two colors: "survival orange" on one side, camouflage on the other. In his view, the force would earnestly try for an essentially nonmilitary outcome; if necessary, it could resort to military measures.

The old and persistent question arises: can the military be so

---

[6]Quotations in this section are from notes taken of a speech by Gen. Carpenter at a conference on "The Future of the United Nations" held at Villanova University in May 1969. Some points were clarified in a later conversation at Kingston.

relegated to servile status, to be used only when all other means fail? Or does its very presence from the start intrude so basically, imposing psychological and organizational requirements and dynamics, that it militates against the success of the nonmilitary means? Is the military a "shield" for the nonmilitary, or is it rather an active organizing factor with sovereign demands, however well masked, or reluctantly invoked?

This question surpasses in importance the improved technical competence which such a college assuredly could provide.

Training vs. Improvisation: A Note

Military men, not surprisingly, emphasize that training and careful advance planning are needed. Major Generals Rikhye and Carpenter tell of occasions, some of them grimly humorous, when snafu was normal, when language differences led to misunderstandings, or needless problems arose over diet, pay scales, military discipline, or attitude toward the indigenous population.

Col. Egge has said:

> I was sent to the Congo by plane, had a blue helmet stuck on my head and told, "Now you are a soldier of peace." I asked what is a soldier of peace, but no one could answer. They said, "Do your best—we have to avoid war." ... [The troops] were trained as military—to kill and to conquer. How on earth can you tell them that now you cannot do that, you are a policemen?[7]

A case can also be made for improvisation, that is, for designing and developing an ad hoc force appropriate for the specific occasion. Those who argue for improvisation acknowledge the problems raised by field men and commanders, but believe improvisation is more a strength than a weakness. Military procedures and discipline are much the same the world over, they claim. While problems are bound to arise, they hold that those problems should be accepted as part of the price of fashioning an ad hoc force designed for the crisis at hand.

They also say that the more people designated in advance for specific functions, and the more organizational charts prepared, the more targets to argue about in the consensus-developing stage. Also, prior organization removes some areas for bargaining.

Whatever the merits of these arguments, the emphasis on improvisation is more congenial to the superpowers' position, because less binding in advance. They will have more cards in their hands to bargain with than smaller powers.

[7]From his speech at the Oslo Conference (November 1968) of the International Peace Academy Committee.

Peacekeeping Plus Peacemaking

Some advocates of peacekeeping recommend that peace force personnel engaged also in development tasks or other serviceable work in such fields as education, self-help or emergency aid.

A major impetus for such proposals comes from the charge, often heard from the Third World, that peacekeeping characteristically will freeze the status quo or forestall basic change. Proponents of peacekeeping quickly reply that they favor peaceful change, but usually they are vague or unpersuasive about specifics.

"Peacekeeping plus peacemaking" is an attractive slogan. Does it promise more than can be delivered? We have already noted the impasse over peaceful settlement proposals, as indicated by the defeat of Lord Caradon's modest call in 1965 for merely a UN study. Much more formidable is the task of effecting a three-way linkage: peacekeeping, peaceful settlement and peaceful change.

Three Models

Proposals have been formulated in terms of three different organizational models:

A. A military agency which includes peacemaking and peacebuilding functions: e.g. proposals by some military veterans of UN missions.
B. A nonmilitary agency only: e.g. many proposals by peace groups.
C. An agency emphasizing peacemaking and peacebuilding but equipped with "lethal but relatively discriminate weapons": e.g. the Waskow plan. He believes that a military agency such as a Scandinavian force may also be required in some situations.

Model A is based on two practical facts: no army engages in military action only, and those "more than military" actions can be either incidental or strategically conceived.

Armies have long engaged in activities other than fighting. The Etruscans built aqueducts around Rome, English armies drew maps of Palestine and India, Spanish armies harvested crops. Quite a few countries, including the US, have taken up "civic action" programs, putting their armies to work in "nation-building" or "counterinsurgency" programs. The Pentagon is enamored of civic action, for example in Latin America where traditional military functions are eroding: to keep the machine going, improve its image, and provide access (both geographical and political) to the "insurgency environment."[8] General William Westmore-

---

[8] For a survey of this field, see Edward Glick, *Peaceful Conflict*, Stackpole, 1967.

land has said that of the "lessons" learned by the United States military in Vietnam, "None is more important than the matter of coordinating efforts of all national agencies, civilian and military."[9]

From another perspective, revolutionary theorists have emphasized the interaction of the military and political in specific ways. Today's guerrilla usually spends more time in teaching and organizing than in fighting.

Several authors are working on books to explore what has been called "the nonmilitary uses of the military," as an aspect of their concern about peacekeeping, drawing on many antecedents from many parts of the world.

Model A Dilemmas

This report is not the place to analyze proposals in detail. It may be useful, however, to point out some dilemmas or insubstantial claims.

For example, the problems of peacekeeping in the Third World can be only partially dealt with by forming a predominantly nonwhite force. While the prospect of whites "helping" nonwhites may be unacceptable to some Third World nations, a nonwhite mission could still become an updated version of the white man's burden.

A Model A peace force which has engaged in military operations, whatever the provocation, will face the problem stated by a Canadian commander in Cyprus:

> I've found that you can get things done by talking here. If you go and ask somebody to stop firing they usually will, for a while at least. But how will I be able to talk to Greeks and Turks if I've been pumping bullets at them?[10]

Another dilemma is comparable to that of an armed domestic police force in a situation of severe community conflict. The police in a quieter time may have used violence rarely; a veteran policemen told the author he has pulled his gun only twice in 20 years. When conflict intensifies and violence increases, the police resort more often to violence. In critical situations they may become a paramilitary force with aspects of an occupying army. Then no "community relations program," even if staffed by dedicated police officers, can overcome or even mitigate the community's hostility to the police. Similarly, some peacekeeping operations may involve a very low level of violence and not

[9]Speech to the 8th Conference of the American Armies, at Rio de Janeiro, September 1968.
[10]Quoted by Geoffrey Carnall, in *To Keep the Peace*. Peace News, 1965.

alienate the indigenous population very much. The dilemma remains for situations of high tension and severe conflict.

Another problem, minimized by Model A advocates, is this: the effect of a military force will be estimated in military terms. When a force is not equipped with heavy lethal weapons, the military factor may not be decisive but it will be there, and will figure in the military and political considerations of nations involved. The military man's image of his role, especially if he is committed to "peacekeeping," prevents him from seeing the baneful and penetrating effects of the military, even if blood isn't flowing or bodies falling.

Common to what we are calling Model B and Model C is the new professional envisaged by Arthur Waskow. He would combine the skills and activities embodied in many peace proposals: those of the policeman, the conciliator, and the teacher-organizer. He describes the trainees:

> The men who would work in such a service would be men of a new profession, with a new career line; and like all professionals, they would have to learn their craft. Such men scarcely exist today, though one can see the ancestry of their vocation scattered in a dozen different places: the American Seabee, the British Bobby, the Cuban militiawoman, the peace corpsman, the Shanti Sena nonviolent policeman, and the Red Cross worker.[11]

Can such Peacemakers make much of a dent on the problems they would be dealing with? Peacekeeping is an emergency action. Paradoxically, almost any problem grave enough to require international action will be bound up with deep-seated problems, probably involving social, political and economic structure. Such problems are not readily amenable to change by improvised or ad hoc or short-term action, especially by outside groups. To cope with them requires more fundamental, sustained decision and action, possibly involving the character of the socioeconomic regime. Positive gains might indeed be achieved, but they may help more in image-building than nation-building.

Advocates sometimes propose development tasks for a mission in order to gain access more readily to a crisis area. If they mean access before the crisis, this hit-or-miss method would be too expensive a gamble on where the next peacekeeping mission would be stationed. In a crisis, the unit might be forced to leave because of changed conditions. If they mean that these activities would make the mission more attractive, this may be true, but then other problems arise, such as the cost of deployment of standby units when not on a crisis mission.

[11] *Toward a Peacemakers Academy*, p. 8.

Waskow would bypass some of these problems by offering the services of such personnel between missions to whatever nation could use them, consistent with their peacemaker function. He appears to underestimate the implications of such a considerable undertaking. What he really proposes is training a cadre of leaders (500 trainess and a $1 million budget in the "early years") and does not spell out very far what a transnational agency embracing these activities would involve.

A lesser problem should be noted: if peacekeepers engage in constructive work, they may encounter the problem the UN faced in Cyprus, i.e. one group claimed the other side was getting more help and sympathy, and that the peacekeepers were not really nonpartisan.

If the peacekeeping force is nonmilitary, and does not harbor or offer exaggerated hopes about the impact of its ancillary work, these problems may prove to be obstacles to overcome rather than decisive objections. Two conclusions may be drawn:

1. Peacekeeping should probably stand on its own feet and be justified on its own terms, however frustrating some of the experience may be. However valuable in certain circumstances, "service" cannot completely cope with problems of conflict in this field.
2. Some aspects of the idea which appeal to its advocates, e.g. work for social change, are the ones which may be regarded with suspicion by those to whom a mission may be sent.

Peaceful Settlement of Disputes

Some experts insist that peacekeeping operations should be linked with procedures for peaceful settlement of disputes. When U Thant reported to the Security Council in May 1967 on withdrawing the UNEF from Egyptian territory at President Nasser's request, he said:

It is true to a considerable extent that UNEF has allowed us to ignore some of the hard realities of the underlying conflict. The governments concerned, and the United Nations, are now confronted with a brutally realistic and dangerous situation.

If peacekeeping results in little prospect for dealing constructively with underlying issues and problems, it may be condemned for bringing about "the pacific perpetuation of disputes."

On the other hand, nations are reluctant to render themselves vulnerable to any *automatic* procedure for peaceful settlement which limits their power to decide and maneuver. If they suspect that the resolution of an issue will disadvantage them, they will persist in their policies. If they wish to resolve an issue, they can find a procedure now, including third parties willing to help.

The problem does not appear to be a shortage of good proposals.[12] A more formidable question is how to cope with the double standard of international conduct: small nations are expected to solve their problems quickly and "reasonably" in the interests of the larger community; big nations, wearily acknowledging their burden of responsibility, nevertheless decide matters in their own interests with scant concessions to the larger community.

Of course, smallness does not guarantee a nation's virtue. For example, it takes two to traffic in arms. The seller, a "have nation" in this regard, can easily be seen as a threat to the peace. The buyer, a "have not," seizes the chance to play the game the way others play it, and quickly cries "big power domination" if they call the practice into question.

Those who press for more progress in peaceful settlement often do so because they openly or covertly advocate new political institutions or an altered international system, in which peacekeeping takes on a much larger significance. National leaders may concede that such changes should come some day, but they function now in a pattern of big power dominance and rampant unilateralism. They will not say "A" if it is a way station to "B" when they believe that "B" is either utopian or irrelevant now.

Nevertheless, it is hard to see why some nations, even from a gross reading of *realpolitik,* should so adamantly oppose attempts to explore and develop new approaches in peaceful settlement. To oppose any such steps could become a political liability. Then such intrasigence may produce a reaction, and provide leverage to move on the larger questions for which the proposals were designed in the first place.

The Nub of the Matter

This report deals with peacekeeping possibilities in a world not yet disarmed or disarming. This survey and analysis, and what it implies, points to these conclusions:

1. Peacekeeping missions by military forces are likely to serve primarily the interests of the superpowers; and threaten to isolate, exploit or dominate smaller and weaker nations, particularly in the Third World.
2. Specialists in this field have generally not taken into sufficient account the rapid obsolescence of the military as an appropriate instrument for organizing peace. As they continue to rely upon it,

[12]See Dorothy Hutchinson, *Toward World Political Community.* Women's International League for Peace and Freedom, 1967 revised edition.

they will alienate many who they hope will be their co-workers and allies in this work.

3. Specialists have also given little thought to nonviolent action: to deal with disorder and violence, resist military or paramilitary aggression, serve as an organizing principle in action and struggle, or as an operational discipline.

4. A breakthrough toward nonmilitary peacekeeping is more likely to occur when states other than the superpowers challenge the existing pattern and strike out on new courses of action. They may be aided not only by specialists and people in key positions, but also by other states less bold but willing to help within their limited powers.

5. Even such a breakthrough can have only limited success, and for a limited time, so long as the present system of armed and warring states continues without substantial tranformation. At best, third parties play a transitional role in major conflicts. While such a role can be helpful, even critical at some point, it is no substitute for an organization of transnational life more viable than one based on the threat of massive destruction.

Two Unexplored Possibilities

Short of radical change in the international system, two other possibilities deserve to be considered carefully:

1. An *Alliance of Disarmed Nations*, willing on invitation to undertake peacekeeping assignments, having developed a new nonmilitary capability in this field.

2. A *World Peace Brigade*, a nongovernmental agency for the same general purpose as the Alliance, committed to nonviolent action in its organization and discipline.

Both could avail themselves of the services of an International Peace Academy, or could adopt or adapt suggestions in the Waskow proposal, for example. Both could be aided by other nations not disarmed, as well as by movements and nongovernmental organizations.

An Alliance of Disarmed Nations

Maj. Gen. Carpenter can envisage a nation—it could be Canada, he says—unilaterally offering its military forces to the UN. Why not go a step further and abolish these forces, then develop a nonmilitary peacekeeping capability? Such a next step seems less drastic than the earlier leap.

Such a nation would have to go beyond neutralism. Austria, for example, scarcely has a military establishment of significance, but is bound to neutrality by its constitution and its peace treaty. Neutrals— without such formal constraints—concentrate on keeping out of the way. A disarming nation desiring to pursue a peacekeeping role would have to "come on strong" to cope with the new and possibly dangerous challenges it would face.

If Canada Took the Lead

The World Peacemakers Association proposal, stating what new policies would be required for Canada, gingerly discusses NATO and NORAD ("no abrogation of treaties or breaking of commitments is involved") and speculates that military alliances such as NATO and the Warsaw Pact may wither away or join forces.

A disarming Canada would necessarily face these questions more directly. Its actions would in all likelihood precipitate serious conflicts with the United States about the DEW (Distant Early Warning) line, military overflights, storage of weapons, strategic plans. Important "non-military" questions would also arise: e.g. about oil, or the St. Lawrence Seaway. In turn, questions would arise in relation to the military plans and policies of the Soviet Union.

To free itself for its new international role, a disarming Canada would choose to face this period of potential serious conflict rather than continue its old policies, which may in time precipitate acute dilemmas anyway. One could argue that the United States would lose immeasurably more than it could gain if it engaged in harsh reprisals. Overt US military action would be highly unlikely. Despite tensions, the US and Canada are bound together by many ties of common interest: political, geographical, historical. These ties could serve well to help overcome the problems arising out of this new proposed relationship.

Canada could then appeal to other nations to join the Alliance, which would in effect become a new version of the World Peacemakers Association. According to a report[13] for 1966, only Iceland and Costa Rica had no armed forces. Thirteen other nations had less than .05% of their population in the armed forces; ten of these are in Africa. Zambia (President Kenneth Kaunda is deeply interested in these matters) had an army of 3000 men, or .1% of its population. Some or all of these nations might decide to make a virtue of necessity and join the Alliance.

Other nations, not disarmed but deeply interested in this new venture, could help: in diplomacy, transport and supply, or finances.

[13]US Arms Control and Disarmament Agency, Economics Bureau Research Report #68-52, December 1968.

Specialists could be drawn from anywhere in the world. Movements and organizations could help: with influence, trained personnel, literature and research, or propaganda. Possibly the Organization of African Unity could become involved in this kind of peacekeeping effort.

The author has been unable to find any systematic study of what unilateral disarmament might mean for Canada and for those with whom Canada works closely. The first tasks are to identify major problems and variables, analyze possible options of such an Alliance, develop scenarios for strategy and initiatives, and estimate what it would take to prevent or minimize the possibility that other powers may try to stymie so bold and powerful a move.

A coordinate task is to develop the idea, functions and possible structure of a nonmilitary peacekeeping capability. What are the nonmilitary equivalents of discipline, and of command and control? What policing skills are relevant? Is there a new technology at hand, or needed?[14] Are there skills to be learned from nonviolent actionists? What legal problems need rethinking: e.g. nonmilitary "intervention"?

It may prove easier to envisage and develop SOPs for such an instrumentality than to comprehend the political dynamics of the situation in which it would be working.[15]

If Canada decides to move in this direction, the payoffs could be immediate and dramatic. Of course, the Alliance could start with any nation or group of nations. Revolutionary developments have a way of starting in unexpected places.

To recapitulate: four key elements in this proposal are
- An Alliance of Disarmed Nations
- New relationship of these nations with their neighbors and/or former military allies
- A new nonmilitary peacekeeping capability
- Treaties or agreements of support by other interested nations.

A World Peace Brigade

The Peace Brigade idea has often cropped up and deserves more study.[16] The founding statement of the World Peace Brigade (1962-1964) said that it aimed to

[14]Betty Goetz Lall, *Regional Arms Control, Peacekeeping and the United Nations*, a Memorandum prepared for the 18th Pugwash Conference on Science and World Affairs, Nice, September 1968, Section 6.

[15]An approach is suggested—though the answers would differ in significant respects—in the collaborative studies prepared for the Peace Research Institute Report *Quis Custodet? Controlling the Police in a Disarmed World*. Washington, D.C., April 1963. Hard to get.

[16]Charles C. Walker, *The World Peace Brigade*. Monograph to be published by the Gandhi Institute, 1969. Also Theodore Olson, "Vision and Failure," in *Our Generation Against Nuclear War*, June 1964.

organize, train and keep available a Brigade for nonviolent action in situations of potential or actual conflict, internal and international . . . [and] against all war, preparations for war and the continuing development of weapons of mass destruction.

The Brigade was first called to what was then Northern Rhodesia, now Zambia. Kenneth Kaunda asked that a force, predominantly African and organized in neighboring Tanganyika, be on call to march into Northern Rhodesia and keep the civil peace if Sir Roy Welensky, head of the Central African Federation, persisted in his designs to forestall an election and prevent Zambia from coming into being. A training center was set up in Dar es Salaam, with a governing board of representatives from the Brigade, the Tanganyikan African National Union (TANU), Pan African Freedom Movements of East, Central and South Africa (PAFMECSA), and United National Independence Party of Northern Rhodesia (UNIP), all bound to a policy of nonviolent action in this common effort.

More than 5000 people (most of them Africans; some from Europe, Asia and the United States) massed near the Northern Rhodesian border. Several sources have said that this was one factor, if a minor one, in the set of forces which produced a peaceful resolution of the issue. WPB Co-chairman Michael Scott and organizer William Sutherland were, as a result, invited as guests of the Zambian government in its 1964 independence celebration.

In the wake of the Sino-Indian border clash in 1962, the Delhi-Peking Friendship March, sponsored by the Brigade, had some impact—though not to be exaggerated—on Indian opinion. (China did not grant visas for the Marchers, after they had walked nearly a year through India.)

The Brigade might intervene in a conflict on its own initiative, but most likely at the request of a constituent group, if it could solve the key problem: access to the theater of action. In the East African project, the WPB received help in gaining access to the conflict through one government (Tanganyika—not disarmed), and another about to become independent (Zambia). It was also helped by a regional organization (PAFMECSA), the Gandhian movement and other smaller movements.

The World Peace Brigade foundered on some of the usual scores—not enough money, too little time and attention by its caretakers, failure to commit key personnel at critical times—but also from a simplistic attempt to transpose national action patterns to the international scene. It also needed more national and regional components, each with a strong base.

Though this venture is now in limbo, the basic idea has much merit. Governments make war, but private groups can have some effect. The efforts of private organizations often pave the way for governmental action.

Detailed and systematic studies of nonviolent action might yield insight and guidelines about strategy and tactics. Geoffrey Carnall writes:

> It would certainly be worth studying the tactics adopted by Gandhi when working in the riot-torn districts of Bengal in 1946-1947. Lord Mountbatten described him as "the one-man boundary force who kept the peace while a 50,000-strong force was swamped by riots." General Sir Francis Tucker estimated the Mahatma's power at the equivalent of two battalions.[17]

Even in military operations, there are times when the best available choice may be seeming impotence: to abstain rather than do something counterproductive. Beyond that, it is likely that people will volunteer for nonviolent action even at peril of their lives. In the mid-1950s, when 72 Indians walked into Goa to demand its return from Portugal, Portuguese authorities machine-gunned all 72 as they continued to walk into the range of fire. Immediately hundreds of Indian *satyagrahis* (nonviolent actionists) volunteered to march again, but the Indian authorities intercepted them to prevent another possible massacre.

If the Alliance described earlier came into being, a nongovernmental group like the World Peace Brigade could help in many ways.

Conclusion

If the United States and the Soviet Union attempt a condominium, using the UN where they can to isolate a conflict or impose a "peace," the underlying conflicts will not be abated.

Many people will nevertheless prefer joint crisis management to eyeball-to-eyeball confrontations. If turbulence grows in the Third World, and new crises appear in the highly industrialized nations, many will welcome anything that promises to keep the lid on the cauldron, and lower the political temperature, even if in extremity it is limited war in the name of limited peace.

On the other hand, such developments, if they do occur, may reveal more clearly the depth of the crisis, and hasten the emergence of previously unexplored possibilities. In times of turmoil and uncertainty, no one can tell who will "pull the plug" (in Herbert Butterfield's phrase) touching off a dramatic chain of events where old certainties crumble and new possibilities appear.

Whether some of the new ventures or proposals recorded here will prosper probably depends upon whether they help prepare the way for the breakthrough to nonmilitary forms of peacekeeping. It is not enough

[17]In *To Keep the Peace*, p. 12.

merely to bring technical competence to systems which are part of the problem rather than part of the answer.

Charles C. Walker

The author wishes to thank the Friends Peace Committee Working Party on Nonviolent Peacekeeping for guidance and criticism:

Marilyn K. Roper, *chairman of the Working Party*
James E. Bristol
F. Miles Day
George C. Hardin
Lawrence W. Scott
Lyle Tatum

Others helped on various phases.

INDEX

Other World Without War Council Publications

1. Robert Pickus and Robert Woito, **To End War, An Introduction to the Ideas, Books, Organizations that can help.** 261pp, 1970 $1.50 The best layman's introduction to twelve war/peace fields, 600 books, over 100 organizations and fifty periodicals. A useful definition of the field and a guide to work for a world without war. Now widely used in college and adult education courses.

2. Albert Camus, **Neither Victims Nor Executioners,** 28pp, 1968 $.25 Camus' classic essay opposing the use of violence to gain political objectives, with an introduction by Robert Pickus relating Camus' themes to the current American peace movement.

3. Allan Blackman, **Face to Face with Your Draft Board: A Guide to Personal Appearances,** 108pp, 1971 $1.00 This book is designed for conscientious objectors and is valuable to all men facing a personal appearance before their draft board. It helps to clarify fundamental beliefs while assisting the reader in obtaining the classification he wants and deserves.

4. Thirty Law Students, U.C. Berkeley, **The Law and Political Protest: A Handbook to Your Political Rights Under the Law,** 115pp, 1970 $1.25 What you can do and what is illegal; covers the full spectrum of forms of political action. Also offers an opportunity to consider current attacks on constitutional democracy.

5. G. Ramachandran and T. K. Mahadevan (eds.), **Gandhi, His Relevance for Our Times,** 393pp, 1970 $2.95 An anthology of Western and Indian students of government applying Gandhian ideas of constructive nonviolent conflict to current problems of international relations, nonviolent theory, civil rights activity and nonviolent resistance to aggression. Selections by Joan Bondurant, Gene Sharp, T. K. Mahadevan, Kenneth Boulding, Charles Walker, Mulford Sibley, R. R. Diwaker and others.

6. Lucy Dougall, **The War/Peace Film Guide,** 56pp, 1970 $.75 Prepared for those working for a world without war, this film guide introduces 150 short and feature films and provides program resources and bibliographical aids designed to help program chairman use the film media to present war/peace ideas intelligently.

7. Geoffrey Nuttall, **Christian Pacifism in History,** 96pp. 1971 $1.25 A noted British scholar identifies five different roots of Christian pacifist thought and argues that combined these teachings contain what should be the modern churches teachings on war.

8. Robert Woito (ed.), **Vietnam Peace Proposals,** 54pp, 1967 $.75 An anthology of peace proposals which sets criteria for judging them. Examined are government proposals, peace organization proposals and the initiative strategy proposal.

9. Ann Stadler and Bev Herbert, **The World Without War Game, A Weekend Exploration of the Realities of World Conflict and the Roads to a World Without War.** $10.00 Includes all the materials you need to organize, plan and carry-out a weekend learning experience for 15 to 40 people. Provided are game rules and props for "The War Game," a simulation of current role playing in society; two narrative readings for three on "The Weapons of War" and "Taking the Initiative for Peace," plus a one act melodrama, and one act skit. Attractively designed and packaged.

Order From:
WORLD WITHOUT WAR COUNCIL, 1730 Grove Street, Berkeley, Calif 94709